Whittingham

To my dear friend, Nancy
Thanks you for all your
help. C. Whitti

CW

Whittingham

The Story of a
Thoroughbred Racing Legend

JAY HOVDEY

THE BLOOD-HORSE, INC.
Lexington, Kentucky

ISBN 0-939049-61-9

Printing in the United States of America
First Edition: December 1993
1 2 3 4 5 6 7 8 9 10

Book and Cover design by Brian Turner

Dedicated to the memory of William E. Shirley,
journalist and friend

"I studied the lives of great men and famous women, and I found that the men and women who got to the top were those who did the jobs they had in hand, with everything they had of energy and enthusiasm and hard work."

—Harry S. Truman

"Experience is the comb that Nature gives us when we are bald."

—Belgian proverb

CONTENTS

A twenty page photo section appears after page 84

ACKNOWLEDGMENTS

Benjamin Franklin wrote, "If you would not be forgotten as soon as you are dead, either write things worth reading or do things worth writing."

Either way, we need a lot of help to do anything well.

At the celebration of his 70th birthday, held at the home of Thoroughbred owner and breeder Louis R. Rowan, Charlie Whittingham took center stage and addressed the crowd at length. He singled out scores of people for special gratitude. He cited small gestures that meant the world to him. He summoned up tales of the past that let everyone know how lucky he was—and how grateful he was to those who had helped him along the way.

I could fill a similar room with those who have made this book come to life. People love to talk about Charlie Whittingham, just as a person may linger over the memory of a great meal or a perfect holiday. Of the dozens who have shared their stories—both written and told—and thereby placed me in the thick of the Whittingham saga, I must express special thanks to Neil Drysdale, Alice Rodich, Bill Shoemaker, Arthur Hancock, Howard Keck, Rodney Rash, Sid Luft, Mary Jones Bradley, Christopher Speckert, Joe Burnham, Aaron Jones, Leon Rasmussen, Janet Johnson Ropp, Joe Hirsch, Noble Threewitt, Francis Risco, Ron McAnally, Tim Yakteen, Laura de Seroux, Gerald Strine, Nelson Bunker Hunt, Ivor Herbert, Charles Clay, Dan Smith, Sonny Greenberg, Christine Picavet, Bob Hebert, Alex Harthill, Brian Sweeney, Jack Robbins, Jimmy Kilroe, Frank Solis, Bob Benoit, W. L. Proctor, and to John Maluvius, Lazaro Barrera and Joe Manzi, racing men no longer with us.

Additional thanks to the people at the racetracks where Whittingham has worked so many of his wonders—especially to those at Santa Anita

Park, Hollywood Park, Del Mar and Churchill Downs. Thanks also to the photographers who have trained their cameras on the Bald Eagle to record his exploits. They gladly learned to live with the glare.

Creating a book requires a dedicated publishing team to counter-balance the wild mood swings and the deadline-defying attitude of a temperamental author. What you have in your hands right now would be nothing more than bytes in a computer memory bank without the quality control of Diane Viert, the research assistance of Matthew Hegarty, Debbie Tuska and Patty Lankford, the design of Brian Turner, and the orchestration and patience of our editor, Ray Paulick.

As for the Whittinghams . . . the story belongs to them. Peggy, a tireless keeper of her husband's legacy, was the driving force behind the book. Thanks to Michael and Charlene, I learned about the father behind the legend. And Charlie. Thank you Charlie. When it comes to horses, you've taught me everything I know. And that's a far, far cry from everything you know. — *Jay Hovdey*

PROLOGUE

At 5:38 p.m. on November 4, 1989, in the melting glow of a warm south Florida afternoon, Charlie Whittingham leaned his lanky six-one frame over the railing of his Gulfstream Park box seat and peered eastward down the track through a pair of Zeiss 10x40 binoculars. In the distance, a quarter of a mile away, three horses and three riders appeared together, banking left and charging headlong into the final 440 yards of the Breeders' Cup Classic. Two of the horses were chestnuts, their red coats muted by the twilight. Whittingham gave them a glance to gauge their progress, then turned his attention to the black colt in the middle. A smile tickled the corners of his fine, small mouth.

"Now we'll find out where Molly put the peaches," he thought. "Come on, you black sonofabitch."

The black colt in the middle—a high-headed, wild-eyed mass of guts and muscle named Sunday Silence—was distinguishable only by a nervous blaze dribbling down his face and the dark green shadow roll wrapped over his nose. He moved like a shark, probing for the right moment to strike, as one red horse clung to the front and the other lurked just behind.

Up in the stands, the ex-Marine sergeant in Whittingham let out an urgent "Now, jock! Let him go!" in the general direction of Chris McCarron. Amazingly, the rider seemed to respond, as if he were actually awaiting Whittingham's command from on high. McCarron gave Sunday Silence a nudge, and the colt lunged for the finish line, ignoring the bone chips coming loose in his right knee. As one red horse weakened, the other came on in a futile attempt to catch the black leader. It was too late, though. Too late to catch Charlie.

From the moment Sunday Silence glided under the wire a confident neck in front of Easy Goer, Whittingham was mobbed. Strange hands reached out to slap his strong, thin shoulders. As he made his way down through the stands, his bald head bobbed through a sea of hairy admirers, a beacon for all to follow. Chants of "Charlie! Charlie!" bounced off the walls and soared into the South Florida night. Everyone wanted a piece of Whittingham—fans, friends and dignitaries alike. When he finally got to the track, Whittingham made a beeline for the real hero, the creature who made it all possible: a mud-splattered, cow-hocked, semi-reject of a Thoroughbred who had just won the most important horse race of the decade.

Standing there, snorting and tossing his head at the center of a chaotic celebration, Sunday Silence at that moment represented nothing less than a four-legged compendium of the Whittingham legend. The black colt had become a concise distillation of the patience, the planning, and the precision that have been Whittingham hallmarks from the beginning of his incomparable journey. Horse racing, a sport that cherishes its past and mistrusts the present, was once again slapped with a cold towel of reality: there is none better than Charlie.

During a career that has spanned parts of seven decades, Whittingham has transformed his corner of the training profession into an enviable pocket of pure commercial craft. While most trainers are held slave to the vagaries of the patronage system, Whittingham fancies himself an artist on open-ended commission.

And the result? Masterpieces by the bushel. Rich prizes galore, of every shape and size, brought to grateful owners in Whittingham's own good time. Santa Anita Handicaps, Arlington Millions, Gold Cups both East and West. One Classic, then another, a Kentucky Derby or two. All of them are panels in Whittingham's own version of the Sistine Chapel. Each horse a brush stroke in the story. Run together, they make up the grand panorama of American racing as it has twisted and turned through the last half of the twentieth century. And Whittingham has bounced around every bend in the road.

After a hardscrabble youth that sent him on his own at age fourteen,

Whittingham began training racehorses in the depths of the Great Depression. Back then, a third-place finish worth ten bucks or so meant enough pocket money to put beans in the belly and a little honey in the mash. He won or went hungry. So he won. And he came through it all with a flint-hard attitude that puts the horse first, and everybody else a distant second.

Still, the Whittingham most people know is a heady bouillabaisse brewed from one part disarming charm, one part wise old sage and one part roughhousing redneck. Add large amounts of gin, stir and then stand back, lest you get in the way of a genuine, U.S. Marine-issue head butt.

After more than sixty years of good times and desert dry martinis, ten champions and nearly 650 stakes wins, Whittingham is still on patrol—and still thirsty. His icy blue eyes, honed on watch in the South Pacific during World War II, continue to scan the horizon for the ultimate animal, the Thoroughbred Charlie describes reverently as "the good horse." He'll stop training, he winks, "when they put the pennies on my eyes and plant me six feet deep."

And so, by happy necessity, the book on Whittingham is incomplete. This is Charlie's story, but only so far. As long as there is a good horse in the barn and a bounce in his step, little things like age won't bother him at all.

"Besides," he'll say every chance he gets, "if they didn't tell you when you were born, you'd never know how old you are in the first place."

CHAPTER 1

FROM SCRATCH

By the age of fourteen, Charlie Whittingham answered to no one but himself. He was on the road, all alone, and riding the rails up the central coast of California. The cold floor of the boxcar spanked his skinny rump as the train wheels chattered. Charlie Whittingham daydreamed about the racetrack, his big brother Joe, and the new pair of overalls he was hoping to buy.

No question, he figured, life at the track will be better than working on a farm, or going to school, or picking lemons in the Sunkist orchards south of San Diego. There would be money, a lot more money than the ten bucks a month he used to make delivering newspapers. There would be good food. There would be action, and there would be girls. He already knew plenty about girls.

Ka-chack, ka-chack, ka-chack went the train wheels, lulling Charlie Whittingham to sleep. The next morning he would wake up in San Bruno, just south of San Francisco, then hoof it to Tanforan Racetrack and show up at the barn where Joe worked, grinning to beat the band. "Hey, buddy, the boss need any help today?" Joe would laugh, and then put his kid brother to work.

On the day Charlie Whittingham was born, in the year of 1913, the circus came to town.

The Sells-Floto Circus, that is. A three-ring troupe of geeks, creatures and high-wire acts that descended upon the bustling little California town of San Diego amid the raucous sounds of bagpipes and calliope. There was Spader the Clown, Maud the Unridable Mule, the Royal Scotch Kilties of Toronto, and—best of all—the Fabulous Aeronautic Horse, a forgiving animal of infinite patience which allowed itself to be harnessed to a helium balloon and floated to the upper reaches of the big top. Fireworks included.

On the day Charlie Whittingham was born, one hundred miles to the north, the Nixons of Yorba Linda were fussing over their two-month-old baby boy named Richard. War was brewing in the Balkans, and Woodrow

Wilson had just been inaugurated as the twenty-eighth President of the United States. Americans were lining up to see *The Squaw Man* at the movies. They were doing a hot new dance called the foxtrot. And, whether they liked it or not, they were paying federal income tax for the very first time.

San Diego was a harbor town of not quite forty thousand souls, poised on the verge of expansion. Mayor Charles F. O'Neall—whose real career was in loans, real estate and fire insurance—was beating the drum for the Panama-California Exposition, planned for two years hence in Balboa Park. The new Spreckels Theatre downtown was the city's cultural hub. The San Diego *Sun* ("Independent—Fearless") was two cents a copy, and on Sundays the funnies included Little Possum Gang, Bear Creek Follies and Jimmie the Messenger Boy. For four dollars you could spend a night at the Hotel del Coronado, buy a round-trip ticket to Los Angeles on the Pacific Navigator steam line, or get a double-reinforced gold crown with a ten-year guarantee from the White Dental Co.

On the day Charlie Whittingham was born, the Reverend Dr. W. H. Geistweit of San Diego's First Baptist Church preached from his pulpit that, according to *Who's Who in America*, the sons of ministers succeeded in life 221 times more frequently than those of any other class of people. In New York, a five-year betting ban was about to be lifted, much to the delight of the horse racing community. At the same time, William Jennings Bryan, who fancied himself America's clarion conscience, denounced gambling as "even more demoralizing than drink and harder to defeat."

Charles Edward Whittingham was born at home on a Sunday, April 13, sharing the date with Thomas Jefferson, who raced his Thoroughbreds at the old National Course near Washington, D.C., in the early 1800s. Charlie was the third of three sons born to Edward and Ellen Whittingham, and came into this world sporting blue eyes, pink skin and a crown of angelic blond hair.

Yes, hair.

The family was newly arrived immigrant stock. Edward Whittingham— he was called Ned for short—was born in 1873, one of four boys and two girls of Joseph and Sarah Whittingham. Ellen, later called Nellie, was born in 1877, the second-youngest of six children brought into this world by Charles and Ann Taylor. Both Ned and Nellie were from Dukinfield, one of a cluster of small English towns in the northwestern counties of Lancashire and Cheshire, not far from the moody Yorkshire moors.

Like most people of the region, the Whittinghams and the Taylors were dependent upon steady work as laborers in the textile mills of nearby Stalybridge on the River Tame. The able-bodied adults among them were weavers, cotton piecers and self-acting minders, a tedious job that required the monitoring of an automated cloth spinning machine called a spinning mule.

Chances are, they did not spend much time going to the races, since the British sport in the last half of the nineteenth century was a pastime dominated by the gentry. Nevertheless, the Yorkshire region to the east of Lancashire and Cheshire was an important corner of the English racing universe. The legendary trainers of the northern counties included John Scott, who won the St. Leger at Doncaster fifteen times, and William I'Anson, whose filly Blink Bonny won both the Epsom Oaks and Epsom Derby of 1857.

Had a young Charles Whittingham been raised in the land of his ancestors instead of in California, he might have found his way to a private stable and worked his way up through the ranks to a position of senior head lad. There he would have languished, unable to penetrate the thick walls of a class system that required trainers to be blessed with independent wealth or a patron of patrician rank. Of course, it is far more likely he would have worked in the mills, minding a spinning mule, or else ended up in the local iron works, breaking his back at the smelting pots.

Charles Whittingham, yet to be born, was spared such a fate by the luck of the draw. His parents were brave souls who coveted a new life and a place where they could stretch out and start over. The men and women of the Whittingham and Taylor clans decided it was worth the risk to pack up hearth and home in order to make a fresh beginning in that vast continent of untapped hope: North America.

Their first landfall was Maine, in an area just south of Portland. From there the winds of meager opportunity took some of them to Canada, some to Colorado, and then on to California, where land was cheap and the weather mild. In 1907—one year after the great Stalybridge flood back in England—newlyweds Ned and Ellen Whittingham found a home in Chula Vista, a tiny community situated between San Diego and the Mexican border. It was rimmed on the west by the San Diego Bay, on the north by the Sweetwater River, and on the rest by acres and acres of fruit trees. By all measures, it was a far cry from Stalybridge.

"There are no unpleasant months, and few unpleasant days," read a San Diego Chamber of Commerce brochure in circulation at the time. "The difference between this and many other parts of our land is that nature seems to work with man, and not against him."

Most of the English immigrants ended up in the groves. Ned Whittingham went to work as a laborer and field hand for the San Diego Land and Town Co., a subsidiary of the Santa Fe Railroad, while Ellen commenced bearing their children. Joseph Whittingham was born in 1908 and William Whittingham in 1910, both of them named after uncles. Then came Charles.

Was life good for the Whittinghams in turn-of-the-century Southern California? Well, it wasn't bad. Ned had a steady paycheck, the "big city" of San Diego was just up the road, and for entertainment, there were Whittinghams and Taylors aplenty. They were butchers and builders and ranch hands and farmers, and most of them were of the same mind as John Wood, Ned's brother in law, who proclaimed, "I am no longer English. I'm an American!"

Ned Whittingham, a full head taller than his diminutive brothers, was a kind husband and father, and well-regarded as a reliable employee. In matters of family he usually deferred to his energetic wife, who ran the household like a sergeant-major. He certainly was not prone to rash behavior, although there was some fleeting evidence of an undiagnosed nervous disorder that surfaced in late 1913.

During the early months of 1914, Southern California was lashed by a series of ferocious storms. Inland communities were ravaged by flash floods. The rail line between San Diego and Los Angeles was blocked by mudslides. San Diego, at the southern edge of the front, escaped catastrophic damage, although the area's major dams came perilously close to overflowing.

Finally, the tempest abated. The evening of Monday, February 23, was cool, calm and a little cloudy. No one gave it a second thought when Ned, still in his work clothes, donned his coat and hat, glanced at his wife and three boys, and left their house on I Street quietly on foot.

In those days, Chula Vista had a population of less than a thousand. When someone disappeared, word got around. The Whittinghams were a popular part of an English enclave that included not only their immediate family, but scores of fellow British immigrants as well. The story of Ned's disappearance made the front page of the San Diego *Sun* under the headline "Man Is Missing; Family Saddened." Everyone feared the worst.

Three nights later, a watchman at the San Diego Lumber Co. dockside yard at the foot of Sixth Street found a coat and hat. They were identified as belonging to Ned Whittingham. Friends and family joined local authorities dragging the San Diego Bay and combing the waterfront. On February 28, a body was spotted floating near the lumber company pier. With the help of a motorcycle patrolman, the elder Joseph Whittingham pulled his dead brother out of the cold, gray water.

Ned Whittingham was still in his work overalls. There was three dollars worth of silver coins in a pocket. A seven-member coroner's jury fixed the date of death as February 24 and labeled the cause of death, "By being drowned. Suicide." He was one week shy of his forty-first birthday. Charles, his youngest son, was only ten months old. And Ellen Whittingham, at the age of thirty-six, was suddenly a widow with three boys under the age of six, totally reliant upon the mercies of her extended family. Her sorrow was palpable, her straits were desperate.

Within two years she married Jack Rowbottom, a quiet, unassuming man of the English-American community who was a close friend of Ned's. Seeking a fresh start, they moved to the mining town of Agate, Colorado, where land was available for homesteading. But eastern Colorado was a hard bargain, and bad luck continued to dog the family. In fact, little Charles—by then they called him Charlie—came terrifyingly close to a fatal injury when he fell on the sharp blades of a field harrow. One of the tines pierced the right side of his neck. Blood spewed everywhere. His mother, who weighed barely a hundred pounds, hoisted her child aboard a horse and rode off to find a doctor. Luckily, the wound missed the artery.

While in Colorado, Ellen became pregnant with her fourth child, presenting the family with a grim financial situation. With too many mouths and not enough to go around there were precious few options, none of them pleasant. Ellen, a take-charge woman of iron resolve, decided to lessen the burden on her other children by taking one of them back to Chula Vista to live with her late husband's relatives. Joe and Willie were young boys able to help around the homestead. That left Charlie, five-year-old Charlie, as Ellen's only choice.

After returning to Chula Vista and giving birth to her fourth son, named Edward, Ellen relinquished Charlie to his aunt and uncle, Alice and John Wood, to live on their ten-acre spread on Anita Street in the town of Otay, just to the south of Chula Vista. Ellen and the baby headed back to Colorado.

Otay was intended to be a flowering suburban community, offering a semi-rural alternative to the growing hubbub of San Diego ten miles to the north. Its name was derived from the Native American word "otahay," which most likely meant "a wide, level knoll" or perhaps "a place of roads." Whatever it meant, it did not translate into great riches for the developers. There was a brief boom in the late 1800s, spurred by the output of the Otay Watchworks ("the only watch factory West of the Mississippi"). But it did not last. By the 1920s, downtown Otay was going downhill fast.

Civic evolution meant little to young Charlie. He was more concerned with life as a barefoot farm boy and getting accustomed to a new set of parents. Alice Wood, the stately, hawk-faced sister of Ned Whittingham, was everyone's favorite aunt. John Wood, portly and proudly mustachioed, grew celery and rhubarb. They married late and were childless, until Charlie came along, that is.

As the years passed, Charlie wrestled with his mother's decision to give him up. The uneasy feelings grew stronger when the Rowbottoms returned to Chula Vista a few years later, but did not take Charlie back into their home. The questions buzzed around in Charlie's head like flies on a hot day. "Didn't my mother want me? What did I do wrong? Why am I still living with Aunt Alice?"

"Charlie seemed more like a cousin to me," recalled his half-sister, Alice Rowbottom Rodich, who was the last of Ellen's five children. "He was a typical boy, full of mischief. I remember asking him for a taste of his ice cream cone. He said, 'Sure, here you go.' Then he spit on it and handed it to me."

In time, Charlie came to understand why his mother had done what she'd done. Ellen Taylor Whittingham Rowbottom had made the hardest choice a mother can make. She gave up her child for the child's own good. In the late 1930s, when Charlie was training horses on the Southern California circuit, his mother became an avid racing fan—at least as far as her health would let her. When her son was in the service, Nellie would hum through her favorite wartime song, "When the Lights Go on Again All Over the World," and then add her own chorus: "And my Charlie comes back home." She died from the ravages of Parkinson's disease in January of 1944, shortly before Whittingham was safely stateside from his tour of duty in the South Pacific.

To no one's surprise, Alice Wood treated young Charlie like a son, and the Otay farm was a good enough place to grow up, even if it did lack an indoor commode. There was a roomy main house, a big barn and corrals, a massive fig tree in front fit for climbing to the sky, and a variety of livestock that included cows, chickens, pigs, horses and a lively part collie named Laddie. John Wood even boarded a few racehorses who needed a place to stay between starts across the border at the downtown Tijuana Racetrack, just five miles away.

Three years after Charlie's arrival, the Woods took in Johnny Whittingham, Charlie's eight-year-old cousin, whose mother died of cancer in 1922. A year apart in age, Charlie and Johnny shared a room and spent most of their time doing chores on Uncle John's farm. Spare time? Not much. There was baseball, duck hunting along the river, and swimming in the ocean. Charlie caddied for pocket money at the nearby San

Diego Country Club. He and Johnny raised pigeons, some to eat, some to sell. Each night the boys would deliver fresh milk to customers in the neighborhood, and every morning they were up early to deliver the San Diego *Sun*. Johnny rode his bicycle; Charlie rode a horse. A horse named Molly.

Molly was nothing more than a plodding old plow horse, but oh, did Charlie love to ride! When the spirit moved him, he would bolt out of Miss Duck's class in Otay's two-room schoolhouse and gallop off to the beach. Or find some friends and race through the arroyos lacing Otay Mesa, south of home. Whoever brought a saddle was the star.

One day Molly propped and Charlie hit the ground hard. The horse landed on him, smashing his left elbow. The bone knit inside a massive plaster cast; but when the cast was removed, the arm would not straighten. No problem, said old Doc Ashcroft, Chula Vista's finest. Doc put a knee to the joint and yanked backwards on Charlie's forearm. The calcification crumbled and the arm was straight—or, at least it was straighter. Charlie's screams could be heard up and down the main boulevard.

Even though they grew up in separate homes, Charlie worshiped his big brother Joe. And by the mid-1920s, Joe was something special. Lean, handsome and athletic, he was the heartthrob of every young girl in the neighborhood. He was soft-spoken, polite to a fault, and exuded the air of a tragic hero. The tragic part, he had earned. While living in Colorado, he and younger brother Willie were horsing around with an ancient muzzle-loading pistol they found in the barn. The boys played tug-o-war with the old weapon until it went off. Willie was killed, and Joe blamed himself.

Joe started exercising racehorses when he was twelve with the idea of becoming a jockey. He won his first real race at sixteen, back in the days when a trainer owned your contract, your body and your soul. Charlie started tagging along to the track, and soon he was walking hots and mucking stalls for Joe's boss, John "Old Man" Stanfield, at Tijuana. When Joe got too big, he started to train, with little brother Charlie at his side. They became racetrack gypsies, packing their few head of horses from track to track on railcars and borrowed vans. They groomed, galloped and walked their own hots, and at the end of the long day they slept in the stalls when they had to. The credo back then was simple. When you won, you got paid. Anything else was just scraping by.

As far as Charlie is concerned, he got his first racehorses in 1930 when Joe was heading off to Ohio and then Canada for the summer. There were two animals plainly not worth shipping, so Joe turned to his seventeen-year-old brother.

"Take 'em, kid. And here's five bucks. Congratulations. You're a horse trainer."

Charlie, ever on the hustle, picked up another nag named Booster Twist from a one-armed trainer who said, "Pay me when he wins." He didn't, but Charlie was able to turn a profit with Joe's old horses by running them up north at the Monterey County Fair and selling the pair for a bit more than $300. When Joe returned to California in the fall, Charlie was sporting a new suit and walking tall. It was plain as the wavy brown hair on his head: for better or worse, young Mr. Whittingham was in the horse business.

CHAPTER 2

SEMPER FI

"I was taught when I was a little boy that if you never lie, cheat or steal you'll be all right. But it's tough when you're a horse trainer not to steal a little here or there."

Peel back the tough hide of Charlie Whittingham and there was always a horse trainer lurking just under the skin, crying to get out.

When he was so broke he slept on a cot in a crackerbox bedroom right next to the stalls, he still wanted to train horses.

When he tried hustling mounts for a collection of low-rent riders, it was only to make enough money to buy and train horses.

Even when things got so bad he turned to growing tomatoes in San Diego or milking cows in Minnesota, he knew he'd soon be back at the track, training horses.

"I don't think Charlie was ever intended to do anything but train horses," said Jimmy Kilroe, the respected racetrack executive who shared forty years of history with Whittingham.

Predestination? Hard to deny, since Whittingham and the world of the racetrack seemed to be such a perfect fit from the beginning. The racetrack of the 1930s was a place with its own set of rules, where a fellow with energy, charm and all-around horsemanship could establish a quick reputation through a betting coup or an eye-catching animal. At the racetrack, an abundance of formal education was extraneous baggage. A dose of sophistication was handy, but not mandatory. Life at the racetrack required hard work and luck. It didn't take long for Whittingham to learn that the harder he worked, the luckier he got.

As a lanky six-footer in his early twenties, Whittingham was as strong as cable wire, built like a steel string bean, and topped off with thick brown hair. He moved with an elastic grace, his arms swinging loosely out from his sides. His voice—a lazy California twang—could shift from reedy thin to deep and commanding, depending upon the desired effect. He was not nearly what anyone would call classically handsome, although there was something decidedly attractive about this tall drink of water with bright blue eyes and ready smile. Most of the time he left behind an audience still chuckling from his homespun homilies.

Whittingham was always on the hustle, looking for ways to make his talents pay. "I could remember anything," he said. "Only had to read something once. I'd read through the track program, then bet anybody to name a horse in any race. I'd tell them the breeding, the color, the owner, the trainer and the jock. Made some money that way, too."

From the moment he went on his own, Whittingham led the life of a racetrack gypsy, hopping from one track to the next with his handful of horses. The problem for Whittingham—for everyone—was money. The America of the 1930s was bound and gagged by the Great Depression. Prices were at rock bottom, but for many it didn't matter. Cash was scarce. Only the fortunate earned steady paychecks. Millions were on the government payroll in such programs as the Works Progress Administration (WPA) or the Conservation Corps, doing make-work labor for little more than room and board. Despite the slim pickings in horse racing, Whittingham considered himself among the fortunate. He was part of a crude but self-sustaining community, while millions of other able-bodied American working men were adrift.

"At least there was always some kind of living on the racetrack," Whittingham said. "You could get something to eat, find a place to live, and maybe pick up a little money. I was lucky I didn't have to go to work for the WPA—we called them two comin', two goin', two shittin' and two mowin'."

The racing world was small and insulated. There were only a few hundred horses on hand at most racetracks. Trainers were lucky if they had more than three or four healthy runners when they showed up in the morning. A twelve-horse string was considered big-time action. No one cared where the money came from as long as the money brought in fresh horses. And to find the money, a man had to go where it flowed.

"Charlie was just like everybody else back then," said Frank Buckley, a jockey's agent from the old days in San Francisco and Los Angeles. "His owners were cab drivers, pimps, bookmakers. Artichoke Joe, Ten Grand Paddy, Big Prick Mike. Mike met his wife in a whorehouse. Everybody knew everybody else and showed up in the same joints.

"Big Tits Judy ran a bar we all went to in Belmont, not far from Bay Meadows. Half the racetrack wouldn't go there because it was beneath their dignity. Red Rydell, Black Cecil, Bobby McRoberts, Charlie Whittingham—we were all regulars. There was another place close to Tanforan called Chip's Serenade. Steaks were a dollar ninety-nine. If you didn't come out of there with a black eye, you didn't have a good time.

"Uncle Tom's Cabin was across the street, another wild place. Charlie walked in there one night and a guy Sunday-punched him the second he stepped in the door. 'Oh, I'm sorry,' says the guy. 'I thought you was somebody else.' Charlie says nothing. He has something to eat, downs a few shooters. On his way out this guy is still sitting by the door. Charlie sends him flying. He's laying there in a heap, and Charlie says, 'Oh, I'm sorry. I thought you were somebody else.'

"One night Charlie was at the Willow Tree, a gambling joint run by a guy named Georgetti. A steward from the track sees him and says to Charlie, 'What are you doing here?' Charlie never blinks. 'Never mind me,' he says. 'You're a steward. What are *you* doing here?' "

In the early 1930s, the border town of Tijuana was the hottest spot in North American racing. Top East Coast owners would ship their stables to the old Tijuana Racetrack, then later to the sparkling new Agua Caliente racing emporium just outside of town. To promote the track, Caliente's Mexican owners offered the first purse worth $100,000. In 1932, they were able to lure the Australian star Phar Lap for the Agua Caliente Handicap, which he won with astounding ease.

"I never got to see Man o' War," Whittingham said. "I was too young. But he'd have to be a helluva horse to be better than Phar Lap. He won that Caliente race running almost all the way around on the outside fence. His rider was convinced the other jocks in there were out to get them. He figured the best thing to do was not give them the chance."

Tijuana offered casinos, nightclubs and showrooms to keep the action going well into the night. Whittingham and his pals enjoyed as much as they could afford, leaving enough in their pockets for a visit to the girls in the Molino Roja, the classiest cathouse in town.

Racing in Tijuana had its drawbacks. Foreigners were required to carry passports if they worked across the border. There were raids by the Mexican authorities at Caliente every Monday morning, just to see who was foolish enough to neglect their papers. The border did not open until six o'clock in the morning. Sometimes it closed as early as at eight at night, effectively trapping Americans on the Mexican side. The Tijuana police were notoriously corrupt, as Whittingham learned on more than one occasion.

"I had my only horse get bit by a snake," he recalled. "I was broke and didn't have the money for the serum. Then a guy came up with two hundred he owed me. I was off and running across the border to get the serum. A Mexican cop stops me for speeding. It was either pay him right there or go to jail. I asked him how much, and he says, 'How much you got?' and takes the two hundred. That horse was a goner."

In 1933, California legalized pari-mutuel betting on horse races. Whittingham was at Santa Anita Park when it opened on Christmas Day 1934. He had two jockeys and no horses. Bay Meadows was up and running the same year. Del Mar began operation in July of 1937, then Hollywood Park made its debut in June of 1938. He was there for the Del Mar and Hollywood openings, training a couple of horses and pushing his jocks. The riders never made him rich, not when the agent got only a few dollars per mount. At one time or another, Whittingham's jockeys included Clyde Turk, Noel "Spec" Richardson, Bobby Coalpits, Keith Stucki, George Burns and Don Lyons. He worked for other trainers, as well, handling the barn chores for Ollie Brown and then Lonnie Copenhaver, who was so hard up he couldn't afford exercise riders.

"Lonnie sat on a stool in the middle of a yard and ran them in circles around him on a long line," Whittingham said. "I'm not sure what they got out of it, but you could get them going pretty fast."

Whittingham squeezed what he could out of the horses he had. He ran a cheap horse named Overstimulate four times during Del Mar's first month of operation. The best he could do was a third-place finish worth fifty bucks. In 1939, he won a few races with an Alfred Vanderbilt castoff named Home Burning. For awhile, Whittingham trained Malicious, a durable old gelding who went from barn to barn while building a popular following for his dramatic finishes. Announcer Joe Hernandez would holler, "And heeeere comes Malicious!" A few minutes later, Whittingham would cash his tickets.

Through trial and error, he was learning everything there was to know about keeping a horse fit and healthy, no matter what the horse's potential. More importantly, he was learning to evaluate ability, for in racing, then and now, there is no room for self delusion. A trainer with the healthiest, fittest horse in the race would die of starvation if that horse was placed with the wrong competition. Whittingham won races and lost horses through the claiming box because he understood where his horses belonged.

It didn't take long for Whittingham to realize he had the right personality to handle high-strung Thoroughbreds. His rowdy social side belied a quiet, sympathetic demeanor around the animals. He found that the more time he spent with his horses, the more he learned about them—how they moved, when they were content, and what made them anxious or uncomfortable. There were no secrets, no mystic potions or poultices that could make a horse outrun his own destiny. And there were no shortcuts, as far as Whittingham was concerned.

"I had to know how to do everything," he said. "Did their teeth, their feet. Cooled them out and did them up. There was only one vet on the whole racetrack back then, and you didn't need him for much. There was some things guys would do to try and steal a race. Some used heroin on the horse's tongue, then they'd taste a little for themselves. Why do you think they called it 'horse'? I never liked to use it, though. The horse was feeling no pain and that's no good. They could break a leg and not even know it. Besides, it made them way too nervous."

Along the way, Whittingham married a young woman he had met in Seattle named June Sturgeon. She was eighteen and he was twenty-one. They started out traveling together, but soon Whittingham headed off on his own, still very much the gypsy. The young Mrs. Whittingham did not bargain for the life of a racetrack widow. The horses took Charlie far and wide—up and down the West Coast and eastward to tracks in Texas, Maryland and a hodgepodge of stops in New England. After about a year June went home to Seattle. Their divorce became final in 1937. June Whittingham later remarried "Bones" LaBoyne, agent for Eddie Arcaro, and settled in New York.

In the summer of 1937, Whittingham showed up for the opening of Del Mar Racetrack with two horses and a cross-eyed coyote he'd bought in Mexico for forty dollars. One night a friend saw Charlie tie up the coyote outside the tackroom where he slept instead of near the horses in their stalls.

"I thought you got him for a stable watchdog," the other fellow wondered.

"I did," replied Whittingham. "But tonight I got ten dollars in my pocket. And I want him where the money is."

Money never stayed in his pocket for long. Whittingham was generous to a fault, perhaps the softest touch around. One time his half-sister, Alice Rodich, encountered a woman with a true tale of Charlie.

"It was the end of a Santa Anita meeting, and everyone was getting ready to ship to Bay Meadows," Alice Rodich recalled. "Charlie was stopping by the house of a trainer he knew while on his way out of town.

"What he found was the trainer's wife and baby, all alone. Her husband had left her high and dry. Charlie asked her, 'What will you do?' She said she didn't know. She had no money. 'Here, this will at least get you a ticket home,' Charlie said, and he emptied his pockets. 'I'm riding with the horses anyway.' "

The early days at Del Mar provided a turning point in Whittingham's career. The relaxed, informal atmosphere of the seaside spa played right to Charlie's nature. West Coast high society let down its hair and rubbed shoulders with the colorful locals. Whittingham disarmed the pretentious with a wisecrack or an off-color joke. He became friends with Bing Crosby, the man behind Del Mar Racetrack, and even played second base on the Ol' Crooner's amateur softball team.

"Bing would serve a big meal every day at his place in Rancho Santa Fe," Whittingham recalled. "I wasn't shy about getting in line. If it wasn't for that, I would have gone hungry."

If it wasn't for Crosby and Del Mar, Charlie may have never met the single most important man in his life.

Horatio Luro began spreading the gospel of the South American Thoroughbred through the American racing world in 1936. By the autumn of 1939, with several successes under his belt, he was in Southern California, training his horses on Imperial Beach just north of the Mexican border. Whittingham, fresh out of runners, was back to hustling a jockey's book at Caliente.

The careers of Whittingham and Luro crossed for the first time in August of 1938. Ligaroti, a horse imported by Luro, was ridden by Spec Richardson, Whittingham's jock at the time, in the celebrated Del Mar match race against Seabiscuit. Ligaroti lost by a nose. But the real news was the slashing and pulling between Richardson and rival jockey George Woolf as they tumbled through the final stages of the race. Both riders were suspended for the balance of the meet.

Whittingham remembers meeting Luro at Caliente during the spring of 1940. Luro recalled their first encounter as taking place either in a Tijuana nightclub or on Imperial Beach. Whatever the circumstances, they clicked from the start. Whittingham was impressed with Luro's suave salesmanship and continental style. Luro saw in Charlie a young trainer of unbridled enthusiasm and boundless energy. Before too long, they respected each other as consummate horsemen with the ability to pick out a proper horse, train it well, and either sell it or cash a bet—or both—depending upon which presented the greater opportunity.

"Horatio called me 'Chuck,' " Whittingham said. "No one had since I was a kid. He'd say, 'Chuck, what I tol' you?' Later I named a horse in his honor, Whatitoldyou."

The two men pooled their slim resources and headed for points north with horses named Dandy, Negra Mia and Bang. Their first stop was Longacres, near Seattle, where Whittingham did the training and Luro wooed owners and beautiful women in equal amounts. They worked their way around the country, with stops in San Francisco, Chicago, Cleveland and New Orleans. By the end of 1940, they were badly in need of fresh stock. Luro arranged a voyage to Buenos Aires, where he would be able to buy horses through his old connections.

"There was just me and Luro and a boatload of schoolteachers," Whittingham fondly recalled. "We didn't exactly lack for company. This one fat gal really had a thing for Horatio. I kept telling her how my friend really liked her, and she spent the whole trip chasing him all over the ship. I had to hide him a few times."

The journey back to America was not nearly so enjoyable. To house the horses Luro had purchased, Whittingham built temporary stalls on board the ship. He spent most of his time tending to the horses and arrived in New Orleans looking much the worse for wear. Of course, it was possible he had yet to recover from the schoolteachers. Soon, the two men were off and running again through Canada, New England and the Midwest. The best of their bunch was a colt named Bronte, a winner at River Downs in Ohio and at the Fair Grounds in New Orleans.

Charlie Whittingham was fiddling around with Bronte and the other Luro horses at the Fair Grounds on the morning of December 7, 1941, when the radio blasted out the news about Pearl Harbor. The Japanese had attacked.

Whittingham and his racetrack pals began pawing the ground like penned up mustangs. They were spoiling for a fight, for God and country. All they needed was a little basic training, a weapon and a target. War was hell, and they were after a piece of it.

They all leaned toward the Marines. Or, at least, they liked the idea of being part of an elite combat corps that ate fire and drank blood. Whittingham was in no mood to go Navy and say goodbye to dry land. If he went Army, he would be a PFC at age twenty-eight, odds-on to be the guy they called "Pops" in the platoon. No, the only real choice was the Marines, where the only measure of a man was the number of nails he could chew and digest at a dead run.

The Corps snapped him up. And why not? Whittingham was a natural-born Marine who fit the profile to a tee. He was fiercely loyal to his closest comrades, contemptuous of establishment authority, and a born survivor to boot. He offered the Corps a pre-toughened psyche, along with a body as hard as an anvil and strong as a bear trap from years of wrestling with ornery Thoroughbreds. He even came with tattoos included: one of Man o' War on his right shoulder and another with his initials—"CEW"—in elaborate cursive on his right bicep.

Whittingham ended up back in Southern California for basic training at the Marine Recruit Depot in Point Loma, across the bay from downtown San Diego. It was a crash course, because the war effort needed live bodies in the Pacific on short notice to shore up defenses against the sweeping Japanese advances. Whittingham managed to learn just enough to kill and maim without getting killed or maimed. He slipped in a quick visit to his mother on a weekend pass wrangled by his brother-in-law, Bert Thompson, and then it was off to Oahu for final staging.

A lot of men came back dead from the Pacific theater of action. As part of the U.S. Marine Corps Second Division, Whittingham figured to have plenty of chances to cash in. But somehow, for some reason, he was blessed with a kind of twisted good fortune that kept him safe from the ultimate harm.

His first assignment was to have been aboard the battleship Lexington, freshly refitted as an aircraft carrier and destined for the Coral Sea. They filled the Marine contingent, though, before they got to the "W" in the alphabet. Had Whittingham been a Barrera, a Fitzsimmons or a Jones, he might have met the same fate as the other Marines who were lost when the Lexington was torpedoed and sunk.

Second prize was the Solomon Islands, a daisy chain of atolls and sand spits just east of New Guinea that was rapidly becoming part of Japan's eastward expansion. One of the islands was Guadalcanal, described by author-soldier James Jones as a tropical landscape of haunting beauty that was, in reality, a "pestilential hellhole." Whittingham's unit hopped from island to island, sometimes encountering entrenched unfriendlies, as the U.S. forces prepared for a major offensive. While stationed on Guadalcanal, the Marines awoke each day to the sight of a huge sign stuck on the top of a knoll that read:

"Admiral Halsey says 'Kill Japs, kill Japs, kill more Japs!' You will help kill the yellow bastards if . . . You do your job WELL."

The bullets missed but the mosquitoes hit Whittingham with a dose of malarial virus. He was sent back to Honolulu to recover. In the meantime, beginning in May of 1942, the Marines of Guadalcanal led the way in America's first offensive of the widening war.

Whittingham—now Sgt. Whittingham—served most of the rest of his South Pacific tour on Johnston Atoll, a key stop on the supply line seven hundred miles southeast of Hawaii. It was tedious duty, with nothing to do but patrol the perimeter of the treeless island, string barbed wire just offshore, and swim in the coral infested waters while the Air Corpsmen maintained the lonely landing strip.

"About the only thing we had for entertainment was the goony birds," Whittingham said. "Thousands of them, all over the place. They were loud, but they weren't really a nuisance unless some of them got caught up in the airplane engines."

Whittingham's stay on Johnston was interrupted by a bout with appendicitis. At the military hospital in Honolulu, Whittingham was comfortably bedded down for a few days rest when a nurse lieutenant ordered him up and about.

"Sweep the floor, sergeant. You need the exercise," the nurse ordered. Whittingham balked. It was bad enough she was a woman, and a lowlife junior officer to boot. But sweep the floor!

"Marine sergeants don't sweep floors," he snapped. The next day he was out of the hospital and on his way back to the island.

Near the end of 1943, Whittingham's tour on Johnston came to an end. He was posted back to Honolulu and placed in charge of a military police unit.

"Knew a fellow there named Frank Wench," Whittingham said. "He had horses back in the States, and he was installing the first air-conditioning units for the military. So he was doing all right. He'd throw parties at his place, and I'd go there dressed in civilian clothes and have some fun mouthing off to the brass. Frank would tell me I'd get myself in trouble doing that one day. But hell, they didn't know who I was. And if they did, so what? What were they gonna do to me anyway?"

Whittingham finally was rotated stateside in the spring of 1944, going through Mare Island north of San Francisco on his way to Camp Lejeune in North Carolina. Soon, he was patroling the streets of neighboring towns, on loan to local police departments. One of the towns was Rocky Mount, the home of Peggy Boone. They were married in October of 1944.

With the war winding down, Whittingham was anxious to resume his career in horse racing. Luro was on a roll in New York, with a good stable of horses and wealthy clients. He had gained a measure of fame with Princequillo, a colt he had claimed for $2,500 and then later won several major events, including the 1943 Jockey Club Gold Cup. But Luro's complicated personal life was beginning to take a physical toll. When Whittingham called, Luro jumped at a chance to put his horses in capable hands and step back from the daily grind.

"Chuck, you come back to work for me," he told Whittingham. "We make a lot of money."

The renewed relationship with Luro gave Whittingham a chance to work with a better class of horse and a different breed of patron. Not that it changed Charlie in the least. When he and his bride arrived in New York in the spring of 1946, Whittingham was a coiled-and-ready combination of Western racetracker and Marine Corps sergeant. Luro introduced Whittingham to the horses and his staff, then caught the first luxury liner to Buenos Aires. Charlie waved goodbye, then fired the whole crew and replaced them with the help of an old Virginia horseman named Jack Skinner.

With Luro's substantial stable, Whittingham was able to add military regimentation to his own brand of thorough horsemanship. The Luro-Whittingham outfit became a model of efficiency. Luro provided Whittingham with the latitude to search each horse for its ultimate level of ability, while at the same time reminding Charlie, "Never squeeze the lemon dry."

"What did I learn from Horatio?" Whittingham has been asked the question many times through the years. "One thing more than anything else—patience. But that's not as simple as it sounds. There's a lot of things can make a trainer impatient. Owners, for one. And himself, or his own empty pockets. You've got to let the horse tell you when he's ready. Listen to anyone else and you're in trouble."

Whittingham, with his eighth grade education, could easily calculate the circular logic posed by Luro's philosophy: the better the horse, the bigger the purse he can win. The bigger the purses, the fewer the starts a horse needs to make to pay his way. The fewer the starts, the sounder and better a horse shall remain. And so on, to wealth and fame.

In many cases, patience was imposed. Most of Luro's best horses in those days were freshly imported from South America. They needed time to acclimate not only to the North American seasons, but also to the new tastes in food and water, and to the different routines in training.

Luro and Whittingham won stakes races with the ace South Americans Rico Monte and Miss Grillo. The least of them all may have been the Argentinean named Talon, who stepped off the boat from Buenos Aires with shaved mane, mottled coat and several ribs showing. By the time he arrived at Saratoga, where Whittingham was stabled with the Luro string, Talon was looking forlorn indeed.

"He came in with a pony, a big old hunter, and there was only one stall," Whittingham said. "Before I got there the boys did up the pony all clean and shiny and put him in the stall. Talon they tied up to a tree. We got 'em switched and Talon cleaned up before Horatio and the owner showed up the next morning."

Luro and Whittingham took their show on the road to Santa Anita during the winter of 1947-48, marking Charlie's grand return to California. They hardly recognized this new version of Whittingham, turning up for the races in tailored suits and fine shoes. He was as generous as ever, though, always ready to reach for his bankroll to help out a hard-luck joe. And after hours, it was the same old Charlie at the Derby Restaurant and the Talk o' the Town, only with a few nasty moves courtesy of the Marines—and a lot less hair. Whittingham blamed his malaria.

Santa Anita Park was enjoying a post-war boom in both business and quality of sport. Top East Coast stables like King Ranch and Calumet Farm were sending horses out West for the winter. They paid special attention to the Santa Anita Handicap, the richest race in the world. The best older horses on the grounds that year included Talon and Endeavour from the Luro string, Double Jay, Autocrat and Flashco. There was the local hero, On Trust, who nearly won a Preakness, and tough old Olhaverry, winner of the 1947 Santa Anita Handicap.

The 1948 Handicap unfolded under cloudy skies on the afternoon of February 28. Dick Ryan, Talon's owner, promised the whole gang a party at the trendy Ciro's Restaurant on the Sunset Strip if his gray horse should win the race. That was fine with Luro, who had recently returned from a South American excursion in the company of Lana Turner. Whittingham worried about the weather—Talon hated the mud—but an early sprinkling merely settled the dust.

"They will have to beat On Trust to win the handicap," said Bill Molter, On Trust's trainer. "Fair enough," thought Whittingham as he gave a leg up to Eddie Arcaro aboard Talon. And that is precisely the way the race played out. Johnny Longden kept On Trust within close reach of the early pace, while Talon lagged at the back of the pack. Nearing the finish, On Trust held the lead from the onrushing Talon. They reached the line as one. Peggy Whittingham, watching from a hillside overlooking the track, was convinced Talon's run was too little too late. She headed home to their rented ranch house on Second Avenue and made plans for a consolation dinner. A little while later the telephone rang.

"Are you ready?" It was Charlie.

"Yes," Peggy answered. "Come on any time. Dinner is in the oven."

"Throw it out. We won! It's Ciro's for us tonight."

Later that year, Luro gave Whittingham his release. Charlie was perfectly content to keep rolling along as a well-paid assistant, getting five percent of the purses. Luro was looking to the bottom line. "You make too much the money," read part of Luro's handwritten letter. "It is time you go on your own." Resigned to his fate, Whittingham broke the news to Peggy.

"I'm not sure where we're going from here," he warned his wife. "But I can tell you, our lifestyle will have to change for awhile until we get going again."

CHAPTER 3

STRONG WOMEN

"Nobody knows where the nose goes when the door's closed."

"**W**here the hell's the light switch?"

It was five in the morning, and Charlie Whittingham was fumbling around in the dark, feeling his way along the wall of a guest room at Llangollen Farm.

"Find the bathroom door," answered Peggy Whittingham. She was still in bed, curled up in a corner of a twin-size mattress. "Step down, turn right, and walk to the end. There's a cord over the sink."

Charlie crossed to the door, opened it and then . . .

"God damn son of a bitch! God damn fucking dogs! I stepped in dog shit!"

Peggy jumped out of bed and managed to find a switch on the wall. There, framed by the bathroom door, Whittingham stood on one foot, naked as a jaybird, scowling down at the foul smear of brown clinging to his toes.

"What'll I do with it?" Charlie demanded. A thought flew across his mind—find the dog, grab it by the neck and use it for a rub rag. Or, better yet, find the owner of the dog and . . .

"Well, stick your foot under the faucet, for goodness sakes, and rinse it off in the tub," Peggy replied, stifling her laughter. "Or stick it in the toilet and flush!"

So began another day in the glamorous, fast-paced, and sometimes seriously weird world of the lady of Llangollen Farm, known to everyone as Liz.

Mary Elizabeth Altemus—later married to a series of men named

Whitney, Person, Lunn and Tippett—was Whittingham's first patron, and perhaps his most important. It was an odd match, one that took some getting used to. He was a mid-twentieth century "man's man" raised on the rough edge of society. She was a Philadelphia belle, an elaborate hostess and financially independent enough to look upon Whittingham as a hired hand if she felt so moved. Yes, there were women in racing, but it was still very much a male world.

Of course, Liz was like no other woman. She was an expert rider and handler of all types of horses. She and Whittingham clicked with a deep and abiding affection for animals. As a famously indulgent dog lover, however, she sometimes took things to eccentric extremes, as anyone who visited Llangollen's canine heaven could testify. Whittingham, for his part, could deal with the hounds as long as Liz held up her end of the relationship as one of the foremost breeders and owners of Thoroughbred racehorses in North America.

With a daring mixture of breeding and buying, Liz maintained that level for nearly two decades, from the early 1950s to the late 1960s, when the vast majority of her best runners were trained by Charlie Whittingham. She liked to call him Sir Charles.

Charlie knew Liz because Liz knew Luro. And Luro knew Liz because she was a beautiful woman with position, money and horses. It was a natural attraction, one that Luro found impossible to resist. Liz, between marriages at the time, dallied with Luro and let him train a few of her horses. Her pet name for the stylish senor was Poontang.

In the winter of 1948, after Whittingham got Luro's letter of separation, it was Liz who stepped up to rescue Charlie. Her Llangollen Farm, in the horse country of Upperville, Virginia, cranked out a solid product. Liz knew her horses, and knew them well. When the farm sent Whittingham a young colt or filly, it came fully equipped with a set of high expectations from the owner.

Theirs was a classic relationship fueled by a healthy amount of creative tension. Whittingham would tell Liz that a certain horse "couldn't beat a fat man up a hill." Liz would tell Sir Charles to can it. She supplied the horses. It was his job to pipe down and train them. And never forget—they were her pets, her babies, her darlings.

"What are you doing?" Whittingham once spotted Liz with a handful of carrots, feeding a stakes horse who had just come back from an exercise at the track.

"I'm giving *my* horse a treat," Liz replied, apparently oblivious to Whittingham's post-exercise routine, which definitely did not include an immediate ration of carrots.

"It might be your horse, but these are my stalls and he lives in one of them."

Whittingham trained them his own way, in his own good time. As a result, between 1953 and 1959, Liz had the best years of her racing life. First, there was Porterhouse, a son of the South American champion Endeavour, who was imported by Liz in 1947. In 1953, Porterhouse became Whittingham's first champion, thanks to victories in the National Stallion Stakes at Belmont Park, the Christiana Stakes at Delaware Park, and the prestigious Futurity Stakes back at Belmont Park in October. Three years later, Mister Gus bloomed into a top five-year-old, setting an American record on the grass and winning major races in New York, Los Angeles and Chicago.

In the winter of 1956, Liz pulled the ultimate folly. She delivered unto Whittingham a horse by the name of Corn Husker and told him to set his sights high, despite the fact that the West Coast Llangollen string already included such proven older performers as Porterhouse, Mister Gus and Social Climber. Corn Husker was a three-year-old gelded son of Endeavour who had run for a $10,000 claiming price at age two, had broken his maiden at three in New York, and had most recently won a sprint race in Maryland. In between, to Whittingham's horror, he was a jumper.

"You're sending me a hurdler?" growled Whittingham over the phone. "Don't bother."

"I'll breed them, you train them," snapped Liz. "Then we'll get along just fine."

Corn Husker was a jumper because Liz wanted to win a steeplechase at

Belmont Park named for Louis E. Stoddard, a close family friend. The leggy Corn Husker rose to the occasion and won the Stoddard, plus one other steeplechase event. Now it was Whittingham's job to turn him back into a flat racing machine.

Before long, Charlie discovered that Corn Husker could run. Really run. Based on Corn Husker's obvious stamina, the trainer formulated an ambitious plan that included nothing less than the Santa Anita Handicap as the ultimate goal. His cause was aided by the early announcement of weights for the Handicap in those days. When the assignments came out in late December for the ninety-two nominees, Corn Husker was given just 104 pounds. Whittingham's next stop was the Caliente future book, where Corn Husker was hung up at a 100-to-1 in the unlikely event he would win the Santa Anita Handicap. Charlie bet all he could afford.

Corn Husker popped with a big race right out of the box, winning the San Gabriel Handicap on New Year's Day, 1957. Liz could not resist an "I told you so." But Whittingham didn't care. "We're still looking toward the big one," he told everyone. Corn Husker's future book price proceeded to plunge.

Eddie Arcaro, nearing the end of his career, was the first-string jockey for the Llangollen horses at Santa Anita that winter. As such, it was his choice to ride either Social Climber or Corn Husker in the Santa Anita Handicap. He wanted Corn Husker badly. But not badly enough to cut off a hand or a foot in order to make the weight. The best Arcaro could do was 109 pounds. "Not good enough," said Whittingham, who intended to take advantage of every ounce.

So Liz and Charlie turned to Ralph Neves, a legendary weight-loser who defied his anorexic lifestyle by owning a popular local restaurant named Talk o' the Town. Neves starved himself down to 105—close enough—and the light weight helped Corn Husker win the Handicap by half a length. As the horse received hugs and kisses from Liz right there in the winner's circle, Neves dismounted, weighed out and announced, "Man, lead me to some food." Charlie, for his part, gave Liz full credit for the Corn Husker coup.

Arcaro was reunited with Corn Husker a few weeks later for the San Juan Capistrano Handicap, although the rider nearly blew the mount when Liz found him still out on the town at four o'clock on the morning of the race.

"You little son of a bitch, I'm taking you off my horse," Liz threatened.

"You're not gonna take me off because there ain't no son of a bitch out there that can beat me riding him," Arcaro shot back.

So Arcaro rode, and won the race, but it wasn't all that easy on just a few hours sleep. "I never screwed it up so bad in my life," Arcaro said. "Must've got shut off a hundred times. He won by a head and it should have been five lengths."

In August of 1955, during the Saratoga meet, the Whittinghams rented a house overlooking Lake Saratoga. It was an idyllic setting, complete with panoramic vistas and private boathouse, owned by a Syracuse priest who used it as a quiet, off-season retreat. As the Whittinghams were settling in, the priest pulled up in a limousine, showered them with red roses, and told them to help themselves to the wine in his well-stocked cellar. Thus consecrated, Charlie and Peggy commenced to enjoy themselves without remorse.

At a dinner party—one of many—Liz arrived with her usual canine entourage. The great Dane was particularly bothersome, meandering among the guests and knocking highball glasses this way and that with his wagging, harpoon of a tail. Liz, ever oblivious, made lovey-dovey sounds whenever the Dane waltzed by.

At eight o'clock, Charlie called for dinner. Peggy walked inside from the screened porch to check on the arrangements at the large round table in the dining room. To her horror, there was nothing set out, only a couple of pieces of pork roast on a plate.

"What's happened to the food?" she demanded of the servant attending the table. "I know I saw it out here earlier."

"Dog ate it, ma'am," the servant replied. "The big dog it was. Left that bowl of cucumbers in sour cream is all."

Peggy broke the news to Charlie, and Charlie confronted Liz.

"Your god damn dog ate our dinner!"

"Oh, good," Liz replied. "He hasn't been eating well lately."

In keeping with her unpredictable personality, Liz fired and rehired Whittingham a couple of times during their decades together. Because of his growing reputation, Whittingham was able to bring in fresh horses owned by a growing supply of rich and influential patrons. They were mostly businessmen and industrialists, but one of them was a woman of considerable means, from a well-regarded family, whose love of horses dated back to her youth, and who just happened to be named Mary Elizabeth. Liz Whitney reincarnate? Not hardly. Mary Florsheim Jones was in a class by herself.

As a fledgling owner, Mary Jones—she had been married to musical star Alan Jones—brought an anemic dowry to her beginnings with Whittingham. She had been dallying with claiming horses, afraid to lose them but reluctant to spend enough money to escape to a higher level. Her stable was down to a pair of sad creatures named Quasar and Lauriebird.

"Moo cows is what they were," Whittingham said. "We traded one of them for a Ribot mare, then sent the new mare to Kentucky, where she was killed in a barn fire. The other one we were lucky to lose for eight thousand."

Mary was devastated. As Lauriebird was led off, a red claiming tag dangling from her halter, Charlie said, "How about a drink?" and took her to the clubhouse bar. "A double?" asked Whittingham. "How about a triple?" replied Mary. The vodka flowed.

"Charlie always said that 'drinking in the daytime ruins drinking at night,'" Mary said. "So we never drank at the races, except that once. Not long after that he found Duncan Junction for me. The first look I got, the horse had these ugly pin-fire scars and saddle sweat marks. He cost me $30,000. I begged Charlie not to tell anyone I paid that much for a horse."

When it came right down to it, Mary Jones knew very little about the finer points of being an owner of Thoroughbred racehorses. Her childhood background was as a spectator at the side of her grandfather, Milton Florsheim, the shoe company founder who also served as a director of

Arlington Park near Chicago. As a result, she was deeply dependent upon Whittingham, right down to such basics as where to sit and where to stand.

"What the hell you doing way up here?" Whittingham wondered when he found Mary at a table near the rafters at Hollywood Park on the day in July of 1967 when Duncan Junction was running in the Hollywood Derby. "You've got a horse in the Derby. You ought to be down there somewhere."

"But Charlie, he's 30-to-1," Jones innocently replied. "I guess they think this is where I belong."

Duncan Junction finished second that day to the Whittingham-trained Tumble Wind, providing a vivid lesson in the good news-bad news aspects of having a horse with Charlie. Shortly afterwards, Duncan Junction was dispatched to Chicago. Jones was there to witness his first start at Arlington Park, which resulted in her first victory as a racehorse owner. To her ever-lasting delight, it occurred in front of her hometown friends and family.

"I literally didn't know what to do," she recalled. "I was so busy talking to people and shaking hands, I didn't realize I was supposed to head straight for the winner's circle. By the time I got there Charlie was fuming."

Charlie would sometimes rage at Mary for one reason or another, but it was mostly just tough-guy steam. She would counter with, "Oh, Charlie, what would you do if you didn't have me to abuse?" After awhile, they became the racetrack version of Oscar Madison and Felix Unger, an odd couple with a "can't live with 'em, can't live without 'em" relationship.

Because Mary Jones did not breed her own horses at first, she relied upon Whittingham as her agent to find runners in the marketplace. Whittingham usually bought a piece of the horse to soothe Mary's nerves. In the beginning, he rooted around in the bargain basement. He found an inexpensive Limelight colt called Lime and another by Command Pilot, a horse he had trained years before. Mary, frustrated when a series of names were rejected by The Jockey Club, finally dubbed the colt "Whittingham" in honor of her trainer.

"If he's any good, he's named after me," Charlie responded. "If he's a bum, I'll say you named him after brother Joe."

Whittingham wasn't a bum. Far from it. The first time he won at Santa

Anita, track announcer Joe Hernandez got so excited as the colt made his move that he boomed, "And here comes Charlie!" On April 11, 1970, two days before the two-legged Whittingham celebrated his 57th birthday, he won both divisions of the Will Rogers Stakes at Hollywood Park. First came Lime, winning by a nose. Then it was Whittingham's turn, but he had to survive a scrape with the rail at the top of the stretch and then run like the wind to catch Colorado King Jr., his stablemate.

Euphoric from her sweep in the Will Rogers, Jones was all ears when Whittingham told her later that summer a horse called Cougar was for sale. Cougar was a Chilean colt of reasonable promise, imported by Joe Hernandez and on the market for about $60,000. When Cougar won a minor stakes race, setting a record on the Del Mar grass, the price went to $80,000. Jones balked. Cougar won again, and then finished a close second to the Whittingham ace, Daryl's Joy, in the Del Mar Handicap. Jones had seen enough. She wrote the check for $125,000, and Cougar was hers.

Legend has it that Whittingham was in for a share of Cougar from the beginning. In fact, it was almost a year later, after Cougar had run up about $400,000 for Jones, that Whittingham made her an offer. Mary said no, way too low, but Whittingham had taken his best shot and was not in the mood to dicker. His loss, he admitted, after Cougar retired with more than a million dollars in earnings.

But if Jones ever is tempted to feel smug about keeping one hundred per cent of Cougar, she need only summon forth the memory of Ack Ack, who went up for sale in January of 1971 when his owner, Capt. Harry Guggenheim, was gravely ill. At the time, Ack Ack was the best horse in the Whittingham stable, rivaled only by Cougar.

"Charlie gave me first chance to buy Ack Ack," Mary ruefully recalled. "The price was $400,000. He offered to go half and half, but his commission was ten per cent. If he was going to own part of the horse, I thought his commission should come off the top and said so. Charlie saw it different. I didn't get Ack Ack."

Ack Ack, carrying the colors of Greer Garson and Buddy Fogelson, was North American Horse of the Year for 1971.

Good times and a bounty of winners dimmed the near miss with Ack Ack. Jones—who later married businessman Bob Bradley—turned into "the luckiest owner I know," as described by Whittingham. Good horses popped up with regularity for Mary and her partners. Her red colors were carried by Greinton, Swingtime, Riot in Paris, Live the Dream, Our Suiti Pie, Exploded, Handsome One and Castilla.

After awhile she was more a pal than a patron, enjoying beer brunches with Charlie at the Bluebird Cafe, or crawling around on all fours in the Belmont grandstand with her trainer alongside, cursing her luck and searching in vain for the winning tickets they had torn up by mistake. Occasionally, the friendship would strain over a horse or a race. Whittingham would unleash a mighty barrage of Marine Corps vocabulary into the telephone. His staff would smile nervously and take cover, imagining Mary shriveling to dust on the other end of the line.

"Ah, but they weren't hearing my end of it," Mary said. "And remember, Charlie likes to show off a bit. He loves an audience. He would talk very badly to me in front of people, then later that night he would innocently ask, 'So, what's new?' " Mary and Peggy became fast friends, in spite of their rude introduction. That was the day Charlie hauled Mary home on their way to a horse sale, little knowing or caring the house was still a mess from the party the night before, and that Peggy was bedded down with what was rapidly becoming the flu. Naturally, the trainer's wife felt obliged to impress the new patron. She also wanted to strangle her husband.

"Far be it for Charlie to give me some warning," Peggy recalled with a grimace. "We had some caviar left over, so that was okay, and there was some chili, too. I warmed it up while I went to put on some makeup. I was feeling awful, then the chili burned. So that was Mary's first meal in our home. Burnt chili and caviar."

Peggy Boone Whittingham was accustomed to such social improvisations. To that point, her life as the wife of a well-known Thoroughbred horse trainer had been a creative blend of social excitement and domestic compromise. Their relationship began with a whirlwind romance and had survived through early years as hotel-hopping vagabonds before settling into a suburban California lifestyle dictated by the routines of the race-track.

In the late summer of 1944, as the Allies fought their way through Northern France and bore down on the Japanese at Iwo Jima, Peggy Boone was a lithe, sloe-eyed nineteen-year-old college girl in the coastal plain town of Rocky Mount, North Carolina. She was the second of five children of Ted and Beulah Boone, local storekeepers and upright citizens. Their daughter was an independent-minded young woman who worked as a secretary for the local chief of police. She reorganized the department filing system, updated sloppy records, and became certified in the use of a .38 caliber revolver. To support the war effort and help bolster troop morale, she once made a stack of her police identification photograph and handed them out to soldiers and sailors departing on the local train.

Wartime Rocky Mount was located in the recreational crossfire between the Marines of Camp Lejeune, the soldiers of Fort Bragg and the sailors of Norfolk, Virginia. As such, things occasionally got a little rowdier than the depleted Rocky Mount police force could handle. Chief Red Thomas was stuck with nothing but old men and 4-F rejects to patrol the streets, so he sent up an SOS to the Camp Lejeune commandant requesting a detachment of military police. Among the assigned Marines was Sgt. Charles E. Whittingham, thin as a rail after his latest bout with recurring malaria. Whittingham did his first shift on the streets of Rocky Mount during the summer of 1944.

Peggy was just back from a stint at Louisburg College studying commercial law when she first laid eyes on the tall, lanky sergeant. He was earthy and charming, more a young Walter Brennan than Errol Flynn. As an MP he was hardly a crimebuster. Drunken sailors and brawling soldiers got a night to sleep it off, then Whittingham would cut them loose. "It didn't take me long to figure out that if I arrested everybody I was supposed to and did all the paperwork, I'd be spending all my time testifying at court martials," Charlie said. "I had better things to do with my time."

Like court Peggy Boone? Heck, that took no time at all. Never mind that she had a boyfriend at sea somewhere in the Atlantic Ocean. Over the howls of her mother and quiet rebuke of her father, she announced their engagement and said her vows, almost all in one breath. They spent two dollars for the license (Peggy's treat) and appeared before a Presbyterian minister in the nearby town of Wilson. The date was October 12, 1944, barely six weeks after they had met.

"I remember looking over at Charlie while lying in bed the next morning," Peggy recalled. "He was still sleeping. I thought to myself, 'Well, I'm not quite sure this was exactly what I had in mind when I dreamed about a husband—this skinny guy who's already losing his hair.' But there was something so appealing about his charm and his self-confidence. He was so sure of himself, so convinced that what he did was always right. I found it to be . . . very sexy."

It took Peggy's parents awhile to recover from the shock, but soon they succumbed to Charlie's charm. "He was like nothing they had ever known," she said. "Not only was he twelve years older than me, he was a divorced Catholic, and a 'foreigner' from California. He said words I'm sure they'd never heard uttered in their home, where if you said 'darn' you got in trouble. Before the war he was some kind of horse trader— that's what I thought he said—and he planned to go back to doing it after the war. Pretty soon, though, my mother was won over. She couldn't do enough for Charlie. Of course, she was still mad at me."

Whittingham provided no handbook for a trainer's wife. Peggy had to make it up as they went along. Her knowledge of horses was zero.

"Oh, look Charlie. What a pretty gray horse," exclaimed Peggy as she looked out the train car window on their way north to New York.

"That's a mule," Whittingham said, shaking his head. "Gal, have you got a lot to learn."

When they arrived on the New York racing scene in 1946, Charlie took it all in stride. Eventually he was dressing like the stylish Luro and spreading around hundred dollar bills from a thick wad in his pocket. Peggy, on the other hand, found New York racing society as strange as the dark side of the moon.

"The first thing they asked you was when you 'came out,' " she said. "All the women talked the same and even had identical handwriting, depending upon which private school they attended. Your background was all that mattered. It never bothered Charlie. He could get away with anything and they would have loved him. He could have drooled in his plate and it wouldn't have mattered! But a woman couldn't."

Although it appeared as if he was having nothing but fun, Whittingham worked as hard in the evenings as he did during the day. He preferred Peggy to stay clear while he networked his way through the racing and society crowds at parties and restaurants. Standing there in her homemade clothes, her youth and her southern accent glaring like a neon sign, she would chat with whomever she could. After awhile, she sensed the cold shoulder. "What have I done wrong?" she asked a sympathetic friend. "Don't you know?" came the reply. "They're all jealous of your youth, especially when they see their husbands talking to you."

Life was unconventional, to say the least. In the first four years of their marriage, while Charlie ran Luro's stable, the Whittinghams shuttled between Long Island in the spring, Saratoga in the summer, back to the Island in the fall, and then off to winter quarters in Camden, South Carolina, or to the Santa Anita meeting out West. Their first son, Michael Charles, was born in April of 1946 in Rocky Mount, where Peggy had stopped on the way back to New York. Charlie went on ahead and missed the blessed event. They lived in hotels, in racetrack cottages and in tiny guest houses on lavish estates. They borrowed furniture, dined in swank restaurants and lived off the roll in Charlie's pocket. Eventually, Luro took Whittingham aside and advised, "Chuck, I think you should open a bank account."

Their daughter, Charlene, was born in November of 1950. In January of 1953 came Taylor, son number two. By then Peggy was spending most of her time juggling boxes and trunks, nannies and pet dogs. The family needed roots, and she found them in Sierra Madre, a quaint little hillside community just north of Santa Anita Park. In the winter of 1955 they rented a modest house tucked into a tree-lined street. They nicknamed it

Sleepy Hollow. The following year, when the owner was looking to sell, Peggy told Charlie they ought to buy. The price was $24,000.

"Where are we gonna get that kind of cash?" Charlie protested.

"We don't need to get it all," Peggy said. "We can take out a mortgage for most of it."

"I don't like to go into that kind of debt," Charlie growled. "I'd rather pay as I go."

"Okay, Charlie, but you realize living in a hotel or renting a place costs more than a monthly mortgage payment?"

In the spring of 1956, the house on Lowell Avenue became the property of the Whittinghams. Peggy could stop her constant packing and unpacking. The children found schools they could stick with. Charlie, of course, still traveled with the horses wherever and whenever he had to, without giving it a second thought, and sometimes Peggy went along. When she did, she pined for the kids back home with the nanny. If she stayed in Sierra Madre, she longed for her husband.

"I called a hotel once in Miami where Charlie was staying and asked for their guest registered as Whittingham. A woman answered the phone. I said, 'Who's this?' and she said 'Mrs. Whittingham.' Great, I thought, now he's letting them use my name. As it turned out, she *was* a Whittingham from someplace in New England. For all I know, she could have been a distant relative, from the family of Charlie's uncle who stayed in Maine.

"That didn't let him off the hook, though. There was a time in Saratoga—we'd been married for fifteen years—when I was talking to a woman who went there every year. When she found out who I was she said, quite surprised, 'I didn't know Charlie was married!' "

CHAPTER 4

MONEY MEN

"Get yourself a good horse, son, and you'll dine with kings."

Charlie Whittingham was heading back to his barn at Bay Meadows one afternoon with Sandy and Buddy Hirsch when they spotted a line of horses being led down the stable road. The horses looked uncomfortably familiar.

"What the hell?" Whittingham recognized every one of them. They were his—or, more accurately, they belonged to Maj. C. C. Moseley, Whittingham's primary patron at the time—and they were being spirited away from Whittingham's shedrow to be taken who knows where.

"Charlie, what's happening?" cried Sandy Hirsch.

"Damned if I know," Whittingham replied. "Guess I'd better find out."

Whittingham knew exactly what had happened, and no one who knew Charlie was surprised. The next morning, as Dr. Jack Robbins made his backstretch rounds, he looked in on Whittingham and found only a few horses surrounded by empty stalls. Robbins was aghast.

"The man wanted me to blister all his horses," Whittingham said in answer to Robbins' amazement. "I told him it wasn't such a good idea. He told me to do it anyway. So I told him where to put the peaches."

Translation? Well, in his own way, using his own bedrock brand of the king's English, Whittingham was telling a wealthy patron that input of a technical nature regarding the handling of his Thoroughbred investment was not welcome. Any further interference, no matter how well meant, would be taken as a vote of no confidence regarding Whittingham's care and management of the investment. Quite simply, the patron needed to learn to live with his role as a quiet, reliable resource of capital, then sit back and enjoy the sport in a ceremonial capacity. Yes, there is money to be made, Whittingham would maintain. But not with me if the patron insists upon constant meddling.

Whittingham's philosophy derives from the same inner strength of character that powers any number of successful professionals: enormous, unflagging self-confidence. Training a Thoroughbred racehorse to run as fast and as far as his natural ability will allow is a strange and difficult way to make a living. But Whittingham never gave a second thought to his odd job description. He simply learned everything there was to learn about the Thoroughbred, cutting away the distractions and the non-essentials, and discovered a modus operandi that could be fine-tuned, but never improved. To question Whittingham's handling of a horse was to question his very soul.

There were supremely successful businessmen who found the Whittingham approach reassuring. Nelson Bunker Hunt, the larger-than-life Texas oil and mineral baron. Charles Wacker, the Chicago trading whiz. William du Pont of the chemical dynasty. Millard Waldheim, Midwestern real estate developer. Arthur Stollery, Canadian mining and cattle tycoon. Howard B. Keck, the president of Superior Oil.

Keck's roots in horse racing went back to the mid-1950s when he bought a group of broodmares from the stable of Elizabeth Arden Graham. By the early 1960s, he had enjoyed moderate success—his best horse to that point had been Bagdad, winner of the Hollywood Derby and second in the 1959 Belmont Stakes—but the performance of his horses on the track was beginning to lag behind their potential on paper. And so he began observing Whittingham from afar.

Within days of the departure of the Moseley horses in the fall of 1964, Whittingham received a call at Bay Meadows Racetrack from a fellow who identified himself as Howard Keck.

"I'd like to talk with you, but I'd rather not do it over the telephone. I'll tell you this much: I'm going to make a trainer change. For my own reasons. Can you be in my Los Angeles office at six o'clock Monday morning?"

Already, Whittingham liked Keck's style. He especially liked his hours. Obviously, here was a fellow workhorse who hated to waste daylight.

"I looked at other trainers," Keck said. "Noble Threewitt, Buddy Hirsch. Hiring Charlie was a sheer guess on my part. But before I hired Charlie I always thought he displayed good judgment in placing his horses where they belonged. It didn't take long for me to confirm that opinion. He knows the ability of a given horse and the ability of the competition. As a result, you never feel you've wasted that horse. You know exactly what you've got."

Whittingham was invigorated by the Keck connection. He shipped south to Santa Anita and polished up a set of fresh webbings and buckets in anticipation of the new arrivals. Unfortunately, there were no champions among them.

"Keck really didn't have much at the time," Whittingham noted. "Then before long everything I ran for him started to win. There was one horse I just threw into a race against Hill Rise—didn't think he had a shot—and he almost won. Made me look like a genius."

Whittingham began to put Keck's red and charcoal gray silks on the map with regularity. Keck's first draft of two-year-olds with Whittingham included Saber Mountain and Drin, both beautifully bred colts with classic potential. But Saber Mountain was too precocious for his tender age, and Drin was a laid-back character who clearly needed a mile or more to display his true ability.

With such an influential new patron to impress, anyone else might have felt the pressure to crank up the Keck colts as soon as possible and win, win, win. Charlie, true to his colors, waited until late in the year before bringing them out for the races, and it paid off. They won six stakes between them in 1966.

Over the years the list of Keck stakes winners grew to more than two dozen. Whittingham and Keck were able to work together like fingers on a strong hand. Keck's passion was breeding, aided and abetted by A. B. "Bull" Hancock at Claiborne Farm. Keck supplied the product then backed off, leaving the development and training to Whittingham.

Occasionally, Keck would appear at Whittingham's barn at dawn and spend a few hours before heading to his office. For the most part, however, Keck stayed in the background, affording Whittingham the privacy he deserved in his trainer's domain.

"He never second-guesses you, never bothers you, no matter what's going on," Whittingham said. Even when Keck was embroiled in other matters—his struggle for control of Superior Oil with his brother, William Keck, or his noisy divorce from his wife and fellow horse owner, Elizabeth—Whittingham saw no ripples with the horses. "I think he likes coming out in the mornings sometimes," Whittingham said, "just to get away from everything else he's dealing with."

Of course, they had their occasional disagreements. "I always wanted to run my horses a little sooner than Charlie," Keck pointed out—a familiar complaint. "But I certainly can't fault him for doing it his way."

His way. Or the highway. Whittingham was an honor graduate of the old school; and the old school taught its students that Thoroughbred trainers must act as if they were infallible. One rule never changed: no matter how successful or rich, no matter what his standing in business and social circles, a patron could never know enough to criticize Whittingham's management. Aaron Jones, whose best runners with Whittingham included La Zanzara and Miss Musket, figured that out early.

"Once you got to know him, you never doubted him when he told you something about a horse," Jones said. "If ever there was a man who could look into the middle of a six-inch rock, it was Charlie."

When the classy colt Ack Ack came West to Whittingham in late 1969, the trainer took one look at him and prescribed a pin-firing for an irritated splint bone. Whittingham did not bother to consult Ack Ack's owner, the respected Capt. Harry F. Guggenheim, who was at that time hospitalized and in the last months of his life. When Whittingham finally reached Guggenheim, the Captain was firm when it came to Ack Ack's shin.

"I don't believe in pin-firing," he said.

"Too late," Whittingham replied.

From early in the game, Charlie became resigned to a rule of thumb that never failed. The better a horse, the more an owner was tempted to interfere. There were exceptions, of course. But only to prove the rule.

In the spring of 1960, Liz Tippett sent a well-regarded New York bone specialist to Kentucky to examine her Derby hopeful, Eagle Admiral. The colt had come out of a work dead lame. After viewing the X-rays, Whittingham and his vet, Dr. Alex Harthill, diagnosed the injury as a slab fracture of the third carpal bone in the knee.

"That's no fracture," chimed in the bone specialist, who was holding the X-rays wrong. "That's his patella. We can just put a little cortisone in there and we can run him."

Unfortunately, the equine patella is situated in the hind leg. Once again, Whittingham was amazed at how some people thought his business was so simple. "Maybe he'll run for you," Charlie said. "But he won't run for me."

Of course, Whittingham is always predisposed to enjoy the patrons for whom he trains. For instance, his admiration for Serge Fradkoff was sincere. No owner of Charlie's ever played the races like Fradkoff, a diamond merchant and Swiss banker who bet thousands and thousands at a time. Whittingham normally shies away from patrons who are heavy bettors on their own horses. Winning and losing is tough enough without the added pari-mutuel pressure. But, as far as Whittingham is concerned, no serious player handled it better than Fradkoff. The stylish Fradkoff barely blinked when Perrault—the horse he owned in partnership with Baron Thierry von Zuylen—was disqualified after finishing first in the 1982 Santa Anita Handicap. The bet was ten thousand.

But Fradkoff, like many of Whittingham's owners, could get frustrated by a lack of forthright communication from his legendary trainer. Whittingham traditionally offers an owner as much as he thinks they need to know. Usually, that includes the date of the race and the post position draw. Any more than that, he figures, would only be misinterpreted.

"Owners are like mushrooms," Whittingham liked to say in his most mischievous moments. "You've got to keep them in the dark and covered with plenty of shit."

During the spring of 1982, Whittingham's operation sprung an innocent little leak, and Fradkoff was getting reports on Perrault's condition as the Hollywood Gold Cup approached.

One morning, about a week before the race, Fradkoff put in a call to the Whittingham stable from his home in Switzerland.

"Charlie, hello," said the effusive Fradkoff. "Are we going to run in the Gold Cup?"

Whittingham, interrupted during training hours, tried to cut it short. "Yep, we're running."

"Well, Charlie, I heard a rumor that Perrault isn't doing so well."

Whittingham smelled blood.

"You did, huh? Well, Serge, I heard a rumor that you're an asshole. But I don't believe every rumor I hear."

Perrault won the Gold Cup.

Because he got results, and because his operation was so thoroughly organized and well run, Whittingham's philosophy of passive patronage went down well with a majority of his owners. Far from taking horses away, they lined up three deep to place their expensive, talented animals in his care. While most trainers spent a healthy chunk of their time hustling for clients, Whittingham could pick and choose. Word was, if you didn't have a stakes horse, don't bother Charlie.

Aaron Jones was already well established in the Northwest lumber business when he approached Whittingham in the winter of 1972. Jones, a rookie to horse racing, had what he thought was a promising colt named Tumalo (after the Oregon town). As far as he knew, Whittingham was the best trainer in the game.

Jones went looking for Whittingham and found him busy at a pile of paperwork in his Santa Anita stable office. Outside, circling on the tow ring or standing peacefully in their stalls, there were horses named Cougar and Quack, Tallahto and Le Cle, Groshawk, Kennedy Road and Belle Marie, every one a top-class animal. Charlie peered over the top of his reading glasses and fixed his bird-of-prey stare as Jones explained that he had a nice colt, that he was getting into the Thoroughbred business, and that he wanted Whittingham to train his horses. If he wouldn't mind.

Whittingham nodded. Or at least he made some kind of movement that signified "keep talking." Jones went on about the colt, then began fishing for some kind of response. Charlie obliged with a "send him on, we'll see what he's got," and Jones had his trainer. Later, he told friends he had approached Whittingham.

"They told me I had no shot," Jones recalled. "Whittingham was too big. He'd never take me on. I guess I didn't know enough to worry, because Whittingham had said yes. Anyway, it didn't take me long to get on his good side. I found out his favorite drink was Bombay gin."

Whittingham has been showered with gifts from grateful owners who find that mere words—plus ten per cent of the purse—are not enough to pay for the thrill of victory in a show-stopping race. He's got watches for every day of the year, scores of crystal doodads, and enough autographed photos from the rich and famous to build a bonfire two stories high.

(Strangely enough, the only photograph that deserves constant display in his racetrack office is the image of Ferdinand giving Whittingham his first Kentucky Derby.)

As a child of unglamorous roots, Whittingham is an avid stargazer and a lifelong fan of the glittery and the famous. Those who have earned public recognition for their accomplishments impress him greatly, whether it be Jonas Salk or Andre the Giant. But if Whittingham ever had a shy moment, no one has noticed. When in the company of mainstream celebrities he is as comfortable as twelve-year-old scotch, disarming them with the same bawdy humor that wears just as well back at the barn.

Nose to nose with England's Queen Mother at Woodbine Racetrack near Toronto, Canada, Whittingham talked horses and asked if she cashed a bet. Actors, to Whittingham, are a kick to be around, because their movies, he figures, lose as often as his horses. He has caroused with His Royal Highness the Aly Khan at Saratoga, glad-handed senators and governors with political aplomb, and slept in with Peggy while Judy Garland rustled up scrambled eggs and bacon downstairs in her Hollywood home. No, says Charlie, she didn't hum "Somewhere Over the Rainbow" while she cooked.

Sometimes Whittingham will allow a relationship with an owner to transcend pure business and slop over into being just plain pals. Garland's husband, Sid Luft, will attest to the time Whittingham saved his skin in a restaurant brawl near Santa Anita. "I said something. Two guys went for me, and Charlie—God bless him—jumped them both," Luft wistfully recalled.

Dana Tasker was editor of *Time* Magazine when Whittingham trained his horses, bought to provide an outlet for stress. As Charlie watched Tasker's knuckles go white and face turn red over a close race one day in New York, he was quick to see the potential heart attack ahead. "Dana," Charlie said, "I think you might want to try a different hobby."

Generation means nothing to Whittingham if you've got the right stuff. Howell Wynne, forty-five years Charlie's junior, was part-owner of Greinton with Whittingham and Mary Jones Bradley when they took the Hollywood Gold Cup winner to New York for the 1985 Breeders' Cup. Problem was, Whittingham was torn over where to run and how much to pay in late nomination penalties. Were he to run on the grass in the $2-million Turf, the ante was $240,000. To run in the Breeders' Cup Classic, worth $3-million, the cost was $360,000. Wynne wanted to roll the dice. He was willing to put up his thirty-seven per cent share of the $360,000.

"I want you to meet my partner," Whittingham called over to Penny Chenery, Secretariat's owner, at a party just prior to the Breeders' Cup. Charlie had Wynne in a hard arm clamp, so there was no escape. "This kid's got balls to his knees. Balls to his knees!"

In the late 1960s, Burt Bacharach was the toast of the popular music business. Anyone who didn't know the tunes "Promises, Promises" or "Do You Know the Way to San Jose?" had been living in a cave. Within two years, Bacharach had two Academy Awards—for the music to *Butch Cassidy and the Sundance Kid*—before Whittingham won his first Eclipse Award. When a mutual friend introduced them at Santa Anita in the winter of 1968, it was celebrity heaven. Bacharach was star-struck by Whittingham, and Whittingham was just as impressed by Bacharach, only Charlie didn't let on. After all, Bacharach wanted to buy a horse. Commerce came first.

Whittingham found a two-year-old named Battle Royal that cost Bacharach $15,000. That spring, during the Hollywood Park meeting, Battle Royal won his first start for the composer while running for a $15,000 claiming price. Bacharach was hooked. Later, Whittingham tried jumping the horse in class and putting him on the turf, but it was no use. Battle Royal was worth $15,000, and that's where he belonged. Back in he went for the claiming tag.

"I'm worried, Charlie," Bacharach said the morning of the race. "You think someone might take him for fifteen?"

"No way," the trainer answered. A few hours later, Battle Royal was claimed.

Bacharach was crushed. "Please, Charlie. Let's buy him back. Offer eighteen thousand."

Whittingham's cool head prevailed, and Bacharach let Battle Royal go. He did, however, follow his every race, up and down the state. One day, Battle Royal turned up in a $12,500 claiming race. Bacharach called Whittingham.

"Come on, Charlie, let's claim him."

Whittingham just shook his head, wondering what it would take to get Burt over Battle Royal.

"He'll lose today. Why don't you wait and you can get him for $8,500 the next time he runs."

Nothing doing. Bacharach was determined.

"Okay, boy," Whittingham sighed. "Bring a check for $12,500 and be there half an hour before the race. We'll claim your horse back for you."

Looking back, Bacharach laughed at his own naivete. "I know Charlie finally gave in just to get me off the phone," he said. "Of course, I didn't realize Charlie probably hadn't claimed a horse in forty years. He didn't even want to fill in the claim slip."

Whittingham and Bacharach became good friends, and a few good horses followed. "Coming from a very highly geared, over-stated business like the music business, or show business—where everything is 'smash, boffo, big hit'—it was always refreshing for me to be around someone like

51

Charlie," Bacharach said. "He never gets too wound up about success, or the grief. A horse runs a fifth of a second off the track record, he's not suddenly 'the best god damn horse in the world.' He's a 'nice' horse."

Advance Guard won three stakes races for Bacharach in 1971, the same year he won his Oscars for *Butch Cassidy and the Sundance Kid*. Later, a colt named Crumbs won a "nice" pot at Del Mar. Charlie would regale Bacharach with old racetrack stories and Marine Corps tales, while charming the socks off Bacharach's wife, actress Angie Dickinson. At the Whittinghams' post-race parties in Sierra Madre, Burt would sit down at the piano and entertain guests. Charlie and Peggy flew to Lake Tahoe to see the composer in concert, then afterwards, at the craps table, Whittingham waved his arms like a conductor, announcing for all to hear, "Hey, Bacharach, look. Nothing to it."

Through most of the 1970s, Bacharach and the Whittinghams were summertime neighbors on the beach at Del Mar. Sometimes, Burt and Charlie would find themselves hip deep in the Pacific, well into the wee hours, taking a brisk swim to settle the booze.

"Hey, Charlie," called out Burt one night as they bobbed offshore, "I want to see Nikkis Promise work. When?"

"Yeah? Well, he's working tomorrow morning. Come to the barn after the break and you can see him work. But you won't show. You can't get up that early. You don't know those hours, lad."

The next morning at eight-fifteen sharp, Bacharach waltzed into Whittingham's office. Charlie looked up and blinked.

"What are you doing here?"

"I came to see Nikkis Promise work, Charlie. You said he was working this morning."

"Oh shit. I worked him yesterday."

It was all part of Whittingham's education of a racehorse owner. Only there was no textbook, no curriculum, and no one ever knew for sure when class was in session. One time, when one of his horses was running, Bacharach made the mistake of asking Charlie the one question Charlie will never answer. At least not directly.

"How about it, Charlie? Do you like him today?"

"Boy, he's in the race, isn't he? And if I've put him in the race, he's got a chance. Same chance as the other eleven horses in there."

Bacharach wasn't any wiser. A few minutes later he encountered Dr. Robert Kerlan, the noted orthopedic surgeon and longtime Whittingham crony. "You're kidding," Kerlan said. "You're the owner, and you don't know! Charlie loves your horse today. Everybody's betting."

Class dismissed.

"There came a time when some of my horses just didn't fit Charlie's stable," Bacharach said. "They seemed to spend all their time training at San Luis Rey"—the training center supervised by Joe Whittingham—"and never showing up at the races. I asked him if it would be all right to move them to another trainer. Asked him! There was something off about that. But that's how Charlie makes you feel. He's a very special man, and you feel a tremendous loyalty to him. It's like you don't want to hurt his feelings."

About the same time, Aaron Jones was grappling with a similar dilemma. Whittingham had shifted a number of Jones' lesser runners to the stable of his son, Michael Whittingham, who was not reluctant to send horses far and wide in search of opportunities. Mike also was trying to establish himself as a trainer on his own. Jones, still fairly new to the business, did not like the way the switch was handled. He sensed a move was necessary. But how did one divorce an institution?

"How did you get your horses away from Charlie?" Jones inquired of Bacharach.

"Well, you pay the bills, man," replied the composer. "You just do it."

When an owner goes south, Whittingham does not put up a fight. He refuses to hold a grudge. In fact, there is considerable evidence supporting the theory that Whittingham never lost an owner that he wanted to keep. "Charlie would never really tell you to leave and take your horses," said one of them. "But he would do things to open the door a crack. And you would part on good terms."

Scores and scores of horse owners have moved through Whittingham's life in his sixty years at the track. From rough and tumble bar owners in the 1930s to the society dames and industrial giants of his flourishing years. However, when it comes to the best horses over the long haul, four single patrons represent more than thirty-five per cent of all Whittingham's nearly two hundred and fifty stakes winners: Liz Tippett, Howard Keck, Mary Jones Bradley and Nelson Bunker Hunt.

The first horse Hunt sent to Whittingham was Dahlia, the richest mare to have raced in Europe. By the time Whittingham got her in late 1975, Dahlia was a real sour gal, as fast as ever but ready for the breeding shed. Whittingham handled her with kid gloves, giving her the time and patience she needed. Miraculously, he was able to engineer one more major moment for Dahlia, a victory in the 1976 Hollywood Turf Invitational over the best male grass horses in California.

Over the ensuing thirteen years, Whittingham trained at least seventeen stakes winners owned entirely or in part by Hunt. Even though Hunt finally divested himself of the last of his international Thoroughbred holdings in 1990—an outgrowth of his battle with U.S. government prosecution over his silver dealing—he still looks back at his racing days with fondness.

"I probably had a hundred different trainers over the years," Hunt said. "No doubt in my mind, Whittingham was number one. And the reason I think he's so good is because he started training when he was so young. He came up the hard way, and that's probably the best way to make a horse trainer."

The owner was a multi-billionaire, a proselytizing Christian and teetotaler; the trainer was a tough-as-nails, gin-drinking, lapsed Catholic. Other than a fondness for good racehorses, the acquisition of hard-earned money, and a decidedly right-wing political leaning, they had very little in common. For his part, Hunt required no particular bedside manner from his trainer. And that was fine with Whittingham.

"Charlie's always a pleasant fellow to be around," Hunt said. "Very social, and obviously well read and self-educated. But if I want laughs and good times, I'll go to a comedian. The last thing I want from my trainer is a line of bull."

Hunt continued: "Years before I had horses with Charlie, I heard it said that Whittingham is the only trainer in the world who can start five different horses in a race for five different owners and make each one of them feel they are getting a fair and equal shake. Later, when I was part of those entries, I found out why. Whittingham wouldn't tell you something he didn't believe. If he thought your horse could be third or fourth, he'd tell you. I've had trainers with fifteen different owners in the stable who told all fifteen they would win the Arc de Triomphe. Charlie's too smart to do that."

When all is said and done, Charlie Whittingham's primary patron through the decades has been . . . Charlie Whittingham. While Peggy was tugging in one direction for Charlie to invest in this house or that property, Whittingham spent his money on the one thing he knew best. Through the years, he ended up owning horses in partnership with dozens of people. Some of them enjoyed having Whittingham along as a security blanket. Others basked in the status of ownership with a Hall of Fame trainer. At least one person thought Charlie might try a little harder if he owned a piece of the animal.

"Ridiculous," said Hunt when he heard it. The thought truly was absurd, especially in light of a race such as the 1981 San Juan Capistrano Handicap, in which Charlie intended to run Obraztsovy, owned by Brian Sweeney and W. T. Pascoe, and Exploded, owned by Whittingham in partnership with Mary Jones Bradley and Nancy Anne Chandler, Howell Wynne's mother.

Sweeney, an owner who enjoyed involvement with his horses, was concerned about the soft grass course at Santa Anita. He suggested to Whittingham that perhaps Obraztsovy should stay in the barn and pass the San Juan. This, of course, was poaching on Whittingham's domain. "He runs," Whittingham said. "If he's still in the barn when they call for the horses, he runs."

Obraztsovy ran, and won, and beat second-place Exploded in the process. Whittingham the trainer had outsmarted Whittingham the owner to the tune of about $25,000.

That is the price Whittingham pays for his stubborn self-confidence. Imagine telling Ted Williams how to hit, or giving Jerry West a tip on his jump shot.

"Bacharach didn't like the way one of his horses ran one day." Charlie was making a point about the division of labor between an owner and a trainer. "He says, 'Well, do you think maybe he needs to be wormed?' I told him, 'Burt, I haven't heard too many hit songs coming out of your piano lately. Maybe you need to get that piano wormed.'"

CHAPTER 5

GIANTS FALL

"Never say anything bad about a horse until he's been dead at least ten years."

In the summer of 1956, the movie version of the Broadway musical *The King and I* opened in theaters across the land. Overnight, bald was beautiful. And on Yul Brynner—the indomitable, polygamous King of Siam—it was downright sexy.

About that time, Charlie Whittingham looked like any other prematurely bald guy with a sad little souvenir of his youth still clinging to the sides of his head. He wore hats, lots of hats, and doffed them to eye-opening surprise when in the company of unsuspecting strangers. Eventually, though, he grew tired of tending to the graying fringe left from the combination of relentless heredity and the lingering effects of malaria. Barbers were incompetent fools, unable to give the slightest comfort. Finally, Whittingham took things into his own hands. He sent Peggy on an errand.

"Can you find me some of those hair clippers they use?"

"Of course. What have you got in mind?"

"You'll see."

Now, Whittingham never has been a man to change course without compelling reason. He finds great solace in the familiar, and he is almost fanatical in his reluctance to part with loyal elements of the past. He continued to bank at Meadowbrook National in New Hyde Park, New York, long after he moved his stable to California. He has sport coats older than his children, and baggy, deep-ribbed corduroy pants that require carbon dating to determine their true age. Peggy once unearthed a formerly fine wool jacket, a gift from Luro, now moth-eaten down to its suede elbow patches. She wondered if maybe it was time to invest in a new version.

"The jacket's fine. Nothing wrong with it," Charlie snapped. "Just get it fixed."

"But Charlie, it would cost less to buy a new one."

"Just get it fixed."

But his hair? Well, face it, his hair had betrayed him, gone into ignominious retreat. Whittingham parted with most of it right away, leaving a short, clipped remnant. Then, when he switched to an electric razor for his beard, he just kept buzzing—up over the ears and around the back of the neck. The effect was liberating. He suddenly looked ageless. In the summertime at Del Mar, Charlie's dome would go a deep, burnished bronze. His thin eyebrows would bleach from the sun, leaving a countenance dominated by two blue eyes, bright as stained-glass windows.

For all it mattered to the horses, Whittingham could have worn a blond wig and danced an Irish jig (which he did, later on, during the celebration of his sixtieth birthday). In fact, the 1956 season marked not only the emancipation of Charlie's hair, but also the beginning of his reputation as a fearless iconoclast who enjoyed nothing better than winning a big race in the face of insurmountable odds.

To that point in his career, Whittingham had established a reputation as an opportunistic horseman who had parlayed his association with Luro into a decent public stable. In California he was called a New York trainer. In New York he was that guy from California. And although he did not win many stakes races—primarily because there were not that many around to win—he was respected for his high percentage of winners.

Deep into cocktail hour, as the Bombay gin drained steadily behind its ornate label, Whittingham would cast the evil eye on his drinking pals—fellow trainers all—and swear what amounted to a blood oath in their general direction.

"I can out-train all you sons-a-bitches," he would vow, fixing his low stare on each one in turn. "I'm going to run right over the top of you."

His drinking pals just smiled. "There he goes again," they thought. "The Marine flying high." The year was 1954, and none of the three other trainers lounging around the room felt particularly threatened. At the time,

Bill Winfrey was preoccupied with Native Dancer, the best horse in America. Buddy Hirsch was responsible for Rejected, the reigning Santa Anita Handicap champ, and a potent string for King Ranch. And Jimmy Jones ran a little outfit called Calumet Farm, the leading stable in the nation. All three were well on their way to the Hall of Fame, while Whittingham was a Charlie-come-lately, on his own for barely five years.

But even then—especially then—Whittingham was brimming with a giddy self-confidence that transcended the reality of his growing stable. He had become a single-minded fanatic who lived by the motto, "Be the best in town 'til the best comes 'round." Smart people remembered when he made promises. People like Sandy Hirsch, Buddy's wife.

"You know," Sandy Hirsch told Peggy Whittingham years later, "we laughed when Charlie said it. But that's exactly what he's done. He went past everyone."

Other than Porterhouse, his best horse of the early 1950s was Mab's Choice, a mare he bought from comedian Lou Costello. The Whittinghams raced Mab's Choice in a fifty-fifty partnership with Robert Howard, the youngest son of Charles S. Howard, owner of champions Seabiscuit, Kayak and Noor. Mab's Choice rewarded them with the 1954 Distaff Handicap at Aqueduct.

Not surprisingly, Mab's Choice also paid off pretty well at the windows— a fat $43.30—and Whittingham loved nothing more than to orchestrate a sweet score. A juicy payoff put another layer of big bills on the bankroll and kept steak on the table. Mab's Choice offered the perfect scenario: lightly weighted in a handicap after three decent, non-winning preps. She had gone without a victory for more than two years, even though Whittingham had been training her for only a fraction of that time.

"You could cash a bet in New York in those days," Charlie once recalled. "You didn't have to have the registration papers in the racing office until you entered a horse. And you didn't have to identify your horse to the clockers."

Whittingham worked all the loopholes when Porterhouse was an unheralded two-year-old in the spring of 1953. He was finally ready to make his debut on May 23 at Belmont Park, thrown in with fifteen other rookies on the straightaway Widener Course. As far as Whittingham was concerned, the race was for practice. Chances are, he was not alone.

"Let's see what we got here," Charlie told Jack Westrope before hoisting him aboard Porterhouse.

A few minutes later, Westrope brought Porterhouse home in seventh at odds 18-to-1. Whittingham skipped down to the track for a debriefing.

"So, what do you think about next time?"

"Well," Westrope replied, "I know we can beat the six that finished in front of me. But I don't know about the nine behind me."

Porterhouse won his next start.

The Whittingham stable was at Santa Anita during the winter of 1956 with a crack staff firmly in place. Ed "Grandpappy" Lambert ran the crew with a gruff, no-nonsense style. He was Whittingham's man in the trenches, and if you crossed Ed you flirted with disaster. The boys in the saddles included Joe Manzi, Huey Barnes, Joe Merriweather and the new kid, Larry Gilligan, who was an apprentice jockey when Whittingham got through with him in the morning.

The upsets started in February when Whittingham sent out Social Climber for Liz in the San Felipe Handicap. Eddie Arcaro had dismounted from an earlier collaboration and told Whittingham that Social Climber would win someday, as long as he was running for a $7,500 claiming tag. Even Charlie was uninspired, cracking wise just before the San Felipe, "He'll probably do a lot of climbing out there today."

Gilligan did the weight—108 pounds to Terrang's 124—and brought the low-headed Social Climber along the rail to score at $111.20.

Out West, the summer of 1956 belonged to Swaps. The red colt made only one mistake in six Hollywood Park starts, and guess who was there to collect? On May 26, in the Californian Stakes at Hollywood Park, Charlie nailed Swaps on the money with old Porterhouse, still going strong at age five. Bill Shoemaker blamed himself for riding Swaps with too much confidence. Whittingham disagreed, pointing out that Swaps had been plagued by a hoof infection and might not have been at full strength. Privately,

Charlie didn't give a hoot how it happened. He got the money.

And then there was that supernatural week at Belmont Park in September of 1956, when Whittingham defeated the budding two-year-old star Bold Ruler, and then, five days later, knocked off reigning Horse of the Year Nashua in the Woodward Stakes. Nashville, talented but unsound, dispatched Bold Ruler, while Nashua fell to a blue-collar working stiff named Mister Gus.

"Mister Gus couldn't touch Swaps all season long," Whittingham told the New Yorkers, twisting the knife. "So then he comes back here and handles Nashua. What's a man to think?"

As the 1958 Triple Crown neared, the racing world had fallen in love with Silky Sullivan. The huge chestnut had become famous for a ferocious finish that brought him from far, far back. His Santa Anita Derby was already a legend. Folks far and wide could hardly wait to see Silky run them all down in the Kentucky Derby.

But first, Silky Sullivan had to get past Whittingham. And Whittingham had a surprise. Charlie sent a dark gray colt named Gone Fishin' to Golden Gate Fields, across the bay from San Francisco, in order to run in something called the Greater Northern California Purse. For a race worth $10,000, it drew considerable attention simply because Silky Sullivan was using it as a springboard to his invasion of Kentucky for the Derby. Bill Corum, president of Churchill Downs, flew in to grease the rails for the Silky Sullivan crowd. Ben Lindheimer was in town from Chicago to promote his big Derby age races later that summer. Then Gone Fishin' up and stole the show, winning by five and a half lengths, while Silky Sullivan could do no better than third.

A trend was definitely in place. Players beware: overlook a Whittingham horse in a stakes race at your pari-mutuel peril. After all, it was the stakes races—the big ones especially—that Whittingham was committed to winning. Everything else was a means to an end, and he made sure everyone knew it.

In the summer of 1962, Whittingham was killing giants again. The scene was Chicago, where Florida Derby and Blue Grass Stakes winner Ridan towered over his opposition for the American Derby. Charlie ambled into town with a striking chestnut named Black Sheep, and proceeded to inform anyone who listened that he would not have come had he not intended to win. Ridan went down by a length and a quarter at odds of 3-to-10.

By 1963, the memory of Mister Gus and Nashville must have been growing dim back in New York. Whittingham, who considered his stable national in scope, had won only two stakes in the Big Apple since 1956. Charlie had become typecast as "that California trainer" once again. "Back East, they think we're still fighting Indians and using Western saddles on our racehorses out here," he would snap when anyone brought up the highfalutin attitude of some New Yorkers toward West Coast talent.

That fall, a blonde beauty named Lamb Chop was putting the finishing touches on a championship three-year-old campaign for Jim Maloney, her trainer, and William Haggin Perry, her owner. The Beldame, New York's most famous race for fillies and mares, appeared to be a mere formality with which Lamb Chop would wrap up her season.

Then Whittingham hit town with Oil Royalty, a five-year-old mare whose finishing kick was a sight to behold. New Yorkers had seen her before— under different management—and neglected to take into account the beneficial effects of more than nine months of Whittingham's care and conditioning. Oil Royalty caught Lamb Chop to win by a nose at odds of 26-to-1.

Things changed, and through the 1970s and into the 1980s, it was Whittingham who had all the giants. The rest of the pack was gunning for him, but they usually missed. His reputation for finishing first, second and sometimes even third in major stakes races became legendary, and downright annoying to the opposition. Fellow trainers and rival owners were frustrated by the obvious trade imbalance; but they grudgingly gave Whittingham all the credit for cornering such a tough market. There was very little luck involved.

One giant Whittingham could never seem to topple, however, was John Henry. From 1980 through 1984, Whittingham's best older horses spent most of their time chasing the popular gelding and ending up second best. John Henry was winning all the races that Whittingham horses usually won. It was especially galling since Whittingham had missed a fleeting chance at taking John Henry into the shelter of his own stable.

In the autumn of 1978, Whittingham was in New York preparing Exceller for confrontations with Seattle Slew and Affirmed. One afternoon at Belmont Park, he was approached by an amiable fellow named Sam Rubin. He was the proud possessor of a one-horse stable—a three-year-old gelding who had suddenly begun to display an affinity for grass racing. Rubin had heard that California offered great grass racing, and that Whittingham ran the best stable in the West.

"Would you be interested in training my horse?" queried Rubin. Whittingham was noncommittal.

"Send him out if you like," Charlie replied. "We'll see."

At the time, the Whittingham empire consisted of a hundred and fifty horses in various stages of training, spread out over two racetracks, a training center and a couple of farms. His clientele included Nelson Bunker Hunt, Howard Keck, Arthur Stollery, television producer Quinn Martin ("The Fugitive" and "The FBI"), diamond dealer Serge Fradkoff, and Mary Jones. To enter this chosen circle, an owner needed to be willing to invest heavily and supply the product, either through buying or breeding fresh horses. Short of that, an owner would be wise not to appear at Whittingham's doorstep unless he had a top-class horse in hand. Whittingham had nothing against Rubin, a self-made millionaire who parlayed door-to-door selling into a worldwide bicycle empire. But Rubin's equine portfolio was regrettably slim.

Nonplused by Whittingham's reaction, Rubin kept John Henry in New York for another season, then connected with another California-based trainer, Ron McAnally. The rest of the story became racing history, much of it at the direct expense of horses trained by Whittingham. Between January of 1980 and August of 1984, Whittingham horses finished either second or third—or sometimes both—to a victorious John Henry no fewer than nineteen times.

Somewhere along the way, Rubin went public with the story of his brush with Whittingham. It made for good copy, especially since it rendered Charlie a flesh and blood mortal who could make the occasional mistake. If it bothered Charlie, he never let it show. All he had to do was summon up the list of people he had turned away for the same reason he left Rubin cold. It was a long list, and it was useless to look back.

"I can't train 'em all, can I?" Whittingham said with a shrug after another beating by John Henry, the one who got away.

There was a stretch, though, when John Henry lost three straight races to Whittingham. The memory brings a bittersweet smile to Charlie's countenance, for even in victory there was a taste of defeat.

The string began in December of 1981 in the first running of the $500,000 Hollywood Turf Cup. John Henry was at the end of a long campaign. He already was a dead cinch to be voted Horse of the Year. He was running because, in McAnally's words, "We couldn't pass it up." In McAnally's mind, the Turf Cup was made to order for John Henry. He would carry equal weights against all comers at a mile and a half over Hollywood's firm turf course. The temptation was too great to resist.

Whittingham countered with fresh horses, two who'd never had their hearts broken by Rubin's gelding. There was Providential, a light-hearted and leggy Irish colt, and Queen to Conquer, a great hussy of a mare with a relentless stretch punch. Providential had been a problem child until Whittingham had his veterinarians remove an undescended testicle. Thus freed from the discomfort, the colt waltzed away with the 1981 Washington, D.C., International to give Whittingham his first victory in that historic event. Queen to Conquer had taken major races at nine and ten furlongs earlier in the year; but as far as Charlie was concerned, it was the distance of the Turf Cup for which she was truly made.

Under the strange floodlights of a late December afternoon, John Henry found himself in a lather and on the lead, using himself up at an alarming rate. Bill Shoemaker sensed something was amiss at the head of the stretch when Ol' John failed to increase his advantage. Instead, Providential easily reeled him in, while Queen to Conquer came along late for second, adding insult to insult. John Henry actually finished fourth, beaten a total of two lengths.

The champ's fans wrote off the loss to end-of-the-season blues. Whittingham, they contended, finally got lucky. "Okay," said Charlie, "I'll do it again. And I'll do it with a whole different horse entirely." Enter Perrault.

This was a great, brooding beast of a racehorse, a real bully boy, with a heavy, powerful head and a self-destructive way of going that made strong men wince with pain. His name was pronouced with full French flair—just like the Perot who would become famous ten years later in U.S. Presidential politics. And, just like the redoubtable Ross, the four-legged Perrault ran with a blinkered conviction and did not really care who or what got in the way. Whittingham admired Perrault for his brute strength and his competitive zeal in the face of intrinsic unsoundness. As far as Whittingham was concerned, Perrault was a match for John Henry in every way . . . except when it came to longevity.

In their first encounter, the 1982 Santa Anita Handicap, Perrault was stopped cold on the first turn, quickly recovered, and still mangaged to beat John Henry by a nose. John Henry, who carried four pounds more than Perrault, was troubled on the last turn, then was floated outward through the final eighth of a mile by Perrault. Whittingham's horse was disqualified; John Henry was given the race.

"If it's any other horse but John Henry, you think my horse would have come down?" Charlie was seething, lashing out and looking for conspiracies. Finally, he turned upon the real culprit, Laffit Pincay, who had pounded away at Perrault with a left-handed whip even as his horse was drifting to the right.

"You'd think a jock would have the sense to notice his horse wearing an extension blinker on the outside," said Whittingham, rubbing his dome in nervous agitation. "You'd think that might tell him the horse has a tendency to get out, wouldn't you? Why in hell didn't he have his stick in his right hand in the first place?"

Perrault, blowing dirt out of his wide nostrils, cooled down before his trainer. By the time they headed back to the barn, Whittingham was mapping his revenge. "Next time," he vowed, "will be different."

"Next time" came around just three weeks later in the San Luis Rey Stakes, a race won by John Henry in both 1980 and '81. This time it was gloves off, equal weights, going a mile and a half over firm ground favorable to both parties. Perrault, ridden by a repentant Pincay, went to the lead from the start. John Henry gave valiant chase, but Whittingham's horse was inspired. At the end it was Perrault by better than three lengths, with John Henry a desultory third. The old champ emerged from the race with an irritated ankle that kept him out of action until the fall; but that hardly fazed Whittingham. Nothing could spoil the taste of the San Luis Rey nor the momentum of Perrault, who went on to displace John Henry as North American grass champion.

Perrault ended the season as a fallen giant himself, betrayed by a torn suspensory ligament in the Marlboro Cup at Belmont Park. He never raced again, and Whittingham never beat John Henry again. Still, the memory of Perrault lived on, in more ways than one.

While on the road in suburban Chicago for the Arlington Million some three years later, Whittingham was on his way to bed after a full evening of fermentation. As he reached the exit of the hotel bar he was hailed by Pete Axthelm, star sports writer and horseplayer nonpareil. There was something Axthelm had been wanting to get off his chest in the worst way.

"Charlie," began Axthelm, "tell me why you ran Perrault in that Marlboro Cup when you knew he was going lame?"

Now, Whittingham hadn't hit anybody for a couple of weeks. Still, he resisted the temptation and drew on another weapon instead. Leaning back and eyeing Axthelm—just as The Almighty might consider one of his lesser creatures from on high—Charlie decided to be amused instead of vengeful.

"Well . . . Pete," he said, letting his words fall like drops of acid rain, "if you know . . . so god damn much . . . about Perrault . . . what color was he?"

Axthelm was cooked. But, proud man that he was, he decided not to back down. Instead, he played the percentages. And the percentages said: "Bay?"

Whittingham knew what Axthelm would say before he said it. "No, Pete. You see, Perrault was a liver chestnut, a very unusual color for a Thoroughbred, and something you wouldn't forget if you knew the first thing about the horse. Good night, Pete."

CHAPTER 6

UNDER THEIR SKIN

"Sometimes you think you've got the fish caught and cleaned, and he slips back in the water."

As far as Charlie Whittingham is concerned, the horse always deserves the benefit of the doubt. He preaches it daily, in word and deed. Listen to the horse and you can't go wrong. Be patient, be kind, and trust in what the horse is trying to say. But it is hard to do, every single day, when there are any number of frustrating Thoroughbred personalities. Even the most experienced members of Whittingham's crew need an occasional reminder.

"Charlie, this is the worst ride I've ever had!" Laura Lubisich grumbled one morning as she rode a sweaty, anxious filly into the Santa Anita walking ring after a two-mile wrestling match. Lubisich was one of Whittingham's strongest riders. She went on to become a successful bloodstock agent with her husband, Emmanuel de Seroux. On this particular morning, however, she was focused on her own survival.

"This is a no-account, common, worthless bitch, Charlie. Don't you ever put me on her again!"

Whittingham struck his familiar pose—feet splayed, shoulders hunched and hands clasped behind his back. He let leak one of his enigmatic Mona Lisa smiles, and, affecting a somewhat hurt tone of voice, disarmed Lubisich without gunfire.

"That's too bad," Whittingham said. "She says nice things about you."

Whittingham's love for animals knows no bounds. Just about every farm creature short of a Holstein heifer has been welcome around his stables at one time or another.

"I finally got rid of the chickens," Charlie admitted. "They were just too dirty, sitting up there shittin' on the feed sacks all day."

Okay, no chickens. But there have been dogs by the dozen and cats galore. And don't forget the goats. Peggy certainly won't.

"Betty, the goat at Belmont Park," she recalled with a groan. "We had just arrived and I hadn't unpacked. Somehow this goat got to my things in the trunk of the car. When we found her she was eating my clothes."

"She also chewed off some of Mrs. Hertz' convertible top," Charlie said, referring to the wife of an important client, John D. Hertz. "Worthless goat anyhow. They're supposed to help calm down nervous horses. Betty would get in a stall with a horse that was okay and pretty soon they would both be weaving all over the place."

It was the Whittingham dogs, though, who stole the show. Moustache was a bulldog who would climb a ladder on cue, especially if newspaper photographers wandered by the barn. Chula was a cocker spaniel, Charlie's first gift to Peggy that wasn't bought in the Camp Lejeune PX. There was Cracker the mutt and Steel the Chesapeake retriever. Tar the black Lab and Atta the German shepherd were Charlie's personal dogs—no barn duty for them.

Everybody's favorite was Toby the Australian shepherd. Toby, the dog who would smile at Charlie's command. Toby was the gatekeeper at the Whittingham barn, and woe be to the visitor who forgot a biscuit tribute. Toby would hound them until they left or borrowed a treat from Charlie. When Toby died, so great was his fan club that Santa Anita commissioned a bronze of his image and placed it beneath the bust of Whittingham in the paddock gardens. Charlie walks past it at least five times a day.

Some people have a gift for communicating with children. Others lock into corporate or political cultures with fluid ease. The different languages come naturally, like a second skin. With Charlie, it is animals. Watching Whittingham "talk" to a dog or a duck or anything else with feathers or fur is a sideshow unto itself. He gets their attention with a quick word or movement, then holds it with a quiet stare. The ability is not unusual—Siegfried and Roy have made millions with big cats—but it is remarkable, especially to those who must use rare steak or tuna to make an impression with a member of the animal kingdom.

The greatest use of Whittingham's link with animals is the way he understands the Thoroughbred racehorse. He suppresses all human feeling and focuses on pure animal instinct. Talk is useless. The only connection is through the eyes and hands. Where is the pain or the discomfort they sometimes try to hide? Why did that filly sweat up today when she had been perfect in the past? Has this colt grown too much for the exercise planned? How does his eye appear different from the glint of yesterday?

Neil Drysdale—the most successful of Whittingham's high-profile former assistants—recalls going stall to stall with Whittingham on afternoon rounds. It was a special time of connection between the men and the animals in their care.

"Charlie would touch them here and there, checking for heat or soreness, what have you. In the summer he would dab on a bit of ointment for the horses who needed it for their skin sores. I think he just likes the feel of them, the closeness."

Peggy Whittingham remembers well the time she witnessed her husband's most tender side as he ministered to a gravely ill racehorse named Sir Ribot.

"It was a staph infection," Peggy said. "Charlie had to go back to the barn late at night, and I offered to go with him. He said fine, but I had to stay in the car. I waited and waited, and finally went into the barn and peaked into the stall. The horse's head was in Charlie's lap, and he was giving it water with a spoon." Sir Ribot survived.

Those closest to Charlie insist there is a hint of mental telepathy in Whittingham's skills. As Dr. Alex Harthill likes to say, "Charlie is at least half horse." But for those who do not accept the telepathic theory of training, and for those who do not believe in the existence of some skin-headed Dr. Doolittle talking to his own special breed of animals, Whittingham's powers can be boiled down to a comfortably familiar concept: deductive reasoning.

That's it. Nothing fancier than pure logic at work. The racehorse is a puzzle searching for a solution. All the clues are there. Whittingham has played Sherlock Holmes to a half century of equine mysteries. He has succeeded because he is able to cut through the clutter and the distractions and come to the singular truth, as a series of eyewitness Dr. Watsons can testify.

"Charlie's great strength lies in his simplicity," said Christopher Speckert, who went on to enjoy his own successful training career after completing a term at Charlie's side. "The rest of us try to overcomplicate things. Charlie will look at a problem and immediately arrive at the proper conclusion, while the rest of us will be circling around, experimenting with this or that, and wasting our time before getting to the same place Charlie's been for days."

Rodney Rash was Whittingham's chief assistant trainer for nine years before going out on his own with a public stable. Certain lessons were burned into his brain.

"Other people can recognize a problem just as early as Charlie can," Rash noted. "But they tend to want to ignore it. Whereas Charlie will say, 'This little problem is going to mushroom and we'll be in deep crap down the road. So we'd better pull up now.' He looks at the same problem from a different angle. It's like putting down a road. If you have rocks where you're putting down pavement then you're going to have a rocky road later. Charlie stops to sweep all the rocks."

And because of that, says Drysdale, the horse trained by Whittingham usually has a better chance of fulfilling its ultimate potential. There may be a delay in short-term accomplishments, but the prize at the end of the day will make the wait worthwhile.

"He has this incredible ability to envision a horse winning a race months in advance, and then gear the horse's program in that direction," Drysdale said. "He'd say, 'We can win the Sunset with that horse.' The Sunset Handicap is in July, and he would be talking in January!"

Whittingham maintains that the key to his success with top-class horses is the proper application of patience. He credits Horatio Luro with driving home the point.

"Never rush a horse, and never let someone rush you," said

Whittingham. "If they do, then maybe you're not the trainer for them."

Luro created a climate in which Whittingham could adapt his own native horsemanship to Luro's South American philosophy. While Charlie worked with the horses, giving them those extra mile works and those deep-conditioning gallops, Horatio would assuage anxious owners with his wit and charm. The results would take care of the rest.

"People are always looking for the secrets to success in this or that," Whittingham said. "There's no secrets to training horses. You've just got to be there and work hard. You better know the horses, and you'd better know what you're doing, or else they'll make a fool out of you fast."

There may be no secrets to the Whittingham style of training, but there are certain attributes that have defined his operation for decades. Nothing is revolutionary. Anyone can do it. The trick is doing it every single day, week after week, month after month, year after year.

Whittingham begins his day early, halfway through the graveyard shift. The alarm goes off at three-fifteen. He'll dress, have his breakfast of Cheerios and orange juice—no coffee—then he will arrive at the track around four. A handful of trainers are on the same time clock. Wayne Lukas is one of them, and so is Noble Threewitt, who used to give Whittingham a lift across the border to Caliente in the early 1930s.

"If he beats me to the barn by a few minutes he'll let me know," said Threewitt, who neither looks or acts two years older than Whittingham. "I tell him I'm at a disadvantage, though. He doesn't drink coffee like I do, and he doesn't need to comb his hair. That's worth a couple minutes right there."

The first thing that strikes a visitor about Charlie's operation is the strict regimentation. Things happen at precisely the same time every single day: horses brushed, workers tacked, riders up, and off they go. Nervous horses go out early to take advantage of the calming shroud of near darkness, or Whittingham may wait until the end of the morning to dispatch them for a private exercise session on the deserted training track.

There are five sets of horses a day, seven days a week. The players work from a script drawn up the day before. If someone wanted to test

Whittingham's clockwork routine, they could stand blindfolded at a certain spot on the grandstand ramp at Santa Anita, or along the stable road at Hollywood Park. Then, on a timekeeper's mark, they could withdraw the blindfold at the same moment each day and Whittingham would be bearing down on them.

Once he began handling a larger group of horses for Luro after World War II, Whittingham found that the rhythms of military discipline fit in well with a racing stable. In such a structured system, everyone has a task, and all the tasks fit together toward a common goal. Both horses and people find a degree of comfort in such a predictable environment.

"Horses like routine," Whittingham said. "Gives them a feeling of security."

Whittingham's true organizational genius lies in his ability to provide each horse with a specially tailored conditioning program within the strict framework of the daily routine. Although there are certain fairly standard features in each program—the two-mile gallops, the depressurizing strolls through the paddock—no two horses will ever be on identical schedules.

Whittingham starts his training early, and not because he likes to wrap things up at nine o'clock to make a starting time at Bel Air Country Club. With five sets of horses, five or six horses to a set, time is desperately precious while training at a racetrack. Usually, track management allows about five hours for training time, minus at least an hour for renovation of the track surface. A Whittingham-sized stable places an optimum on every available minute. Charlie is always at the barrier bright and early, chomping at the bit to fling open the gate to the track at five-thirty sharp. Or five twenty-nine if possible.

"He threw an awful fit one time in Kentucky when they were five minutes late opening the track," recalled exercise rider Pam Mabes. "And we only had two horses to train!"

Whittingham is a passionate believer in fresh air and open spaces. He gives his horses as much as is possible in the cramped world of urban horse training.

"The longer you can have them outside their stalls the better," he said.

"It's not natural keeping them all penned up like we have to. I'll have them out as long as I can. Graze some of them in the afternoon, too."

Whittingham always works his horses over a freshly harrowed track. In order to accomplish this, he must find ways in which to warm up his workers prior to the opening of the track after the periodic renovations. At Santa Anita, he sends the workers to the training track to loosen their muscles. At Hollywood, he has them brought out of their stalls a few minutes earlier to walk, then his riders jog down a pony trail that rims the racetrack. At Del Mar, he sends his workers on a ten-minute walk from his barn to the grandstand paddock, where they circle for another twenty minutes until the track opens. Only Whittingham—and a few of his most devoted disciples—goes through such an elaborate workout ritual.

"It boggles my mind why other trainers don't follow Charlie's lead," said Chris McCarron, one of the few jockeys that Whittingham trusts enough to work his horses on a regular basis.

"From a rider's standpoint," McCarron noted, "when you are on a horse going over a course that has been chopped up from fifteen minutes of workouts—as opposed to a course that is smooth and virgin—you feel horses bobble. They don't get a hold of it, and they tire more. You think, jeez, this kind of thing has got to lead to injury."

Whittingham prefers to train and run his horses on firm tracks as opposed to loose, deep surfaces.

"A deep track can be tough on soft tissue—ligaments and tendons," Charlie said. "Real hard tracks you're going to get fractures, sure. The worst is a track that changes from day to day. It's like going from the wet sand to the dry sand at the beach. Do it enough and you'll hurt something."

Whittingham avoids training and running over wet tracks as much as possible, although he will give a horse a chance to prove himself to be a mud freak. Stardust Mel, a lanky gray gelding owned by Marjorie L. Everett, was the star of the wet California winter of 1975 for the Whittingham stable, winning both the Strub Stakes and the Santa Anita Handicap over terrible terrain. Ack Ack could handle the mud—some said his speed dried it out as he ran—and so could Sunday Silence.

More often, Whittingham prefers to wait out wet weather, because wet weather brings an increased rate of potential injuries. Based in California, Whittingham never has too long to wait before the storms pass, although sometimes his patience can be tested.

"One winter at Santa Anita, it rained for twenty straight days," recalled Richard Lundy, Whittingham's assistant from 1977 through 1981. "The weather was bad almost the whole meeting. Charlie only won about three races. But he didn't let it bother him. He kept the horses in the barn, then took them over to Hollywood Park and won thirty-five races."

When it comes to the use of medications, Whittingham is apolitical. If the substance is legal and it helps without masking serious pain, he will consider using it for the good of the horse. "Charlie's basically a Christian Scientist with medication," said veterinarian Jack Robbins. "There's no vet who ever gets rich off him."

A young trainer once claimed a horse from Whittingham, an unusual situation since Whittingham runs so few claimers. When the horse won his next start, then his next start, the young trainer shook his head in amazement. "Heck, all Charlie needed to do was give the horse a little Bute," he said. Bute, short for Butazolidin, is an anti-inflammatory drug perfectly legal in most North American racing jurisdictions, but perfectly unnecessary for that particular horse, as far as Whittingham was concerned.

On the other hand, he will not hesitate to explore all possibilities when a horse has lost form. Ferdinand, Whittingham's Kentucky Derby winner in 1986 and Horse of the Year in 1987, was heralded far and wide as a champion who competed without drugs. Then Ferdinand went off his game in the spring of 1988. Whittingham's vet detected a trace of blood in the trachea after a losing effort. Charlie decided to give Ferdinand a dose of Lasix, a legal diuretic (in most racing states) that lowers the blood pressure and in some cases helps reduce the chances of exercise induced pulmonary hemorrhage, a common occurrence in Thoroughbreds.

Ferdinand went flat as a pancake. "That will happen sometimes with Lasix," Whittingham explained. "It knocks them out, saps their energy.

Sometimes they're better the second time they get it. But Ferdinand wasn't. I stopped it and went back to the drawing board."

It may sound archaic, but Whittingham insists the Thoroughbred is best served not by modern medicine or the latest machinery, but by a reliable routine of meticulous attention in an atmosphere of peace and quiet. He takes the term "caretaker" very seriously. The Whittingham barn is not exactly quiet as a church; but it is an island of serenity compared to some of the manic, disorganized stables where music blares from radios and the crew is usually in a chaotic uproar.

"It wasn't always that way," said Michael Whittingham, who started working for his father in the mid-1950s and went on to a training career of his own. "He used to have a pretty volatile mix of people working for him, especially at Belmont Park. They'd end up in loud arguments settling their beefs. And my dad was pretty intense. He wanted something done, you did it right now or you'd hear about it."

The atmosphere in the Whittingham stables began to change in the early 1970s when women came to work at the racetrack.

"That really cracked me up," recalled Charlie's daughter, Charlene. "We'd get into these big arguments at home about women working at the track. Dad would say he'd never have women working for him. It just wasn't a place for them, he'd say. Then a few years later there he was, all those exercise girls. They called them Charlie's Angels."

They did indeed, and because they worked for The Man, they all had their moments of celebrity, depending upon which member of the all-star lineup they galloped regularly. In those days there was a stakes horse in nearly every stall.

Charlie's earliest women riders included the eccentric, unpredictable Mary Meglemre, who kept everyone amazed with her tall tales. Jacque Hendricks hailed from a well-known family of trainers and later became one herself. Janet Johnson, from Washington state, had a velvet touch on horseback and held Whittingham's trust for fourteen years.

Like Johnson, Laura Lubisich started with Whittingham in 1974. She came to him with Maryland trainer Del Carroll's recommendation on her resume, which was enough for Charlie to say, "You're hired." Mary Morton, an aspiring jockey, worked for Joe Whittingham at San Luis Rey before jumping to Charlie. Christine Picavet, who became a successful equine artist, could boast among her previous employers the great French trainer Francois Mathet.

"For the most part, I found girls to be more reliable than men," Whittingham said, explaining his newfound, liberal attitude. "They don't beat horses half to death or ride them into the ground like those frustrated jockey boys. As a rule, they're lighter, so that helps on the wear and tear. And they show up every day, instead of being out drunk or chasing women all night. Only they're not always on time."

One morning, Whittingham simply could not take any more tardiness. The track was about to open, the horses were saddled, and a couple of the girls were maybe two or three minutes late.

"Charlie fired us all on the spot," recalled Picavet with a laugh. "We'd been creeping in thirty seconds later every day, and he'd had enough. I thought, 'My God, now what?' But before we could think what to do, he hired us back again. He didn't have anyone else to ride the horses. After that we started showing up earlier . . . at least for a while."

Whittingham allows his riders considerable leeway in the handling of their particular horses. It is up to the rider to discover the best way to make a horse gallop with a smooth, efficient stride. He requires very little feedback from the rider. When the boss asks "How'd he go?" a short, direct answer is preferred. Whittingham lets them know when he sees something he does not like.

"I like them to ride quiet," is how Whittingham describes the job.

"Don't let him catch you yanking on a horse or being tough with its mouth," Johnson said. "That's the worst thing you could do. He wants his horses kind and willing to work, not afraid."

"Charlie is a very trusting man when it comes to what we did with the horses," Picavet said. "As long as you did not abuse the horse. Then he was very firm. But I don't remember him lacking of praise."

Whittingham trains by the stopwatch as well as by the eye. If a rider came down there way too fast or too slow, there would be hell to pay.

"Yeah, Charlie would yell, letting off steam, and I would take it seriously," Johnson said. "Later I'd be down at the end of the shedrow, sitting on a bale of hay bawling my eyes out because I'd let Charlie down. After awhile he'd come walking up and say something like, 'What's up, girl?' He'd forgotten about it completely."

Along the way, Whittingham got a reputation for low pay. He justified his wage level by pointing to the monthly bonus checks drawn from the money in the pot holding about one per cent of the stakes winnings. At the end of good months—and most of the months since 1967 have been good months—everyone would be reasonably happy. But there were some ripples.

Whittingham actually dealt with a wildcat strike in 1968, back when Francis Risco was a rookie groom. Risco had been on the job for less than a year when early one morning he looked up and realized he was the only one doing a lick of work. The other grooms were standing around, trying to get up the courage to go to Whittingham for more money.

"What's going on out here?" boomed Whittingham as he emerged from his office to witness the sudden stable shutdown.

Risco and another guy were pushed in Whittingham's direction. They were provided with very little negotiating strategy, other than to say they were being paid less than the grooms working for other top local trainers.

Whittingham seethed, but he knew he had to get the barn up and running again or the morning would be wasted.

"You guys go on around to the other outfits and find out what they pay," Whittingham said. "I won't top them, but I'll at least match them. Okay? Now get back to work."

Risco and his co-workers asked around and discovered, to their surprise, Whittingham's pay was already in the ballpark. They returned to him with the news.

"All right then, this is what I'm going to do," Whittingham said. "I'll give you a raise of five dollars a week, and I'll start paying five dollars for every schooler and ten dollars for every runner."

The men were bowled over by their windfall. Then Whittingham lowered the boom.

"And if you ever, EVER hold me hostage like that again, you will all be down the road!"

"I'm not surprised they tried," said Laura Lubisich. "At a hundred and twenty-five a week, we weren't getting rich. That's why there arose such jealousy among us for the best mounts in the morning. The better your horses did in the afternoon, the more you could earn."

"We even thought about a strike," said Picavet. "I'm not sure it would have done any good, though. I think it was Charlie's attitude that we should feel lucky to have such a job. He could never understand when I would ask for a day off to go skiing, or something else.

"He'd say, 'Why would you want to go and do something like that, girl? Look around . . . you've got a whole world right here at the track.' "

CHAPTER 7

BREAKING THROUGH

"The pole is slippery from top to bottom. I ought to know. I've been up and down it a few times."

Scotland was a gray horse Whittingham trained for W. M. Ingram, whose business was tombstones. And Liz—by then she was married to Col. Cloyce Tippett—Liz loved gray horses. She loved them so much she was jealous when she saw one that wasn't in her nest.

"Get that gray beast out of my barn!" Liz demanded. Charlie scowled.

"Your barn! Last time I looked those webbings said 'CW'. I'll decide who stays and who goes."

The year was 1961, and, in reality, it was the state of the Llangollen runners that brought forth Tippett's ultimatum, not Scotland's pigment. After nearly eight years of uninterrupted success with the likes of Porterhouse, Mister Gus, Social Climber, Nashville, Royal Living and Divine Comedy, Charlie and Liz had hit a dry spell. But such a lag was not uncommon for a racing operation fed by its own breeding production line. It happened with regularity to the very finest stables. Furthermore, it always has been a sure way to test the relationship between an owner and a trainer who have enough trouble communicating even in the best of times.

"Show me a winner who can lose," Charlie would say, "and I'll show you a real winner."

In the face of Tippett's demands, Whittingham put up a brave front. He realized, however, that his stable would be gutted if Liz pulled out, since he was down to only a handful of animals owned by other clients. Years later, he counseled his ambitious assistants on the dangers of relying too much upon the patronage of a single owner, offering such sage advice as: "They can wake up one morning and fire you, and then your tit would really be in the wringer."

Peggy, who tried to keep her distance from Liz-storms, wanted her husband to stick by his guns in the showdown with Tippett. "She's just trying to control you, Charlie. Back down on this and she'll think she owns you."

"You know what it means, though, if she leaves," Whittingham replied. "It'll mean quite a change in our lifestyle."

What? No more summers in Saratoga? Parties 'til dawn? Martinis by the gallon?

"Well, we've been through ups and downs before," Peggy answered, "and I've never noticed much difference."

So Charlie dug in his toes, and Liz hit the road. She yanked her horses in February of 1961, turning them over to trainer Tommy Doyle, a former Irish jump rider who was earning a reputation with the fast young California horses bred and owned by Ellwood B. Johnston. Overnight, the Whittingham barn became a lonely place. And Charlie won exactly one stakes race in all of 1961, the Del Mar Handicap. With Scotland.

Within months, Liz was singing the blues. She had nothing but bad luck with Doyle, who later went on to train champion mare Typecast and dozens of stakes winners for other clients. "When will Charlie take me back?" she pleaded to Peggy.

Whittingham was in no hurry. He was busy building up a new clientele, determined never to bank on one major owner again. The barn grew with new blood. John Gaines, C. C. Moseley and Robert Hibbert jumped on board. Then, after allowing Liz to dangle in the wind for almost two years, Charlie finally relented and took on a few Llangollen horses in the winter of 1963.

That same spring, on April 19, the foaling barn at Llangollen Farm sent forth the news that Imitation, a twelve-year-old daughter of Hyperion, had given birth to a healthy dark bay colt sired by Endeavour, Tippett's grand Argentinean stallion. The little guy received the name Pretense. Four years later, he became the focal point of Whittingham's first truly great campaign.

American racing in 1967 was not immune to the unrest in the world at large. National Guardsmen lined the stretch at Churchill Downs on Derby Day, shoulder to shoulder, their M-1s ready to defend against a threatened disruption by local demonstrators. Back home in California, the staunchly right-wing Whittingham growled about protesters and railed at long-haired hippies, chucking them all in the same pot with Commie pinkos and bleeding-heart liberals. He held forth on race relations, allowing that Governor Wallace might make a pretty good President, and that South Africa might have it right after all. But most of all he thought about the horses, a stable so full of proven class and raw talent that even Whittingham himself popped goose bumps whenever he pondered the immediate future.

It was a powerful package. Nothing on the West Coast even came close. And few Eastern stables could rival Whittingham's public assemblage of famous owners and their horses. There was Liz Tippett's Llangollen Farm and Tippett's Virginia neighbor, Leila Ellis. There was William du Pont of Foxcatcher Farm, Ralph Wilson and his Buffalo Bills, Howard B. Keck of Standard Oil, and John R. Gaines of Bold Bidder fame. And there was Mary Florsheim Jones, the shoe fortune heiress and a lifelong horse lover.

By the end of the year, Whittingham would be looking back at the best season of his career. For the first time, his stable earnings would break the million-dollar barrier. He would finish third in the national standings behind Eddie Neloy and Allen Jerkens, the top dogs of New York. Amazingly, the final tally could have been better, so much better, in fact, that Whittingham himself indulged in a rare moment of "what if" as 1967 drew to a close.

But that is getting way ahead of things. In the beginning, there was unbridled optimism. Whittingham's mantra—"Hope for the best and plan for the worst"—seemed a waste of breath. Who could blame him? As Whittingham made his rounds at feeding time on the afternoon of January 1, 1967, going stall to stall and evaluating each animal with unobtrusive precision, this was what he saw:

First, there was Pretense, who was about to become the horse Whittingham always thought he could be. Patience was paying off with the dark bay colt who was built like a battleship. He was unraced at two and started a dozen times at three before he finally gave Charlie the chance to say, "I told you so!" by winning the Palos Verdes Handicap at six furlongs on Santa Anita's opening day, December 26, 1966. It was a pretty scary sight, considering the fact that this was a horse bred to go two miles.

"He's typical of the Endeavours," Whittingham would say when Pretense came up. "You could bring him in a bar and he'd sit and watch you all night." Which is exactly what Whittingham did with his dogs, anyway.

Next in the Llangollen pecking order came Tumble Wind, a drop-dead handsome son of Restless Wind. Tumble Wind was Paul Newman in horsehide, and a genuine Kentucky Derby candidate to boot. The long-legged, perfectly proportioned bay colt was already a good one at age two. Whittingham couldn't wait to get him rolling at three.

Drin was the "other" four-year-old, by Hollywood Derby winner Bagdad from one of Howard Keck's million-barrel-a-day female families. An honest stretch runner who nearly always fired, Drin was the kind of animal Whittingham admired.

Saber Mountain, another Bagdad colt from the Keck nursery, was a reclamation project with a potentially huge upside. He had "Kentucky Derby" writ all over during the winter of 1966, but a broken knee dashed those dreams. His comeback was close, real close, and Whittingham was getting all the right signals.

Charlie continued his stroll, and stopped at the stall of Spinning Around, a three-year-old filly by Fleet Nasrullah who was a pleasant surprise waiting to happen. Swoonalong and Maintain, accomplished mares with class from the past, gave the stable depth in the distaff division. And there was Ultimate, also owned by Tippett, imported from Europe and ready to prove his worth on turf.

But the real star of the show was a South American horse who had the

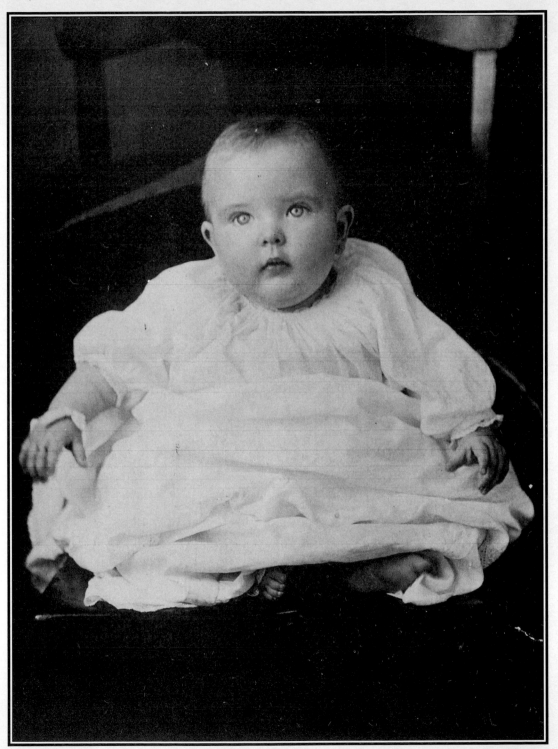

'We all go out the same way we came in,' says Charlie. 'Nothing but asses and elbows.' Ah, but what cute elbows.

Courtesy Whittingham Family

The Otay nine. Charlie (front right) played second base.

Photos courtesy Whittingham Family

Edward and Ellen Whittingham. Charlie lost one, longed for the other.

Johnny and Charlie, barefoot cousins, pose with Laddie.

A hands-on Whittingham struts with a flashy colt named Bang while at Longacres with Luro in 1940.

Luro and Whittingham admire their work after Dandy comes through for a nice Longacres payday.

Longacres Photo

Charlie got extra mileage from the reliable Bounding Home at Old Tanforan in the pre-Luro era.

Haase Photos

From the islands of the Pacific to the hills of North Carolina, Sgt. Whittingham was on the job.
Rocky Mount Police Dept. Photo

Hell on wheels in Honolulu.

Whittingham (front left) on the beat in
Rocky Mount. Ralph Heres (front right)
was his best man.
Photos courtesy Whittingham Family

Charlie (center) playing possum with
fellow Marines on Johnston Island.

An MP's work is never done. Whittingham gets the drop on a pair of dangerous comrades.

Nancy
Thank you
for all your
help.
Peggy

While Peggy worked for the police she learned the ropes. Charlie called her his pistol packin' mama.

Charlie and Peggy (left) celebrate Talon's Santa Anita Handicap with Luro (right) at Ciro's in Hollywood.

Photos courtesy Whittingham Family

Feeding time for baby Charlene and young Michael.

Whittingham on his own, training one morning at Santa Anita.
Santa Anita Park Photos

Porterhouse, Charlie's first champion, with Arcaro aboard and Liz of Llangollen accepting the prize.

Liz loved her grays, whether or not they won the big money.
The Blood-Horse Photo

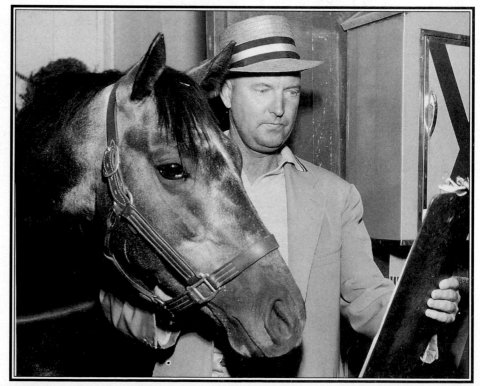

This one could run. Charlie and Gone Fishin' strike a pose for publicity.
Hollywood Park Photo

Whittingham with future Santa Anita Handicap winner Corn Husker and future trainer Joe Manzi.

Four Footed Fotos

A typical Whittingham hand for a big race. 'I've got 'em surrounded.'
Santa Anita Photo

SABER MOUNTAIN A♣

PRETENSE A♠

DRIN A♥

A demon for precision and order, Charlie patrols the tow ring at his Belmont Park barn, circa 1957.
Giles Wright Photo

Taylor Whittingham
(above, and right, on pony)
takes Turkish Trousers to the
track as Uncle Joe and father Charlie
look on.   *Thoroughbred of California Photo*

Burt Bacharach and Angie Dickinson matched star power with their trainer.
Thoroughbred of California Photo

Howard Keck stayed in the background while his horses made the noise.
Inger Drysdale Photo

Cougar and Mary Jones Bradley were a match made in horse racing heaven.
BLS Photo/Courtesy Mary Jones Bradley

Racing visionary Jimmy Kilroe designed and promoted many of the races Whittingham liked to win.
Milton C. Toby Photo

Michael Whittingham made his own name as a big-race trainer.
Shigeki Kikkawa Photo

Neil Drysdale's done his mentor proud.
Inger Drysdale Photo

Whittingham and Shoemaker were a tough team to beat when the stakes were highest.
Inger Drysdale Photo

Whittingham finally discovers a head harder than his own, on display at Santa Anita.
Four Footed Fotos

So this is Derby bliss. Team Ferdinand makes Whittingham history at Churchill Downs.
E. Martin Jessee Photo

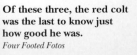

Of these three, the red colt was the last to know just how good he was.
Four Footed Fotos

Neither rain, nor mud, nor Easy Goer could stop Sunday Silence on his Derby mission.
Skip Dickstein Photo

But Whittingham watched the Triple Crown fade away when Sunday Silence lost the Belmont.
The Blood-Horse Photo

Charlie compares haircuts with Woody Stephens and Shug McGaughey.
Skip Dickstein Photo

'A mile in one forty-five! What was that #%*@#% rider thinking?'
Skip Dickstein Photo

Dagmar the goose would do the tango if Charlie showed her how.
Brant Gamma Photo

Charlie and Peggy—a lot more ups than downs in an extraordinary life together.
Photos courtesy Whittingham Family

The children, grandchildren and great-grandchildren assemble in the fall of 1992 for Beulah Boone's ninetieth birthday. Peggy is flanked by Michael (black hat) and Charlene (blonde hair, vest) beside her husband, veterinarian Helmut von Bluecher.

potential to stop the game cold. He was already a legend in his own land, a four-legged Evita with a spotless record and a fanatical following back home in Buenos Aires. Whittingham paused an extra few moments to contemplate Forli, as the chestnut colt buried his muzzle deep in the dark green feed tub. "Perfect," thought Whittingham. "Sweet Jesus, he's perfect."

Everyone seemed to agree. Writing that spring in the *Thoroughbred Record*, turf historian B. K. Beckwith fell under Forli's spell after a guided tour from Whittingham. "You keep absorbing him," wrote Beckwith, "and a voice sounds within you saying that, while there is no such thing as perfection in man or beast, this individual comes close to it."

Forli had been imported by A. B. "Bull" Hancock Jr. and divvied up by a syndicate formed from the inner circle of horse racing's most powerful establishment figures. Leslie Combs, Michael Phipps, Paul Mellon and James Cox Brady were among those in for a piece of the $960,000 pie. Keck was involved, as well, so it was no surprise when Forli went straight into Whittingham's care after clearing quarantine in late 1966.

In fact, Forli was Charlie's first horse of international repute. Later on, Forli would be followed by the likes of Tobin Bronze, Kilijaro, Exceller, King Pellinore, Caucasus and Dahlia, all of them well known before reaching America's shores. But until Forli came along, the Whittingham stable was fueled primarily by runners he had developed from the ground up. Here was this red monster, a full-blown celebrity, dropped into Whittingham's lap with the challenge: "Okay, Charlie. Let's see you move up this sucker if you think you're such hot stuff."

The collaboration of Whittingham and Forli made sense. What better keeper for the pride of Argentina than the man who traced back to El Gran Senor himself, Horatio Luro? When it came to Forli, Whittingham applied everything he had gleaned regarding Southern Hemispherics, including the most important component of all: a healthy respect for time.

It is the ultimate irony of the Thoroughbred racing game that the calendar became so powerful. This is especially true in light of the fact that horses have no sense of time at all—unless you count feeding, or foaling, or the seasonal effects of estrus. Otherwise, one day is pretty much like another in the claustrophobic world of the racehorse.

Whittingham knew this from the moment he began fussing with his paper route pony. He learned that a horse, left on its own, is under no particular time restraints to grow into maturity or recover from injury or illness. A horse will back off from aggravating an ache or pain, a split hoof, or a bruise. Then a week, a month, maybe a year later it will be fine. Who cares how long as long as the problem is gone and the animal survives? The sooner the better, of course, or else the herd is long gone, leaving stragglers to the mercy of big cats and bears.

In horse racing, on the other hand, time marks everything, from foaling dates to championship campaigns. People lose money when horses don't perform in a given frame of time, and therefore the pressure mounts. "When? When? When will he run again?" To the eternal frustration of many an owner, Whittingham came to terms early with the tyranny of time. No matter what his situation—whether scuffling for a meal at pre-war Del Mar or riding high at Luro's side—Whittingham learned to train by the simple motto, "Either you wait on them, or they'll make you wait."

Such patience was a gamble. Some owners would not wait, and their horses disappeared into other hands. But Whittingham operates with a special arrogance. Given enough rope, he is convinced he can bide his time, produce a better version of the same horse, and thereby wage a long and profitable campaign. Simply stated, if the owner would shut up, Charlie would put up.

There was a tremendous temptation to run Forli early in 1967. After all, the grandson of Hyperion had raced only seven times in Argentina. He arrived within a month of his victory in the classic Carlos Pellegrini at San Isidro. For a purchase price of nearly a million dollars, the new owners had every right to be anxious.

But they also knew Whittingham. They had seen him rest Porterhouse year after year and bring him back glowing and ready to kill. They had watched him work quietly with an unsound four-year-old maiden named Royal Living, then three months later send him out to win the San Juan Capistrano Handicap at a mile and three-quarters—in course-record time! And they listened when he said there was too much racing of two-year-olds. Economics of the game be damned! As far as he was concerned, a Thoroughbred was not full grown and fit for the stress of training and racing until he was at least four, maybe closer to five.

So Whittingham waited, taking full advantage of the six-month difference in Southern Hemisphere racing, where the angle of the Earth on its axis flipflops the seasons from the north. Forli was foaled on August 10, 1963, which was the same as being an early February foal in the United States or Europe. "He's barely three," Whittingham protested to those who badgered him about Forli's first start. "Let's give him a chance."

Forli spent the winter and early spring of 1967 as the show horse in the Whittingham stable. People dropped by just to bask in the new-penny gleam of his glowing copper coat. Charlie played the proud impresario, standing aside so visitors could admire the well-mannered colt. Occasionally he would say, to no one in particular, "Isn't he beautiful?"

In the meantime, that tough lug named Pretense was doing all the heavy lifting. He was an unlikely hero, especially in the context of the 1967 Santa Anita stable roster. In addition to the regal Forli, the racing scene included Buckpasser, the reigning Horse of the Year, and Native Diver, the most popular Californian since the days of Swaps. Before the Santa Anita meet opened, Pretense was not even as recognizable as his stablemates, Saber Mountain and Drin.

After winning the Palos Verdes, Pretense banged his head against Native Diver in the seven-furlong San Carlos Handicap, then lost to Buckpasser in the nine-furlong San Fernando Stakes. He was third both times. Liz Tippett moaned when her baby got beat, but Whittingham took the setbacks in stride. Pretense was being trained for the long haul, where the real money was stashed at the end of ten-furlong rainbows.

He was, however, bearing out on the turns, losing valuable ground that could come back to haunt him someday. Whittingham made two adjustments: he added a prong to the right side of the ring bit, and he strapped on a set of half-cup blinkers. Then he sent Pretense looking for Native Diver.

In the world of American sport, the 1960s was an era of heroes and anti-heroes. Fans and the press whipped up rivalries—sometimes artificial, sometimes real—between Babe Ruth and Roger Maris, Arnold Palmer and Jack Nicklaus, Bill Russell and Wilt Chamberlain. In California racing, the lightning-fast Native Diver was the good guy and Pretense was the bad guy. Before too long, the bad guy was always winning.

Whittingham viewed front-running Native Diver as a fairly simple puzzle just waiting to be solved. "You need a horse who can run with the rabbits and chase with the hounds," he said. "Stay close to him early. Don't let him get that breather around the turn. Hook him there, and you got him for sure." Trouble was, there were few horses who fit the bill. Until Pretense came along, Whittingham never had the weapon to deal with Native Diver's speed over a distance of ground.

When it finally happened, the crowds were stunned. In the San Pasqual Handicap, at only a mile and one-sixteenth, Pretense did not just beat Native Diver. He tied him to the quarter pole and left him for dead. The next morning, a jaunty fellow with a snap brim straw hat and half a cigar stuck in the corner of his mouth turned up unannounced at the Whittingham barn.

"Who the hell was that god damn black son of a bitch you turned loose yesterday?" he growled. Whittingham fought back a self-satisfied grin and introduced Pretense to Buster Millerick, the trainer of Native Diver.

To be fair, a break in the weights helped tip the scales toward Pretense that winter. He got fourteen pounds from Native Diver in the San Pasqual, seven pounds in the San Antonio, and seven again in the Santa Anita Handicap. Still, Tippett's colt won them all impressively, cracking Native Diver's resolve around the final turn each time before pulling clear in the stretch. Exactly as Whittingham planned it.

"Bring on Buckpasser!" Liz proclaimed in the wake of the Santa Anita Handicap. "We'll be going where he's going. And when he's ready to run, we'll be ready to meet him."

By then, Whittingham was accustomed to the outrageous Lady of Llangollen. Whenever Liz got on her Buckpasser kick, Charlie would rub his bare scalp, fishing for a way to stop the crazy talk before someone took it seriously. "Why wake a sleeping grizzly?" Whittingham wondered. "Buckpasser is just fine where he is."

In fact, Buckpasser was hurting. Hoof problems plagued him all winter long in California. His last race in the West was the San Fernando. By the time Pretense won the San Antonio, Eddie Neloy had written off the winter for Buckpasser. His ambitions went no further than making the Metropolitan Mile back in New York on Memorial Day.

Whittingham's long-range plans for Pretense included a Hollywood Park campaign during the summer and then forays to Chicago and New York in the fall. But first, the colt made his final start of the Santa Anita winter meet on March 11 in the San Juan Capistrano in an attempt to complete a sweep of the Santa Anita Handicap and San Juan. Charlie and Liz had done it ten years earlier with that converted jumper named Corn Husker.

Pretense ran his race but could do no better than a third-place finish behind a couple of tough seven-year-olds, the Argentinean Niarkos and an upstart from Washington named Biggs. By then, the opposition was hoping Whittingham would give them—and Pretense—a break. Anyway, it was Charlie's habit to back off after running a horse in the San Juan, especially if that horse was at the end of a tough series of races. Pretense certainly fit the bill, having run seven times at Santa Anita against the best horses in the West.

But Whittingham had never trained a horse quite like Pretense before. Certainly, he was in a class with Porterhouse; and Porterhouse was a champion who won short or long for five campaigns and beat Swaps in the bargain. Charlie gave Pretense a thorough evaluation after the San Juan, then put him on a plane to Florida with his younger stablemate, Tumble Wind, whose goal was the Florida Derby. Pretense would run in the Gulfstream Park Handicap on March 25, two weeks after the San Juan.

Now, Whittingham always has tailored his training to suit the horse—light or heavy, fast or slow, well-spaced or rat-a-tat-tat. But when a big horse and a big race are coming together, there are only a few variations on his basic themes of mental and physical fitness.

If a horse has not raced in a while—say a month to six weeks or more—there will be a stern work of one mile seven or eight days prior to the race, then a quick little spin to open the pipes right on top of the race. However, if the horse has been in steady training and racing without wavering in performance, or if the mile work was not what Whittingham wanted, he will use a five-furlong work four or five days prior to the race. A clocking of one minute, give or take a tick, is usually all that Charlie requires.

On the morning of March 21, Whittingham watched in growing fury as exercise rider Chuck Russell took the 1,200-pound Pretense through five-eighths in :58 2/5 over a surprisingly fast surface. Afterwards, Charlie cooled down with a good yell in Russell's direction, then put on a happy face and gave the workout a sunny spin:

"He really didn't look like he was going that fast."

And . . .

"If I didn't have a watch on him, I never would have realized it."

And . . .

"To look at him now, you wouldn't think he did anything."

And then, four days later, Pretense won the Gulfstream Park Handicap by two and a quarter lengths, beating the 1966 Belmont Stakes winner, Amberoid.

Whittingham gave Pretense an easy April, cranked him up again in May, and put the big colt through a Hollywood Park campaign every bit as tough as the one at Santa Anita. Charlie grumbled as Pretense spotted Native Diver weight the next four times they met. "Why'n hell don't they just put the grandstand on my horse and be done with it?" he said, waving an arm in the general direction of Hollywood's chief handicapper, John Maluvius. After running third in the Californian under 130 pounds (a weight determined by prize money won), Pretense went on to take the Inglewood (128) and American Handicaps (131) in a breeze. He was also second in the Sunset Handicap, giving the winner twenty pounds, but it was the Hollywood Gold Cup that Whittingham will never forget.

At the time, the Gold Cup was California's richest race, worth $162,100. Whittingham never had won it. He wanted it badly because, well, it was California's richest race. That was inspiration enough.

"It's not how many races you win that counts," Whittingham would say, over and over, "but that you win the good ones."

The 1967 Gold Cup went wrong at the start, when O'Hara stumbled and threw Milo Valenzuela. The well-trained O'Hara continued on his merry way, running with the pack just in back of the pacesetting Native Diver. The Diver was oblivious to the commotion and comfortably unhurried. But Pretense was another story. Hounded by O'Hara running alongside, Johnny Sellers rode Pretense gingerly and failed to challenge Native Diver around the final turn. That made all the difference.

Up in the stands, Whittingham gripped his binoculars until his knuckles went white. "Goddammit, jock, kick that loose sonofabitch out of there and get away from him," Charlie seethed through clenched teeth. It was a helpless feeling. And Charlie—a man who could make good horses do great things—hated feeling helpless. By the time O'Hara left Pretense alone, it was too late. The riderless horse crossed the line first, with victorious Native Diver lapped on. Pretense was five lengths farther back.

Whittingham did not let the Gold Cup bother him much longer than his second bone dry martini that evening. Bad luck was one thing—perhaps the only thing—he could do absolutely nothing about. There was also a twisted dash of irony to the whole affair. O'Hara was owned by Jock Whitney's Greentree Stable—the same Jock Whitney who, as Liz Tippett's first husband, gave her Llangollen Farm as a wedding present in 1930. "Today we got the Flying Fickle Finger of Fate Award," Whittingham said with a shake of his head. He was a big fan of the late sixties television show "Rowan & Martin's Laugh-In."

Besides, if there was any good luck floating around, Whittingham needed to spend it on Forli, not Pretense. Forli finally made his American debut on May 16, a quiet Tuesday early in the meet, when Charlie unleashed the Argentine to win the Coronado Stakes on Hollywood's brand new grass course. Six months of acclimatization paid off with an easy win over so-so stakes horses. Bill Shoemaker was geared down at the finish, while the Forli syndicate breathed a collective sigh of relief.

Whittingham's work was just beginning, however. Forli had been smarting from tender shins, a nagging condition that probably cropped up at the end of his South American career. The stress of the Coronado only made things worse. Dr. Jack Robbins, who had worked for Charlie as far back as the days of Talon, pin-fired the red colt in hopes of accelerating the healing. Superhorse had a chink in his armor after all.

The rest of Forli's racing career was an exercise in frustration. On July 8, four days after Pretense won the American Handicap, Hollywood Park staged an exhibition race for Forli. Playing all the angles, Whittingham let the track brass think the race could propel Forli into the July 14 Gold Cup. Fat chance. In spite of the fact that he won by eight and a half lengths, Whittingham was not about to rush this million-dollar baby. So he waited, and waited, and iced the shins, and waited some more. Figuring a turf race would be better for Forli's dicey legs, Whittingham circled the July 29 Citation Handicap at Arlington Park and shipped the colt off to Chicago.

Fragile as he is, the Thoroughbred racehorse still does some amazing things. What Whittingham witnessed in the Citation stamped Forli as a horse for all time in Charlie's mind, the epitome of the "coulda-shoulda-woulda" champion who never really got the chance to prove his true greatness.

At some point during the final quarter mile of the Citation, the long bone between the knee and the ankle of Forli's left front leg began to fracture. He might have taken a bad step during the rough trip. Maybe he was flinching from a pain in the right. At one point he even brushed the inner rail. That may have been the cause, but more likely it was the affect of the suddenly weakened limb.

Whittingham sensed something was wrong, because Forli was not exploding like the Forli he knew. From his perch atop the colt, Bill Shoemaker also felt the change. Yet Forli ran on, undaunted, and still managed to finish a close second to the roan colt Dominar. Before that day, no one had dared mention Dominar in the same sentence with a horse like Forli.

In the box next to Whittingham, Bull Hancock slammed down his binoculars and let loose a barrage of strong language. "Bull was never a very generous loser," Whittingham later observed. A few days later, once Forli's cannon bone was stabilized, Hancock's sons—Seth and Arthur—showed up to van the colt back to Claiborne Farm in Kentucky. Arthur, never having met Whittingham before, did not know quite what to expect. But if he was waiting for Whittingham to moan and whine over the loss of Forli, he had the wrong guy.

"You're a big, strong son of a bitch," pronounced Whittingham as he focused his bleary eyes squarely on the tall, lanky Arthur. "But all I'd need to handle you is a few Marine tricks. C'mere. Just try and choke me." Whereupon Whittingham, grinning like a schoolboy at play, gave Arthur a three-quarter speed demonstration in hand-to-hand combat.

"I had a recollection of Charlie from my youth," Hancock said. "I have a picture in my head of Charlie and Shoemaker playing croquet on our lawn at Claiborne. The time at Arlington, though, was my first encounter with him as an adult, and he tries to disable me. I immediately liked Charlie Whittingham."

Forli's downfall was not the only dark spot of the year. In fact, the grand season of 1967 was starting to take a decidedly dismal turn. Earlier, Saber Mountain had won a small stakes race, then broke down while training and could not be saved. Drin, who won the Strub Stakes during the Santa Anita meet, also went wrong, although he made it to the farm.

At least Tumble Wind was still going strong. He missed the Triple Crown after a bad race in the Blue Grass Stakes, but he came back like gangbusters during the summer, winning the Hollywood Derby by six lengths in the best performance of his career. Then, just one week after Forli's Citation disaster, Tumble Wind smacked a shin while running against Damascus and In Reality in Arlington's American Derby. He was pulled up and finished last, bringing his campaign to a close.

Even Pretense, the indomitable workhorse, was nearing an end. He was beaten on the square by Handsome Boy in the Washington Park Handicap on August 19, giving away just six pounds. In the Benjamin F. Lindheimer Handicap on Labor Day, Pretense finished fourth behind three lightweights. The Arlington invasion had become Whittingham's personal Pearl Harbor. Pretense ran once more, trying the United Nations Handicap at Atlantic City on September 20, and finished seventh. His next stop was back in California . . . on an operating table to relieve the damage of a fractured splint bone.

It was the worst of endings to the best of years. Whittingham's runners earned $1,038,208, nearly twice as much as his best previous season. Even though he was still known primarily as the Bald Eagle of California, he had penetrated the upper ranks of America's training elite. Now, the test was simple. Could he do it again, and again, and again. Looking back on Forli, Drin, Saber Mountain and Pretense, Whittingham shrugged and answered as only he knew how.

"Good horses are like grapes. They come in bunches."

The harvest had just begun.

CHAPTER 8

LEG UP

"What do you expect from a guy who wears a size three hat?"

In early February of 1969, Harry Silbert waltzed up to Charlie Whittingham and said from behind his cigar, "Shoe's ready to come back. Got anything for him?"

"Wait a week," Whittingham replied, "and we'll bring him back in style."

Whittingham made good on his promise. On February 11, an otherwise unremarkable Tuesday afternoon, the sports world zeroed in on Santa Anita Park, where Bill Shoemaker was returning to competition after recovering from the most serious injury of his career. More than a year before, on January 23, 1968, he had sustained a fracture of the femur of his right leg when apprentice jockey Juan Gonzalez caused an accident with a careless move on the stretch turn at Santa Anita. The healing process took so long there were times Shoemaker thought his riding days might be over. But here he was, back in white pants and black boots, with butterflies filling his stomach.

Shoemaker appeared to the roars of the paddock crowd wearing Liz Tippett's Llangollen silks. Whittingham hoisted him aboard a filly named Princess Endeavour, then headed for his seat. A few minutes later, Charlie was not the least bit surprised when Princess Endeavor won by two and a quarter lengths. Nor did he expect anything less when, later that same day, Shoemaker rode Racing Room to a length and a quarter victory in the feature race, again flying the Llangollen flag. All Racing Room did was equal a track record.

As darkness began to fall beneath the foothills of the San Gabriel Mountains, Shoemaker rode once more that unforgettable afternoon.

Whittingham was through for the day, but that did not stop Shoemaker. He won the last race on the program aboard a horse named Jay's Double. Three-for-three after 384 days on the sidelines.

The grand comeback of 1969 was only one of many highlights in the unique relationship between Whittingham and Shoemaker. Their bond goes back to the early 1950s, when Shoemaker was a snaggle-toothed prodigy and Whittingham was hustling to establish himself. They began to really click in the mid-1960s when Shoemaker was Charlie's rider of choice for the best horses owned by Tippett and Howard Keck.

Their golden years were the 1970s, when Shoemaker was in his forties and Whittingham's stable was headquarters for nearly every good horse in the West. In 1970 and '71, the Whittingham-Shoemaker combination won forty-three stakes races. Their total for the decade was 144. Then, during the 1980s, when the whispers started that Shoemaker should retire, Whittingham stood by "my man Shoe" as often as he could. Charlie's faith was rewarded at Churchill Downs in May of 1986 when Shoemaker brought Ferdinand home first in the Kentucky Derby.

"Charlie's always been a good friend," Shoemaker said. "Still is. It wasn't until I started training that I realized how tough his job was. And just how good he was."

Whittingham and Shoemaker were notorious drinking buddies, closing down many an airport or hotel bar while on the road winning big races. Whittingham would launch into his war stories, complete with the gory details of throat slittings and hand-to-hand combat. Shoe would wrinkle his nose and laugh. "Charlie," he would say, "you're so full of shit. You know you didn't carry anything but a pocketknife over there. Didn't you have a desk job?"

They still go around and around, despite the fact that Shoemaker was rendered quadriplegic in April of 1991 in a car crash. After a lengthy hospitalization and rehabilitation, Shoemaker returned to the racetrack and his training career in the fall of '91, only to be greeted in the Santa Anita paddock by Whittingham.

"It's about time you went back to work," Charlie said with a grin.

It was difficult for Whittingham to come to grips with Shoemaker's injury. Approaching the age of 80, Charlie did not really need another reminder of man's fragility and ultimate mortality. But as Shoemaker came to terms with his paralysis, Whittingham followed suit. One morning, more than a year after the accident, Whittingham asked Shoemaker if there weren't times he didn't get just plain pissed off at his rotten turn of luck.

"Doesn't do any good to get mad," Shoemaker replied. "Anyway, what am I gonna do if I do get mad at somebody . . . bite them?"

Whittingham loved the answer. Wished he had come up with it himself, in fact. Deep inside the damaged body, Whittingham still recognized the same old Shoe. And Shoemaker never forgot a thing about Charlie.

"Charlie never likes to work his young horses out of the gate," Shoemaker said. "He thought it would get them too stirred up, and he's probably right. It didn't make things any easier for us jocks, though. You'd be on a first-time starter for Charlie, and as you walked toward the gate you got the feeling the horse was seeing it for the first time. They would fall out of there all tangled up. Sometimes it was all you could do to stay on. Of course, by their next start they were much better."

Whittingham, from the beginning, put Shoemaker in a class by himself. "He had such good hands," Charlie pointed out. "He was so easy on them, but they ran like the devil for him anyway. As small as he was, he could still make a big old hunter do whatever he pleased."

"Shoemaker was a significant component of Charlie's success while I was with him," recalled Neil Drysdale. "A horse would always move up in condition after Shoemaker rode him."

Whittingham treated Shoemaker as an equal. His kidding was laced with affection, never derision. And Shoemaker collected Whittingham stories for pleasure.

"In the sixties the jockey wasn't paid his share of the purse automatically," Shoemaker said. "You had to bill the owner, just like the trainer always has. I walked up to Charlie in the paddock one day and told him Liz Tippett owed me a bunch of money and I needed his help getting it.

Charlie didn't have much sympathy. 'Stand in line,' he said. 'She owes me more than you.'

"He must have been something when he was younger, because he could get pretty wild when I knew him," Shoemaker went on. "There's one time I'm sorry I missed, when he got into a fight with some sailors in a Mexican restaurant on the other side of the racetrack. I guess they got him down and held him while one of them wrote something on his head with lipstick.

"We had some great times when I rode for him. Other than the Derby, the most fun might have been when Mary took me off Cougar for the Hollywood Gold Cup, and I won the race anyway."

In 1973, Shoemaker had fallen out of favor with Mary Jones, in spite of his two years of success aboard Cougar. Jones was distressed by Shoemaker's performance aboard her horse in the Turf Invitational that May. She wanted Whittingham to find another rider for the upcoming Hollywood Gold Cup, and Whittingham wanted to leave well enough alone.

The local press—primarily Gordon Jones of the Los Angeles *Herald Examiner*—was having a feast at the owner's expense. "Shoe Gets the Boot" read one headline. Like a modern-day Pontius Pilate, Whittingham washed his hands of the whole affair. He arranged for Laffit Pincay to ride Cougar and gave Shoemaker a consolation prize named Kennedy Road.

"They were pretty tough on Mary," Whittingham said. "Booing her and all when she walked into the paddock. And then Shoe goes out and wins the race with Kennedy Road. I had a feeling he'd run big, though. I wasn't exactly giving Shoe an empty wagon."

Whittingham would socialize plenty with riders like Eddie Arcaro, Ralph Neves and Don Pierce. They were all part of the racing fraternity, and Charlie was at heart a fraternity guy. In public, though, Whittingham would strike a pose of mild contempt. "What good's it do to tell them anything," he'd say in mock frustration. "You see that little rise leading out to the track. When they get to that spot, whatever you've said runs right out the back of their heads."

As far as Whittingham was concerned, it was okay to give riders and their agents a hard time because Whittingham had been there before. He knew what it was to hustle and plead for a crumb from a reluctant trainer. He became convinced very early how few riders really made a difference, and how most of them just got in the way. None of the jockeys he represented ever won a Kentucky Derby or a Santa Anita Handicap. If he could help it, as a trainer, none of them would keep him from winning one, either.

Whittingham has never felt obligated to share his plans for a particular horse, no matter who might need to know. A jockey's agent is making a mistake if he approaches Charlie with an innocent, "Will you be running that horse next week?"

"None of your god damn business."

"Charlie will drive agents crazy sometimes," said Scott McClellan, a second-generation agent who grew up in Charlie's vast shadow. "Most trainers, they work a horse a half, a couple of five-eighths, then three-quarters, blow them out and enter. Charlie gets up to three-quarters, then he works a mile. Then another mile, then maybe another mile! Pretty soon you've got no idea what he's gonna do with this horse.

"Then, one day, he'll walk up behind you, squeeze your arm above the elbow—just enough to hurt a little—and say, 'I put that filly in.' And smile. Maybe you've taken a call, maybe not. Charlie doesn't care. He always knew you'd wait if you were smart. If you weren't smart, he could always get someone else. And you were screwed."

To hear Whittingham tell it, jockeys always have been a necessary liability along his road to success. Many a horse won in spite of a ride. Sometimes, he allowed, you could slap a pair of goggles on a sack of potatoes and get the same quality of performance as you did from the real thing.

To that end, Whittingham rarely gives jockeys much serious thought. They are a component in the puzzle of the race, but nothing more. And once on board they are out of Charlie's control. Whittingham is frustrated by things that are out of his control, but rarely are they worth an ulcer.

Occasionally, he will take a little extra time with a rider. He has given any number of young jocks valuable exposure and experience. Corey Black, Aaron Gryder, Steve Valdez and Rudy Rosales have been among them. One day at Del Mar he was seen giving a detailed lecture to an eighteen-year-old apprentice just before a race. Caught in the act, Whittingham explained, "He's young yet. He's still got a chance to be a smart rider."

Usually, Whittingham will just stand in the paddock, shooting the breeze and eyeballing his horse. Bill Shoemaker, when he was riding for Charlie, would take a few golf swings with his whip, saying even less than the trainer. Laffit Pincay, another Whittingham regular, will stand, hands on hips, and grapple with his own thoughts in Spanish. Whittingham rarely bothers to interrupt. Guys like Eddie Arcaro, Milo Valenzuela and Howard Grant were going to do whatever they wanted out there, no matter what a trainer said, so Charlie didn't waste his breath. Most of the time he'd simply say, "Hurry back." If they did, they followed instructions.

"I finally figured out why Charlie never gives any instructions," Shoemaker said. "If he doesn't, and you screw up, then he can say it was all your fault."

Pincay came on the scene in the mid-1960s in Chicago and immediately moved to the big show in New York and California. Whittingham provided Pincay with his first win in a race worth $100,000 in 1967. The name of the horse was Drin.

"After that, I started riding whichever horse Shoemaker did not ride for Charlie," Pincay said. "They said Shoemaker had the choice, but I know it was Charlie who told Shoe which one to ride. It didn't matter to me, though. Most of the time I would end up winning on the other one anyway."

Pincay represented brute strength and Shoemaker was the soul of finesse. Between the two, Whittingham had it covered. And he had the horses to lure the riders away from other trainers.

"I love riding a good horse for Charlie," Pincay said. "Good horses do not all feel alike. Some are not conditioned enough. They win anyway, because they have so much class. But Charlie's horses always have so much power. You can tell they are ready to perform.

"That's why he always tells you not to worry about going wide," Pincay went on. "He doesn't want you to get stopped trying to get through. That's a great feeling for a jockey, to know you can lose some ground and still the trainer says you will have enough horse to get the job done."

Like Shoemaker, Pincay has a long history of highs and lows with Whittingham horses. He has been aboard four of Whittingham's fourteen winners of the San Juan Capistrano Handicap, the longest major grass race in America. He rode both Cougar and Greinton when they won Santa Anita Handicaps after four-month layoffs.

Pincay also has had a front-row seat for some of Whittingham's greatest disappointments. He was part of the Miss Musket debacle when she was humiliated by Chris Evert in their 1974 match race. Pincay's left-handed whipping caused Perrault to drift out into John Henry just enough to be disqualified after winning the 1982 Santa Anita Handicap. And there was a series of races aboard the hard-luck Greinton in 1985 that had Whittingham checking his blood pressure.

First, Greinton had a shot at a million-dollar bonus if he could add the Sunset Handicap to his earlier wins in the Californian Stakes and Hollywood Gold Cup at Hollywood Park. The race set up like a piece of cake. Only four horses lined up against them. With a quarter of a mile to run, Greinton and Pincay had dead aim on the pacesetter, Kings Island. Whittingham was counting the money. But as hard as Greinton tried, he could not get by. The million went down the drain by a lousy head.

Later that year in New York, Greinton and Pincay were blocked and hemmed in for most of the Marlboro Cup until, deep in the stretch, they finally wormed loose. Greinton was steadily grinding them down, but it was simply too little too late. They finished fourth, beaten barely a length.

"If I could ride one of those races again, though, it would be the Million," said Pincay of the 1985 Budweiser Million at Arlington. "That is one time I should have stayed inside with a horse of Charlie's and tried to get through."

Instead, a frustrated Pincay made his move wide after finally clearing another horse who had been in the way for most of the race. While Pincay got unscrambled, a big English gelding named Teleprompter slipped through inside and opened a daunting lead. Greinton lowered his head and went after the leader, but the story was still the same. Second, beaten less than a length.

"The thing about Charlie, he is very loyal," Pincay pointed out. "He maybe gets mad at something you do, but he never takes you off the horse. When Perrault was disqualified, I didn't lose the mount. Another trainer probably would have taken me off."

Whittingham explained without resorting to sentiment. "Take off a jock for something like that and you miss the chance they might learn from their mistake."

Chris McCarron first crossed the orbit of Whittingham at Laurel Race Course in November of 1972. McCarron was seventeen, learning the ropes from a Maryland trainer. He was more than a year away from his first mount as a professional jockey. Whittingham was at Laurel with Cougar, the best grass horse in the land.

"One afternoon in the paddock here comes this big, gorgeous brown horse wearing four thick, white polo bandages," McCarron said. "His tail was long, and up over his back. He was prancing and dancing, and just looked magnificent. I thought, 'Wow, there's a California horse!' "

Seven years later, Whittingham provided West Coast newcomer Chris McCarron with his first California victory in a major event when he put the rider aboard Balzac in the Oak Tree Invitational. McCarron made a daring move to take the lead entering the far turn and went on to beat the champion mare Trillion.

"When I first knew Charlie I wasn't really awestruck . . . until I had been around him for a while. Then I started going through the media guides and kept seeing 'Whittingham, Whittingham, Whittingham.' How in the world can a guy win a race twelve times? I couldn't believe the way one trainer could dominate the biggest races on such a tough circuit."

Before long, McCarron began to understand. As he rode more and more horses for Whittingham, he also shared in the morning exercise chores.

"I'm always amazed at the variety of training methods there are at the track," McCarron noted. "They can be so different, and yet they all can work. But when you analyze it a little more deeply, you can't really say they all work as well as Whittingham's way, simply because Charlie has been so much more successful than all the rest. You can't ignore the stats.

"Charlie has an extreme sense of attention to detail," McCarron went on. "He leaves no stone unturned when it comes to finding out what might make the horse a happier camper. He wants to know just how hard a horse was blowing immediately after a work, for instance. If a horse tires pretty badly and doesn't gallop out real strong, Charlie will watch the horse walking back and notice whether or not he's having a hard time recovering from the exercise, or maybe he's recovering very quickly. He will make his assessments from there. He notices everything."

McCarron also found out that you question Whittingham at your peril. In 1988 he was aboard a filly named Fitzwilliam Place, all decked out and ready to roll for Charlie in the Gamely Handicap at Hollywood Park. McCarron had ridden Fitzwilliam Place before and found her to be a difficult filly to read. On this particular day, however, the signs were not good. McCarron got the attention of the official veterinarian, who briefly examined the filly and then ordered her withdrawn from the race. By the time McCarron returned to the paddock tunnel leading to the jockeys' room, Whittingham was there—going ballistic.

Nothing could have insulted Whittingham's professional pride more deeply. It was the ultimate public humiliation, to have a jockey and a racing official decide one of his horses was not fit to run in an important stakes race. Whittingham unleashed a verbal torrent that would have made a Marine drill instructor proud. At the end of the tirade, the trainer vowed to McCarron, "You'll never ride another horse for me again."

"I didn't go around his barn very much for quite a while after that," McCarron said. "If I showed my face too much it would have been a constant reminder of the incident. I would have liked an apology—the way Charlie scolded me wasn't very pretty—but I decided to take the whole thing with a grain of salt. As far as I was concerned it was water under the bridge. I wanted to forget about it, and give him time to forget, too."

Three weeks later, Fitzwilliam Place won the Beverly Hills Handicap. Aaron Gryder, an eighteen-year-old with barely a year and a half of experience, was in the saddle. McCarron finished third aboard Chapel of Dreams.

"Ironically, I had all kinds of trouble in that race and still only got beat a half length," McCarron recalled.

By the following winter, McCarron was out of Whittingham's dog house and back aboard horses. During the spring of 1989 he latched onto a full-figured filly named Claire Marine, who was owned by Whittingham and longtime horse partner Sidney Port. McCarron and Claire Marine won five stakes races together and lost a sixth by a nose. The one they lost was the Gamely Handicap. The winner was Fitzwilliam Place.

As the 1989 Breeders' Cup Classic approached, McCarron was waiting in the wings behind Pat Valenzuela as Whittingham's backup rider for Sunday Silence. Valenzuela, talented but troubled by substance abuse, had been the colt's rider from the beginning. Then, less than two weeks before the Classic, Valenzuela tested positive for cocaine. McCarron was at Whittingham's barn bright and early the next morning to work Sunday Silence, while Valenzuela ended up with a sixty-day suspension. In the showdown at Gulfstream Park, McCarron followed Whittingham's instructions to the letter. He merely waved the whip at Sunday Silence as they held off Easy Goer to win the Classic. The race clinched the title for the Whittingham colt as Horse of the Year.

"I hated to let Charlie down like that," Valenzuela said later. "He'd stuck by me, had faith in me, and put me on Sunday Silence in the first place. I just hope I can make it up to him someday."

Whittingham never keeps track. He's got better things to do than worry about who owes who what and how much around the racetrack. Anyway, there are better ways to settle debts—a little bit at a time.

Through the first half of 1983, Shoemaker was riding a French horse for Whittingham by the name of The Wonder. The French horse could run. He had already won three respectable stakes races, and Whittingham was thinking in terms of the Arlington Million later that summer. But first, The Wonder was scheduled to compete in the American Handicap on the Fourth of July.

Unfortunately, another top horse Shoemaker had been riding was also gunning for the American. He was faced with a familiar dilemma—two horses out there and only one pair of hands. For most jockeys, the decision would have been agonizing. For Shoemaker, it was worth maybe a moment's thought.

"I'll stick with Charlie," he said. "He's stuck with me for a long time."

The horse he gave up was John Henry.

CHAPTER 9

FLYING HIGH

"He who hoots with the owls by night can't soar with the eagles by day."

The big, black Labrador retriever took one whiff of his pie-eyed master and skulked to the far side of the room. "Old Tar's mad at me now," mumbled Charlie Whittingham as he headed for his bed at the Cockatoo Inn. "Knows when I've had too much, he does. Can't stand the smell, can you boy?"

Tar sank his head on his paws, looked up at Whittingham and sighed. By morning, the smell would be mostly gone. Tar would drag his two-legged pal back to the barn at Hollywood Park, where Whittingham would be off and running again, on his way to another day at the very pinnacle of the American racing business. It was 1971, midway through a campaign full of pressure and prestige, steak and martinis, and enough pure drama to satisfy even the most jaded racing fan.

The year before, at the age of fifty-seven, Whittingham finally had achieved the goal he'd seemed destined to reach for so long he couldn't remember. The 1970 season ended with Whittingham astride the racing world, the leading North American trainer on the money side of the ledger with stable earnings of $1.3 million. He had reached the top of that slippery pole. Now the trick was keeping the claws sharp and strong and then hanging on for all his might.

The 1970 season would be hard to surpass. Whittingham had trained eleven different stakes winners for six different owners. His domination of California grass racing was relentless, with depth as well as breadth. In 1970, Whittingham horses finished first and second in the Del Mar Handicap and the Carleton F. Burke Handicap at Santa Anita. He swept both divisions of the Will Rogers Handicap at Hollywood Park, and ran a remarkable first, second and third in both the Oak Tree Invitational at Santa Anita and the Lakeside Handicap at Hollywood. In fact, California's only major grass race *not* won by a Whittingham horse in 1970 was the Sunset Handicap. As if to remind "Chuck" of his roots, Horatio Luro descended upon Los Angeles to win that race with One for All, owned by John A. Bell III.

Of the forty Santa Anita stalls under Whittingham's thumb as the 1971 season commenced, four of them held priceless treasures. There was Daryl's Joy, the New Zealand star who had lost nothing in translation to Southern California conditions. He won both the Del Mar Handicap and the Oak Tree Invitational in 1970. There was Turkish Trousers, a highly strung three-year-old filly who was being touted by Whittingham as the best in her class. And there was Cougar, the enigmatic Chilean horse dubbed "Cougar II" by the *Daily Racing Form* because of a pre-dated domestic runner with the same name. Whittingham's Cougar was soon to prove himself one of a kind.

Finally, there was Ack Ack, who had come to Whittingham at the end of 1969 as the last remnant of Capt. Harry F. Guggenheim's racing empire. Publisher, aviation pioneer and a giant in New York racing circles, Guggenheim had known Whittingham since the early 1950s, when the captain's Turn-to was a worthy rival of Porterhouse. Ack Ack was well known from his wins at one mile in the 1969 Derby Trial at Churchill Downs, the Withers in New York and the Arlington Classic in Chicago while he was trained by Frank Bonsal.

After being switched to Whittingham, Ack Ack did not miss a beat. He won the 1970 Los Angeles Handicap at Hollywood Park on a disqualification, dazzled his audience at Del Mar by setting a track record for five and a half furlongs, then he took a curtain call at Santa Anita in the fall by winning the Autumn Days Handicap on the grass. It was obvious to everyone that Ack Ack had the ability to take every sprint race in sight during 1971. The opposition could only pray that racing secretaries would slow him down with the lead pads last carried by Swaps and Native Diver.

Whittingham had other ideas. Outrageous ideas, in fact. He saw something in Ack Ack that was too absurd to put into words. He envisioned the colt as a mature five-year-old, at peace with his prodigious speed and ready for a different challenge. Whittingham sifted through Ack Ack's pedigree and found such names as Alsab, Royal Charger, Turn-to and—what's this?—none other than Princequillo, courtesy of Horatio Luro. All of them stirred together spelled uncommon endurance, an untapped resource of latent stamina. A master plan was brewing in Whittingham's blueprint mind. Ack Ack, the sprinter supreme, could and would be trained for the riches of distance racing.

"It was always the most impressive thing I noticed about Charlie while I worked for him," recalled Neil Drysdale, who was Whittingham's assistant trainer from 1968 through 1974. "One of his great attributes is being able to determine what a horse is capable of. He can visualize precisely what a horse is going to do later on, and therefore he can be very single-minded in going for that goal."

The ability is rare. Such insights have led to great rewards in the stock market and real estate. Instead, Whittingham's powers were finely tuned to Thoroughbreds, and Thoroughbreds alone. In Ack Ack, a tough colt who stood his ground and demanded strong handling, Whittingham saw a genuine look of eagles—and dollar signs.

"Whittin'ham says he's going to win the Santa Anita Handicap with Ack Ack," whispered Pete Wilson, a jockey's agent who could spot a conspiracy at a hundred yards. "He's getting down in the Tijuana future book. I would suggest you do likewise."

At first, Whittingham kept his cards close to the vest. Ack Ack embarked upon his 1971 campaign in a conventional and entirely predictable manner, carrying 129 pounds in the Palos Verdes Handicap at six furlongs. The track was still sticky from recent rain, Ack Ack drew the inside post, and Jungle Savage beat him in a race that amounted to a four-story billboard for Whittingham's ultimate intentions. Six-furlong events in early January were not particularly important, Charlie was saying. Richly endowed ten-furlong races in March and July were the real targets.

The wet weather of early 1971 broke and mid-January temperatures gave Southern California a summertime shine. On January 16, when Ack Ack appeared for the San Carlos Handicap, the mercury reached a record eighty-four degrees. Ack Ack, still disguised as a sprinter, played the part to the hilt. He blazed the first half mile in less than forty-six seconds to leave track record-holder King of Cricket in the dust, then tacked on a third quarter mile in just under twenty-four seconds. Approaching the end of the seven furlongs, Ack Ack seemed spent, and Jungle Savage was gaining. Bill Shoemaker kept busy as a worker bee in order to win by about two lengths. After the race, Whittingham told everyone it was time to stretch out. Ack Ack would be braving the world beyond one mile for the first time in his career.

In the meantime, the horse had been quietly for sale. Capt. Guggenheim, gravely ill, was entertaining offers somewhat more realistic than the million-dollar reserve he had placed upon Ack Ack at his dispersal auction in late 1969. Whittingham, at that point deeply committed to his remodeling of Ack Ack as a distance runner, had no intention of letting the horse slip through his fingers. When Guggenheim died on January 22 at the age of eighty at his estate in Sands Point, New York, the executors turned up the heat on the sale of Ack Ack. Needing a buyer from his stable of patrons, Whittingham placed a call to Cougar's owner, Mary Jones.

"How much, Charlie?"

"We can get him for four hundred thousand and I'll take half."

"Hmmm. In that case, don't you think you should toss your commission in the pot?"

Whittingham told Jones what to put in the pot and hung up. It was a risky move, since he already had committed to buy Ack Ack for the designated price. He quickly dialed E. E. "Buddy" Fogelson—oilman, philanthropist, Thoroughbred breeder and husband of Academy Award-winning actress Greer Garson. Fogelson's first major foray into horse racing had come in 1938 when he bought Dauber, winner of the Preakness.

(Later, after Ack Ack was such a success, Fogelson liked to recall the day

Dauber set foot on California soil. He broke loose from his handlers, scampered off down the road and injured himself in the process. Fortunately, Fogelson was having better luck with Whittingham, winning stakes with Noholme, Jr., Bargain Day and Colorado King Jr. even before Ack Ack came along.)

Finally, a deal was struck. Whittingham, who considered Ack Ack on the verge of becoming the best he had ever trained, was anxious to secure a healthy chunk of the horse. Strapped for liquid assets, he agreed to apply his sales commission plus training expenses toward a one-third share in Ack Ack. The balance, Fogelson told Whittingham, would be payable whenever the trainer came up with the money. Arrangements went right down to the wire, with funds transferred to the Guggenheim estate at the last minute in order to clinch the transaction. On January 30 the announcement was made: Ack Ack had been sold for a half-million dollars (a well-rounded figure that obviously included commissions). More significantly, he was staying put in the Whittingham stable.

One week later, the Fogelsons were at Santa Anita to watch their new baby in action in the San Pasqual Handicap at a mile and one-sixteenth. They were giddy with anticipation. Greer Garson, an effusive animal lover, already had anointed Ack Ack her knight in shining armor. But the dream nearly turned into a nightmare. Ack Ack stumbled so badly at the start he almost went to his knees. Shoemaker held on, Ack Ack righted himself, and still they were able to make the lead. Up in the stands, Whittingham gripped his binoculars and searched for any sign that serious damage may have been done. Ack Ack opened a long lead down the backstretch. His advantage was cut in half around the turn. Then, as was his habit, he began leaning left through the stretch. Eddie Belmonte, riding the Eastern colt Delaware Chief, allowed himself a fleeting moment of hope. But Ack Ack had enough to win by three-quarters of a length.

Whittingham rushed to the track to inspect his investment. There were superficial cuts on the right front foot, obviously sustained in the tangle after the break. Everything else seemed in place, although Whittingham did not rest easy until Ack Ack had cooled out and was walking soundly later that night. By the next day, Whittingham knew they had dodged a high-caliber bullet. Ack Ack's advance would resume on schedule in the San Antonio Stakes three weeks hence.

In the meantime, Whittingham gave Ack Ack a few morning trips to the gate to erase the memory of the San Pasqual. Eugene "Snake" McDaniels, Ack Ack's groom, fussed with the foot until it was perfect. Whittingham had a feeling Ack Ack's next race would be his best race yet.

Greer Garson spent the morning of February 27 on the docks of Long Beach, serving as the principal celebrity during the welcoming ceremonies for the luxury liner Queen Mary, soon to be converted to a hotel and tourist attraction. Garson wrapped a line around a sturdy dockside cleat and said a few words, then raced across town to Arcadia in time to watch Ack Ack win with ease. The San Antonio went by in the blink of an eye, as Ack Ack left the gate as if launched by springs. The field, thoroughly discouraged, never got close. With the slightest urging, Shoemaker could have squeezed a track record out of the mile and one-eighth. Instead, he won by three and a quarter lengths, mindful of Whittingham's words, "They never pay by the clock."

The only horse on the horizon with a chance to derail the Ack Ack express was stabled right down the shedrow. Clearly, if Ack Ack had become the best older horse in North America, Cougar was pounding along hot on his heels.

It was a perfect scenario, pulled straight from a Hollywood script. Two rivals on the same team, different as night and day. Ack Ack was the All-American boy, a no-frills straight-shooter who plunged ahead without considering the consequences. Cougar, on the other hand, was an elegant artiste, mysterious and unpredictable. He was all long lines and refined, almost effeminate next to the power pack that was Ack Ack. On the right side of his brown rib cage, hidden from public view by saddle blanket and girth, was a splash of white, a symbol, perhaps of Cougar's quirky individuality. Ack Ack, a traditional bay, allowed himself no such indulgences.

Francis Risco, Cougar's Peruvian groom, discovered the horse to be a trusting creature who never seemed to have a bad day. Cougar sucked down his feed like a Hoover upright. He napped like a prizefighter on the day of his races. And, according to Risco, he even displayed an occasional sense of humor, affecting a preference for his native Spanish at odd moments.

Cougar had speed—certainly not Ack Ack speed—but he seemed more comfortable when allowed to warm into a race before rising to the challenge. Whittingham cultivated in Cougar a dynamic finishing kick, one that could reach out and grab all but the most superior front-runners. As 1971 began, Cougar had yet to win a race in four tries for Whittingham and Jones, including a soggy failure in the Man o' War Stakes at Belmont Park. The New Year changed all that.

On January 1, 1971, Cougar disregarded an uncomfortably soft Santa Anita course and won the San Gabriel Handicap. Three weeks later, brim full of himself, he went to the lead soon after the start and trotted home by six lengths in the San Marcos. In the subsequent San Luis Obispo, at a mile and a half on soft grass, Cougar and Shoemaker dogged the slow progress of the determined Daryl's Joy and could not find quite enough to get by. Whittingham, one-two again, knew what he had to do next.

He had to run Cougar in the Santa Anita Handicap, Ack Ack and all. Cougar already had proven his worth on dirt, both at home in Chile and on American soil at Del Mar, when he set a track record just prior to his purchase. The equation was simple, posing few variables. Either Ack Ack would be able to sustain his speed the mile and a quarter of the Handicap, or he wouldn't. Either Cougar would be able to catch Ack Ack, or he wouldn't. Rarely is a major horse race so easily distilled to its essence— before it has been run.

Francis Risco and Snake McDaniels went horse-for-horse for $100. Whittingham stayed away from such intramural arguments, but he had few doubts about what would happen. "Ack Ack's got all the speed, and speed kills," he told anyone who had failed to pay attention.

Through the first part of the race, Figonero—winner of the 1969 Hollywood Gold Cup—attempted to press Ack Ack and wear him down under his 130 pounds. Ack Ack shrugged off Figonero on the backstretch and disappeared into the distance. Whittingham shifted his binoculars back to Cougar and frowned. The South American was throwing his head in reaction to the dirt smacking his eyes and face. Laffit Pincay, who was riding Cougar for the first time, gave up the idea of saving any ground. He wheeled his horse to the outside, away from the flying clods. In a flash, Cougar leveled off and began passing horses.

Deep into the stretch, Ack Ack still was in a race of his own. But Shoemaker was on guard. He knew the last furlong would be the toughest. Sure enough, Ack Ack began showing signs of weariness just as Cougar started one final charge. "I never thought Cougar would catch Ack Ack," Whittingham said. "But he did well to make it as close as he did." After ducking left and then right from Pincay's whip, Cougar regained an even keel and was only a length and a half behind his stablemate at the end.

"I ain't bettin' you no more," McDaniels told Risco, figuring Ack Ack was fortunate to have won. Whittingham vowed to keep Ack Ack and Cougar out of each other's way for the rest of the year.

The end of the the Santa Anita meeting in April of 1971 was appropriately punctuated by Cougar's one-sided romp over reigning Horse of the Year Fort Marcy in the San Juan Capistrano Handicap. It was stakes win number fourteen for Whittingham at the Santa Anita meet. Amazingly, Whittingham appeared to have reduced a difficult, frustrating sport to absurd simplicity. Horse racing—at any level—was not supposed to be this easy. Charlie's grooms and exercise riders strutted through life like lords of the backstretch. Neil Drysdale was looked upon as the right hand of God, and Bill Shoemaker personified the stable's indomitable spirit. Could these people do no wrong?

If there was a weakness in the 1971 Whittingham portfolio it was among three-year-old colts. The barn was dry as a bone, with the exception of Restless Runner, a useful sprinter-miler owned by Liz Tippett. Whittingham's winter and early spring monopoly of Southern California received passing attention in the national racing press, and then the focus switched to the Triple Crown. Charlie stayed home.

Good thing, too, because 1971 was fairy tale time on the Triple Crown trail. Canonero II, the enigmatic Venezuelan, won the Derby and the Preakness, then drew a crowd of 82,694 to Belmont Park for his defeat in the Belmont Stakes. Back in California, Whittingham shook his head and remembered how this same Canonero couldn't even warm up West Coast two-year-olds when he was in town during the 1970 Del Mar meet.

The California scene shifted to Hollywood Park, but the song remained the same. Whittingham first and sometimes second, the rest nowhere. Turkish Trousers, a real live wire who rarely submitted to a proper morning gallop, reeled off seven straight stakes wins, five at Hollywood alone. Ack Ack wrenched an ankle, so Cougar stepped in to win the Californian Stakes on the dirt. When Ack Ack came back, he came back in high style to win the Hollywood Express, a minor entertainment at five and a half furlongs. Cougar responded with his best race of the year, an operatic performance in the Invitational Turf Handicap—sponsored by Ford's new Pinto line—in which the Big Cat came from twenty-five lengths behind under 127 pounds to beat Fort Marcy by a neck.

"It's been a long time since a horse gave me a finish like that," admitted Shoemaker.

"He's never run a better race in his life," said a frustrated Elliott Burch of Fort Marcy. "But what can you do with Shoemaker and Whittingham?"

"What do I need with a Pinto?" cracked Whittingham. "I've already got a Cougar."

Charlie also was putting in overtime at the bar of the Cockatoo Inn just a few miles from the track, where he camped out on racing nights during the Hollywood season rather than commuting across town to Sierra Madre. Whittingham was in a familiar groove—first training, then the races, evening rounds at the barn, and back to the Cockatoo for martinis, dinner (Tar would join him at the table), more cocktails, and a few hours sleep. Then it was back to the track before dawn.

By midsummer, things were going almost too well. Charlie was flush and everyone knew it. "Friends" appeared out of the woodwork for a helping hand. Charlie never said no. For a while, it was hard to remember just how tough horse racing could be. Suddenly, the game had become as easy as downing a cold lager. And Whittingham mistrusted anything that came too easily.

Without a steady diet of diverting challenges, Charlie grew bored. His humility never slipped, but he did spend more and more time hooting with the owls. "Some guys play golf. I drink. It's my hobby," he would proclaim. Holding court in a corner of the Cockatoo, he would pound down deadly dry gin martinis, regaling his audience with tales from the old days, while pals would try to keep pace. W. L. Proctor, the rugged Texan, drained warm cognac and needled Charlie about his hard times on the hustle. Lazaro Barrera, alight with the glow of a tall Cuba libre, kept insisting that Whittingham was Mexican, born in Tijuana, not Chula Vista, and in truth was named Rodriguez.

Then Whittingham would growl once more that he could "out-train all you sons-a-bitches" and slide quietly under the table. They'd load him into a car and drive to peaceful Lowell Avenue in Sierra Madre, where Proctor would keep the engine running while Barrera helped his *borracho* buddy to the door. Tar would answer, up on his hind legs and spoiling for a fight. Barrera would use Charlie's body as a shield, then escape into the night.

Whittingham's incredible self discipline finally hit a limit. The celebrations grew dangerously habitual. His training did not suffer, but his routine was corrupted. And above all, his routine was his strength. Typical of Whittingham, he knew when to pull up. With the aide of Dr. Robert Kerlan, Whittingham found a quiet hospital for a brief detoxification. For a few days he trained from bed—a strange sensation—with Drysdale executing orders in the field.

The horses never missed a beat. Ack Ack answered Cougar's blast in the Invitational Turf Handicap by winning the American Handicap on July 5 in front of 51,299 Hollywood Park fans. All he did was carry 130 pounds to a local grass course record. Shoemaker insisted his horse was sapped at the end. But no one was fooled. The jockey was campaigning in his own way to limit further weight penalties. Whittingham went on record saying he thought 130 pounds should be the most a horse should have to carry. Their pleas met with blank stares. Everyone was focused on the potential fireworks of a second Ack Ack-Cougar showdown in the Hollywood Gold Cup on July 17.

Though his opinions regarding weight on racehorses have often seemed self-serving, Whittingham has remained constant as the North Star in his attitude. Of course, he usually trained the horses assigned the highest weights, so he has been able to accumulate plenty of data from which to draw those conclusions. Whittingham maintains that heavy weights—in the range of 126 pounds and up—can wear a horse down, risk injury and sap condition in disproportionate amounts. Rivals carrying lighter weights derive unfair advantages, no matter how inferior they may appear to be on paper when compared to the highweight. And, says Whittingham, since the people who assign weights have no practical experience with the consequences of weight-carrying, anything they say about "bringing a field together" and "making the race a good betting contest" is nothing but a load of steaming manure.

Whittingham also bristles at the idea that racing, and racing alone, seems intent upon penalizing its brightest stars by bringing them down to the level of the bit players through the artificial requirement of weight carrying. On a given day, says Charlie, any top horse can throw in a bad race for a hundred different reasons. Why increase those chances by making him lug twenty more pounds than the next best animal in the race? A racing secretary would insist that the great weight carriers became great stars and energized the sport. Charlie, ever obsessed with longevity, replies, "Yeah, maybe. But for how long?"

Jack Meyers, the man with the dirty job, emerged from his backstretch office with 134 pounds attached to Ack Ack's name—the most ever given a horse at Hollywood Park—and 130 pounds on Cougar.

"If it's up to me, Ack Ack will not run." Those were Whittingham's words when he heard 134. It made him feel better to say them out loud. Two days later, Ack Ack spoke for himself with a mile work in a rapid 1:39 3/5. Whittingham said Fogelson would make the final decision; and Fogelson, a member of Hollywood Park's board of directors, said run.

Actually, it was easier for Whittingham to swallow Ack Ack's weight than

Cougar's. For Ack Ack, the Gold Cup would be the last handicap of the year. The only other race on his schedule was the Woodward Stakes in New York, in which all older horses carried the same weight. Cougar, on the other hand, still had handicaps on his dance card. A good race under 130 pounds would be more penalizing than rewarding in the long run. Whittingham was convinced that either of his horses could win the Gold Cup. He decided it should be Ack Ack.

Just in case, Whittingham entered Ack Ack, Cougar and Burt Bacharach's recent stakes winner Advance Guard for the Gold Cup. "You never know," he liked to say. "Them other horses in there could all drop dead." He did declare for all to hear that "I'll probably run only one." Two days before the race it was apparent which one it would be when McDaniels brought Ack Ack over to the grandstand for a schooling session in the paddock. Cougar, dozing peacefully back at the barn, was conspicuous by his absence. Whittingham clued in Martin Kivel of the Pasadena *Star News* on Friday, then put in scratches for Cougar and Advance Guard late Saturday morning. The racetrack, fearing a fan backlash, withheld delivering the information to the public until 4:45 p.m., less than one hour before post time.

Not surprisingly, there were boos and sour grapes spread among the 47,923 fans who showed up for the Gold Cup, most of them led to believe they might see a thriller in the spirit of the Santa Anita Handicap. Whittingham could have cared less. Besides the fact that he answered only to his owners—and his own conscience—he was weak and dizzy from the effects of the flu and a 103-degree fever. Drysdale and Whittingham got Shoemaker's saddle—all thirty-six pounds of it—anchored safely on Ack Ack's broad back, then sent him out to make history. The fans, calmed by the sight of their hero, also were treated to an appearance by Cadiz, winner of the 1963 Gold Cup, who led the parade to the post with mane and tail all decked out in red and white ribbons. Some smart aleck suggested Cadiz should have stuck around for the race, as well. Even at age fifteen, he may have been the class of the victims lining up against Ack Ack.

Indeed, the opposition was helpless, their tactics reduced to cheap tricks and scrambling for second. Jesus Guadalupe, aboard the quick colt Judgable, broke fast from his inside post and began yipping and yelling in Ack Ack's ear. Shoemaker glanced over in disgust and took a long hold, while the Fogelson runner toyed with Judgable going past the stands the first time. Around the clubhouse turn, Judgable folded and Guadalupe developed sudden laryngitis. Ack Ack was long gone, 134 pounds and all. With an eighth of a mile to run, Ack Ack was still six lengths in front. He began to lean left, as usual, and Shoemaker kept scrubbing away. They glided under the wire almost four lengths clear of Comtal, the longest price in the field at 71-to-1, significant only because the track had added a rare exacta to create pari-mutuel interest in the one-sided slaughter.

Through the first half of the year, Whittingham was on a pace to break the single-season earnings record of $2.4 million set by Eddie Neloy in 1966. Then, without warning, reality returned. The near seamless success of 1971 began to fray. Whittingham, who held a lifetime pass on racing's roller coaster, simply buckled down and dealt with each piece of bad luck as it came along.

It started on Hollywood's closing day, when Cougar was caught at the end of the two-mile Sunset Handicap by a former claimer named Over the Counter. A sixteen-pound difference in the weights had something to do with it, especially since the margin was only half a length.

The following week, shortly after the stable shipped a hundred miles south to Del Mar, Ack Ack suffered an attack of colic that came close to being fatal. "We couldn't get anything through him," Whittingham said. "It was a pretty tough week before he was in the clear." Veterinarians Jock Jocoy and Joe Cannon teamed around the clock with the Whittingham crew to relieve the blockage and pull Ack Ack through.

Cougar, now on center stage alone, went east in September to run in the United Nations Handicap at Atlantic City. The entourage was greeted by heavy rain and a soft course that spelled doom for the high-stepping South American. Every time he planted a foot, it took twice as much energy to pull it loose. At the merciful end of the race Cougar was sixth, twenty-one lengths behind Run the Gantlet.

Then came the Woodward.

Although he had recovered from the colic, Ack Ack was in no shape to re-enter training and travel three thousand miles and adapt to a different track and climate. Enter Cougar, who was feeling frisky after the disaster at Atlantic City. Whittingham and Jones decided that the Belmont Park event was as ripe for Cougar's stretch kick as it was for Ack Ack's blinding speed. Cougar, Francis Risco and exercise rider Emilio Iglesias were dispatched to Long Island and bedded down with Buddy Hirsch at Belmont. Whittingham would follow on the day before the race.

Everything was going as smooth as glass on the morning of October 1 as Peggy and Charlie Whittingham strapped themselves into their first-class seats and prepared for the flight to New York from Los Angeles International. Then came the annoying news. There would be a delay— "an indefinite delay"—while something mechanical was checked on the plane. To soothe the restless passengers, the bar in the first-class cabin was declared open.

By the time the flight arrived at JFK Airport it was the wee hours of October 2, the day of the Woodward. Charlie and Peggy, feeling no pain, piled into an airport cab and gave Hirsch's address to the leery driver. A few miles later, Peggy eyed the passing neighborhoods with suspicion. "Charlie," she said, nudging her husband. "I think we're being taken for a ride."

Sgt. Whittingham snapped into action. "Stop the cab!" he ordered, and grabbed the cabbie by the scruff of the neck. "Don't try pulling the long way around on me, buddy. We know these streets backwards and forwards. Used to live here, ya know. Now take us where we told you, and do it just like I say!"

Within minutes, the Whittinghams burst into the tranquil Hirsch household, flopped down on the master bed and called for the party to begin. "It's too late to plow. I came to play," announced Charlie. "Let's go right to the Bloody Marys!"

About the same time, Mary Jones was stirring out of a restless sleep at the International Motel near the airport. It was raining, a worst-case scenario that could turn Cougar into a wheel-spinning basket case on the sandy Belmont main track later that day. What rotten luck. They had made three trips east with Cougar and encountered three miserable storms. As far as Jones was concerned, the Woodward was nothing less than a chance for her Big Cat to seize the momentum toward Horse of the Year. She had done the calculations: Cougar had won major races on both dirt and grass. He was 2-and-0 against Fort Marcy, the reigning Horse of the Year. True, Cougar had lost his only encounter with Ack Ack. But Ack Ack was finished for the year, and here was Cougar, bright and fit and ready to fulfill the tradition that demanded a Horse of the Year candidate perform well in the East. The Woodward was everything.

Contrary to the legend growing around him, there was nothing Whittingham could do about the weather. He looked in on Cougar, got encouraging words from Risco and Iglesias, then retired to Buddy Hirsch's Belmont stable cottage for a little hair of the dog that had been biting him since the delay on the tarmac back at LAX. At the races that afternoon, Whittingham was in rare form, playing cordial usher to New York acquaintances in the box seats. He assured them, one and all, that Cougar would beat the living daylights out of this sad little bunch of local crows. They should just be glad he hadn't brought Ack Ack. Then he got serious.

"I think he'll be okay," Whittingham told Mary Jones after watching a few races. "The track's pretty tight." In fact, the heaviest part of the storm had missed Belmont Park. Cougar came out glowing and prancing, poniless and full of beans, looking as good as he had all year long. Whittingham watched him skip across the track in the warm-ups, then took the rubber band off his bankroll. Cougar entered the gate on the Belmont backstretch at odds of 4-to-1.

"We were borrowing money to bet more," Mary recalled. "That's how confident we were."

He was in the race from the start, closer than usual but cruising like a dream. Shoemaker kept Cougar clear of the spraying sand and began his move to the leaders around the gently banking far turn. Up ahead, the Puerto Rican star Tinajero was on the lead but looking weak. Cougar came to him on the outside as they left the three-sixteenths marker and went by in a hurry. Unfortunately, he also leaned inward, barely clearing Tinajero. Eddie Belmonte, the piccolo-voiced New York favorite, screamed and reined back hard on Tinajero. Shoemaker straightened Cougar and barreled to the finish line, five lengths clear of second-place West Coast Scout, who caught Tinajero in the last yards. Immediately, the stewards called for an inquiry.

While the judges mulled their decision, the Cougar party were told to assemble for a photograph in the winner's circle. Against his better judgment, Whittingham gathered his group. Shoemaker scowled down from the horse. Charlie sensed his jockey's trepidation and feared the worst. Jones took up her customary position at Cougar's shoulder, clutching his left rein and forcing a smile. A few minutes later, the picture was rendered an unhappy memory. Cougar was disqualified and placed third, behind Tinajero.

"Here," said Whittingham, flashing $3,000 worth of win tickets at Risco. "How's that for a souvenir." Risco had bet $100, a week's wages, but so had Charlie.

Instead of sulking, Whittingham took the initiative. "At least we showed 'em who the best horse was," he said. Everyone thought he meant Cougar, of course, and he did. Sort of. Forget about the disqualification, he insisted, and look at the finish. Cougar was in a class by himself, and Ack Ack is more than a cut above Cougar. Whittingham challenged the Eastern press to exercise sound logic, confident they would come to only one conclusion: Ack Ack was, by all measures, the Horse of the Year.

"Ack Ack would have won the Woodward by a hundred yards," Whittingham maintained. Only Mary Jones put up any argument.

The good-natured sniping between owner and trainer continued three weeks later in Maryland, where Cougar was gearing up to run in the Washington, D.C., International on October 25. Both Whittingham and Jones spent most of their time worrying over the weather and the prospect of soft turf at Laurel Race Course. But they did take time out to entertain the locals when prodded to discuss the merits of Cougar and Ack Ack:

M. J.: "You know Cougar would have beaten Ack Ack in the Woodward, Charlie. Why don't you admit it?"

C. W.: "I'll spit in my beer if he would have!"

M. J.: "Could it be you're saying that because you own one-third of Ack Ack, and you don't own any part of Cougar?"

C. W.: "Buddy Fogelson owns Ack Ack."

M. J.: "Not very convincing, Charlie. Not very convincing at all."

When another storm lashed the mid-Atlantic states over the weekend, turning the course to mush, Whittingham and Jones pulled the plug and scratched Cougar from the field. On Monday, Run the Gantlet required 2:50 3/5 to win the mile and a half International, a time almost twenty-seven seconds slower than the course record. The following Saturday, Cougar was back home in sunny California, winning the Oak Tree Invitational by five lengths.

The following January, at the Waldorf Astoria Hotel in Manhattan, spot-lights bounced off Whittingham's gleaming skull as he accepted the very first Eclipse Award as Thoroughbred racing's outstanding trainer of 1971. Ack Ack was hailed at Horse of the Year, champion sprinter and best older horse. Turkish Trousers was accorded honors as the best three-year-old filly. Cougar was shut out, but Charlie told Mary Jones, "Don't worry. He'll get his turn."

CHAPTER 10

WHAT PRESSURE?

"You've got to climb pretty high in the tree to get the ham."

Tap City. Whittingham has been there. Living on the cuff. Waiting for a score. The memories keep things in perspective. Charlie once owed Bing Crosby ten dollars, and Crosby, a fellow with plenty of money, called in his mark.

"Let's see," said Whittingham, scratching his head. "If I don't pay you the money, you're unhappy. If I pay you the money, I'm unhappy. I guess I'll have to make you unhappy."

Whittingham was sharing a San Francisco apartment in shifts with five other guys during the Tanforan season. It was the early 1930s, and the rent was next to nothing, but it might as well have been ten thousand a week for all they were able to scrape together.

"The landlord was getting on us to pay up or get out," Whittingham recalled. "Highball Kelly had the room in his name. The landlord sees him in the lobby one morning and says, 'Mr. Kelly, I'll give you two days to pay the rent.' Highball says, 'That's very nice of you. We'll take the Fourth of July and Christmas.' "

Early 1950s, Golden Gate Fields, and Whittingham was batching it on the road while Peggy stayed home with the little ones back in L.A. Charlie relied on Buddy and Sandy Hirsch for wheels to the track. His stable was paper thin. "Loan me a hundred," he said to Buddy one day. "I'm running one in the last race I like. But don't wait around for me. I'll get home one way or the other."

Later that night, Whittingham waltzed in and threw a wad of money on the bed. "There you go," he said. "Horse paid a hundred dollars." Sandy

Hirsch remembers it like it was yesterday. "It seemed from that moment on," she said, "Charlie stayed lucky."

Still, there were times when the feed man went away empty-handed after presenting Whittingham with a bill. "I'd lose sleep for nights when something like that happened to me," recalled Noble Threewitt, who trained alongside Whittingham from the beginning. "But Charlie would just say, 'Don't have it today, but you know I will.' Then he'd never give it another worry. Or at least that's how he acted."

Pressure descends upon a Thoroughbred trainer from a dozen different directions. The most successful among them can juggle the elements and rise above the constant clamor. The best of them are able to focus on their horses and listen to their own instincts. Those who fail fall victim to distractions, and to a fundamental misalignment of priorities. Through the years, Whittingham has rendered a complicated craft down to its essentials, then practiced them to perfection: Find a horse, care for the horse, win the best race that horse can win. Everything else is frosting.

The pressure sustained by a Thoroughbred trainer is vastly different from the pressure imposed upon the athlete in action. The athlete is under the gun only for the duration of the event, whether it be the blink of a high jump or the four quarters of a football game. But the trainer's work—like that of the coach or the manager—is tactical rather than physical. Their challenge unfolds in the days and weeks leading up to the event. There are countless hours in which to agonize, second guess, and cultivate a nightly ritual of nervous sweats.

So many things can go wrong. A trainer relies on a variety of skilled and semi-skilled help in handling the animals. Any one of them can wrap a bandage too tight, drop a hoof pick in the bedding, or doze off on watch and miss a sudden attack of colic. An exercise rider can work the horse too fast or too slow, lose a stirrup or fall off completely. The blacksmith might trim a foot too close or hit the frog with a nail. The veterinarian can blow a simple injection and burn a vein, or maybe forget a prescribed medication entirely.

The strength of Whittingham's organization under pressure has enabled

Charlie to set goals for himself that other trainers never would dare consider. One of them was the 1973 Santa Anita Handicap.

At the end of 1972, Whittingham had won his third straight money title. In the East, a massive two-year-old named Secretariat was a star on the rise. Richard Nixon, Whittingham's contemporary and fellow Southern Californian, was re-elected President in a landslide over George McGovern. And a petty burglary at the Watergate Building in Washington, D.C., was beginning to work its way into the American consciousness.

Cougar, the "Big Cat" from Chile, was the reigning king of the Whittingham stable. While Secretariat was being crowned Horse of the Year, Cougar wrapped up 1972 with his second straight win in the Oak Tree Invitational on November 1 to be hailed as North America's grass champion. Whittingham continued to marvel at the consistency and soundness of the South American, in spite of Cougar's peculiar knees-to-the-sky kind of stride.

"He's got that funny, high way of going," Whittingham pointed out. "And he does it very quickly."

Not quickly enough, however, to have conquered California's biggest prize—the Santa Anita Handicap. Cougar was second best to Ack Ack in 1971, then second again to Triple Bend in 1972. A third try was inevitable. But would he emulate Seabiscuit, who lost the race twice before winning in 1940? Or would Cougar go down as a latter-day Texas Sandman, who finished second, fifth and seventh in three unsuccessful tries?

Whittingham mapped out a daring plan and let word of it leak out a little bit at a time. It was his intention to bypass the traditional preliminary races leading up to the Santa Anita Handicap. Instead, he would train Cougar hard and long, and bring him up to the March 10 event without the benefit of a traditional prep. The racing press scoured the chart books for a precedent. The best they could find occurred in 1957, when Sunny Jim Fitzsimmons produced Nashua at the top of his game for the Gulfstream Park Handicap after an absence of four months and three days.

Whittingham knew the drawbacks. "Training a horse like that is harder on them than running them," he contended. "A horse can go sour, and you've got just as much of a chance at hurting them in a workout as in a race." Still, the pros outweighed the cons. By staying on the sidelines, Cougar could avoid picking up a crushing weight assignment for the Handicap. As a practical matter, he would be out of the way as his new stablemate, the Canadian colt Kennedy Road, was developing into a star for Whittingham. Finally, Whittingham knew it could be done because he had done it before—with Cougar.

In the early summer of 1972, Cougar was bothered by a bruised foot. Whittingham gave the injury plenty of time to heal, then brought Cougar back in October to win the mile and a quarter Carleton F. Burke Handicap on the grass at Santa Anita. It had been just ten days shy of four months since his previous race. Granted, the competition in the Santa Anita Handicap would be tougher than it was in the Burke. But the horse was the same. And Whittingham figured he had the key.

As the winter of 1973 progressed, Cougar's workouts became special events. He was put under the clock every five days, rain or shine, with exercise rider Emilio "Poppo" Iglesias at the controls. In late January, Whittingham began to send Cougar on a series of longer, more demanding moves, beginning with a mile and eventually stretching out to the full Handicap distance of a mile and a quarter. Iglesias, Whittingham's most trusted exercise rider, would indulge Cougar's habit of standing and gawking around, then off they would go on another trial run.

"Cougar could be a little moody," Iglesias recalled. "But Charlie said, 'Just be patient. He'll let you know when he's ready.' Once he got going, he was very kind to rate. Didn't take nothing. Then Charlie wanted him to really finish strong that last quarter mile. No matter what the final time looked like, every one of those works had a great last quarter."

Along the way Cougar lost his rider. That winter at Santa Anita, Bill Shoemaker went down in a hairy spill at the top of the stretch when another horse broke a leg. Shoemaker fractured his right thumb and resigned himself to missing the mount on Cougar in the Handicap. Whittingham, never at a loss for top riders, called on Laffit Pincay, since Pincay had ridden Cougar in the 1971 Handicap when they were beaten by Ack Ack.

On March 1, after the third race of the afternoon at Santa Anita, Cougar worked a mile and a quarter with Pincay in the saddle. Cougar never really leveled out until the final quarter mile, then he finished like a runaway freight train. Still, Whittingham wanted more. Five days later, he paired Cougar against Quack for a dramatic afternoon workout in front of more than eighteen thousand weekday fans. If Cougar was the star of Southern California at the time, Quack was the heir apparent. As pure training art, the workout beat any of the nine races on the program that day. At the end of a mile, Cougar and Pincay caught Quack and his rider, Don Pierce, although Quack was a shade in front at the finish line. This time, Whittingham was satisfied.

The race itself offered Charlie at his vintage best, with his horses testifying loud and clear. Kennedy Road, ridden by Pierce, slipped clear of the field at the head of the stretch and appeared on his way to victory. Cougar, head high and knees churning, suddenly materialized from deep in the pack to give chase. Through the final two hundred yards, the two horses raced side by side and even brushed slightly. Up in the stands, Whittingham's smile broadened. At the end, it was too close to call.

"I was hoping for a dead-heat," said Poppo Iglesias, who was also the regular morning rider on Kennedy Road.

"Either way, doesn't matter," said Whittingham, who headed for the winner's circle wearing a smile. Even when the stewards launched an inquiry into the contact between the pair, Whittingham shrugged and grinned. "I can't lose, can I?"

Cougar's nose was down and Kennedy Road's was up, which made the difference. The inquiry found no reason to make a change. Whittingham was hailed as a genius for his handling of Cougar, and a greedy son-of-a-gun for running one-two again. Charlie took a ration of credit, but mostly he praised the animal for tolerating the rigors of the intense training schedule. Mary Jones, beaming at the post-race press conference, wondered aloud, "Where did your other horse finish, Charlie?"

"Up the track," he replied, referring to the longshot, China Silk.

"Oh, too bad. So you didn't get first, second AND third."

Year after year, the high-pressure, big-money races have drawn Whittingham like a bear to a honeycomb. He was low on ammo when Arlington Park inaugurated the Arlington Million in 1981 as the first seven-figure Thoroughbred purse. But he was back to win it the following year with Perrault, and twice more in the ensuing eight years. When the Santa Anita Handicap offered a million-dollar purse for the first time in 1986, Whittingham felt it was only right that he be first in line. So he showed up to win it with Greinton.

In 1975, when the Oak Tree meeting came up with an early version of the Breeders' Cup Classic—a $350,000 affair called the National Thoroughbred Championship—Whittingham won it with the broad-beamed Argentine mare Dulcia at odds of 7-to-1. The following year the race was renamed The Champions, but the result was the same. Whittingham had the grass horse King Pellinore primed to beat a field of North America's best runners on the main track.

Racing historians hold a special place in their hearts for the 1970s, and so does Whittingham. Competing at the top of the game, both East and West, Whittingham led all trainers in stable earnings five times during the decade. The sport was blessed with a galaxy of heroes—Secretariat and Forego, Ruffian and Spectacular Bid, and, in Europe, Nijinsky and Mill Reef. Sometimes they would collide, as they did in New York in the fall of 1978, when two American Triple Crown winners met in the final major race of the year, the Jockey Club Gold Cup at Belmont Park. Whittingham, never one to miss a good time, was there in force with a horse named Exceller to challenge both Affirmed and Seattle Slew.

It rained without mercy the week of the Gold Cup, but Whittingham paid it no mind. Instead, he huddled beneath the shedrow with Francis Risco, who was now Exceller's groom, and they concluded that their racy bay horse would need to grow wings to be doing much better. Would this be their chance to avenge the Woodward of 1971, when the two men tore up their tickets on the disqualified Cougar? Whittingham thought so, and Risco believed it, especially after he heard from a not-so-neutral third party—Angel Cordero, who would be aboard Seattle Slew.

"Cordero came by one day and said it was Exceller who had the only chance to beat Seattle Slew," Risco recalled. "Not Affirmed. Nobody else. Just Exceller. And he knew the horse, because he had ridden Exceller the year before."

The rain continued, turning the track into a watery, brown gruel. Nelson Bunker Hunt, Exceller's owner, offered his trainer an out.

"It looks pretty bad out there, Charlie," Hunt said. "I'll understand if you think we should scratch."

"Nothing doing," Whittingham replied. "We're here. The horse is right. We're running."

Their images were dim through the dark gray mist, but halfway through the race one thing was certain. Exceller would need to draw on his deepest reserves to catch Seattle Slew, who was splashing along more than 20 lengths ahead of Hunt's brave horse. Whittingham peered through the gloom and saw what he wanted to see, as Bill Shoemaker, aboard Exceller, began steadily making up ground on the leader. Shoemaker cut the final corner and suddenly appeared just to the inside of Seattle Slew. Then Seattle Slew answered in kind. Exceller edged away and Seattle Slew fought back until he was almost on even terms as they approached the wire. But in the end it was Exceller, his head low and covered with mud, who held on to win by a nose.

"See," said an exhausted Cordero as he lugged his saddle past Risco after dismounting. "I told you he was the only one."

Whittingham always will take a chance when the horse is right and the race makes sense. But he also knows when to fold his cards, or stay out of the game entirely. Three straight years, from 1970 through 1972, Whittingham took a horse to Laurel Race Course in Maryland for the Washington, D.C., International. Each year he withdrew his horse because of the dangerous, rain-soaked ground, even though a victory would have clinched a national championship, first with Fiddle Isle and then with Cougar. After awhile it became a local joke. "Who did Charlie bring to scratch this year?"

In 1972, when Cougar was at the peak of his game, Whittingham was just one dry day away from running in the International. He walked the course the morning before the race and found the ground promising, although far from ideal. The homestretch was firmer than the backstretch, while the inside was holding up better than the outside. Couger, unfortunately, would have to make his move on the outside.

Then, early on the morning of the race, the trainer barged into Mary Jones' motel room with the bad news.

"It's raining. Raining like hell."

"No, Charlie, not again." Mary had gone through the same thing with Cougar in 1971. Frankly, she was tired of paying for these fruitless Maryland excursions. "I don't believe you."

Whittingham threw open the door. Jones could see the steady drops glistening in the light of the motel parking lot.

"You want to come with me to scratch the horse?" he offered.

"No thanks, Charlie. I'm going back to bed."

In those days the International was a major event. There was no competition from the Breeders' Cup or the Japan Cup for talent from abroad. The race was hyped as racing's version of the Davis Cup in tennis or the Ryder Cup in golf, with lavish attention paid to the American "team." Of course, Whittingham knew racing was the furthest thing from being a team sport. In scratching Cougar from the 1972 field, he cut through the rah-rah rhetoric and simply pointed out, "The bettors would have made him favored, and they'd all have wound up in the commode."

At the same time, Whittingham allowed how maybe Cougar should have gone to New York to run in the Jockey Club Gold Cup instead, and how he likely would have won the race without taking a deep breath. Sigmund Sommer, the owner of Gold Cup winner Autobiography, bristled when he got wind of the remark. He told his trainer, Frank Martin, to propose a match race. The terms would be a mile and a quarter on the main track, a hundred thousand dollars a side, winner take all.

Of course, the last thing Whittingham wanted to do was remake Cougar into a match racing animal. He knew a horse needed early speed to be competitive in a match. Ack Ack never would have lost going head-to-head. Even the versatile, aggressive Pretense would have been ideal. But the moody Cougar never warmed up until half the race was run. For a hundred thousand, it was the world's worst bet.

"Anyway," said Charlie, "I don't think Mary wants to put up a hundred grand for anything."

In the summer of 1974, Whittingham hummed a different tune when Jimmy Kilroe came calling with the idea for a $350,000 match race at Hollywood Park—a hundred thousand a side plus one hundred and fifty thousand from the racetrack. Charlie gave the green light to a one-on-one between Miss Musket, the filly he trained for Aaron Jones, and Chris Evert, the reigning queen of New York who was owned by Carl Rosen of the Puritan clothing line and trained by Joe Trovato. Some suggested at the time that Whittingham readily endorsed the match in order to please two of his clients, Marjorie Everett and Buddy Fogelson, both members of the Hollywood board of directors. Not likely, said Charlie. But the race did loom as a promotional coup. Furthermore, it was an opportunity for the sport to mute the tragic memory of Ruffian's fatal injury sustained in her match against Foolish Pleasure in 1973.

"When they came to me with the match race proposal, I really didn't know what to do," Jones recalled. "I asked Charlie what was expected of me. He recommended we call the challenge. It was his opinion Miss Musket would beat Chris Evert. That was good enough for me. I felt that if you've got a horse you want to champion, you'd better act like it. Anyway, I knew Charlie wouldn't spend five cents of my money unwisely, let alone a hundred thousand dollars."

Whittingham had a right to feel invincible that summer. In early July, it was announced that he had been elected to the Racing Hall of Fame. During the Hollywood meet alone, his horses had won the Vanity Handicap, Hollywood Gold Cup, the Californian and a half-dozen lesser events. Miss Musket had rebounded from her only loss of the season to win the Hollywood Oaks. The only dark cloud had passed early in the meet when Linda's Chief—purchased for $2 million by Jones in late

1973—crashed into the rail during the Los Angeles Handicap and suffered fatal injuries.

In spite of her Hollywood Oaks win, Miss Musket still may not have been at her best. She was a long, lean filly, nervous and prone to worry, and she had gone through a strenuous season. Her record was brilliant—every bit the equal to that of Chris Evert. On paper, the race appeared to be even. Miss Musket had the home court advantage; Chris Evert was proven at the mile and a quarter distance. The New York filly also had the real Chris Evert in her corner.

Whittingham decided to lean on Miss Musket's natural speed to take the initiative. In a radical move—at least for Whittingham—he decided to put blinkers on the filly. Normally, blinkers and fillies did not go together, as far as Whittingham was concerned. Such confining, focusing equipment was fine for a lazy colt, according to Charlie. But fillies tended toward the excitable. If anything, Whittingham demanded his fillies be surrounded by nothing but calming influences.

In the case of the match, however, Whittingham was being tactical. He wanted Miss Musket to be off and running and in control of the race from the very start. Two years earlier, Whittingham had watched in admiration as Convenience beat Typecast in their quarter-million-dollar Hollywood Park match race. Typecast had tried to stay with her quicker rival, but Convenience, trained by W. L. Proctor, had the sudden moves at all the right times and won narrowly.

Aaron Jones and his wife, Marie, invited fifty friends from back home in Oregon to join them at Hollywood Park for the Hollywood extravaganza. Unfortunately, the race turned into a one-sided romp. Miss Musket, ridden by Laffit Pincay, swerved shortly after the start and was never able to use her speed as Whittingham intended. Chris Evert, under Jorge Velasquez, seized the advantage and led all the way. At the top of the stretch, Pincay gave Miss Musket one last, desperate whack with his whip. The filly had no response, prompting Pincay to mercifully ease her into a common gallop as Chris Evert disappeared into the distance, her tail swishing a fond farewell. The official winning margin was recorded as fifty lengths—an unfair stigma for the loser, perhaps, but a more or less accurate reflection of Chris Evert's domination.

As far as Trovato was concerned, he had just out-trained a freshly minted Hall of Famer. "I didn't change anything with my filly," said Trovato, age thirty-seven at the time. "But the other man did."

Whittingham, as usual, took the defeat with aplomb. "I guess I'd better stay out of match races," he said immediately afterwards. "Maybe she sulked. I know she didn't run like she can." Later, after he was satisfied Miss Musket emerged from the experience unscathed, Whittingham tried to console Jones the only way he knew how, chest out and proud. "If we run against that other filly three times, our filly would beat her twice. They got theirs today." Whittingham went home and packed a bag to leave for the Keeneland summer yearling sale, where he bought sons of Forli and Ack Ack. Jones and his family retired to the Hollywood Park Hotel and their post-race party, which was getting underway in a suite of rooms named with a racing theme.

"We were in the Pincay Suite," noted Jones with more than a little irony. "Only Pincay did not show up."

Three weeks later, Whittingham was in Saratoga Springs, New York, cradling his plaque at the induction ceremonies for the Hall of Fame. The match race was ancient history. There were better memories to celebrate. Long gone days back in Tijuana with brother Joe and Old Man Stanfield, on the road with Luro, playing the big room at Belmont Park. But, in truth, the proceedings were woefully insignificant when considered in light of the events of August 8, just two days before, when Richard Milhous Nixon announced his resignation as the 37th President of the United States in the wake of the Watergate scandal.

Whittingham, timing his remarks to the moment, thanked the assembled crowd at Saratoga and dryly observed, "I guess I'll be the only Republican elected to anything this year."

CHAPTER 11

PRICE OF FAME

"I'm as confused as the little boy who lost his bubble gum in the chicken coop."

"**C**harlie, Charlie, what am I gonna do? I outlived all my money." It was a good line. Whittingham smiled, and without a second thought he dipped into his pocket to peel off a few bills for another old-timer who was down on his luck. It might have been Willie Alvarado, Apples Tabor or any one of a hundred guys still clinging to the game, forgotten by everyone . . . except Charlie.

"If all the racetrack people Charlie gave money to suddenly paid him back, he'd have more than he'd know what to do with," said Alice Rodich, Charlie's sister.

Whittingham's generosity sometimes comes attached to a subtle bit of wisdom, free of charge. A young woman on the Boone side of the family once approached Charlie and Peggy for advice—and possible help—in switching career paths. Her deepest desire was to become a veterinarian. But was it too late to start toward such a goal?

"I'm afraid I've waited too long," she said. "I'll be thirty by the time I finish all the schooling."

"So what," was Charlie's rejoinder as he wrote out the check. "You're going to be thirty anyway."

To witness Charlie Whittingham walking through a crowd at the racetrack is to watch a small-town politician at work. Making his way from the saddling paddock to his box seat in the clubhouse section favored by owners and trainers, Whittingham will brighten when he sees an old, familiar face. He will stop to chat with anyone who pulls him up, just as long as he has had time to dispatch a runner to make his bet. He will leave a trail of wisecracks and colorful sayings that send people away smiling and wondering if they would ever understand what Charlie meant.

To one fellow: "Sam here looks like he's down to the last button on old Job's coat."

To another: "Everybody's crazy but me and thee . . . and I'm not so sure about thee."

And to a routine query: "Of course I'm running that horse Sunday. What do you think I got him for, a watchdog?"

Whittingham's reputation as a notoriously soft touch for any hard luck tale stands in direct contrast to the uncompromising Marine sergeant people see when he runs his stable. Neither does his kind and gentle side necessarily jibe with that brawling barfly of his younger days, or with the outdated prejudice that colors some of his harshest vocabulary.

"That's just Charlie," said Arthur Hancock. "He's no different from a lot of people at the track. But I don't think he'll ever lose too much sleep over being politically correct."

"His bark is a lot worse than his bite," said veterinarian Alex Harthill, who has seen Charlie do plenty of both.

Like Archie Bunker, the lovable bigot from TV's classic 1970s comedy "All in the Family," Whittingham's words usually are drowned out by his deeds.

"How prejudiced can the man be," said Laura de Seroux, a former Whittingham exercise rider, "when he had a black man as his stable foreman for more than thirty years, and kept him on the payroll long after he couldn't do anything else but sit in a chair? Charlie would have stepped in front of a train for him." She was referring to Ed Lambert, who first joined Whittingham in the early days in New York.

Whittingham saves his greatest contempt for those who squander opportunity or talent, no matter what their race, creed or color. Nothing frustrates him more than to see a horse with potential that goes untapped. The same holds for humans. When Taylor Whittingham died at the age of twenty-one from a self-inflicted gunshot wound, one painful thought kept bubbling up through his father's grief.

"All his talent and all his education," Whittingham said. "What a waste."

If he allowed himself to dwell on the past, Whittingham could find plenty of tragedy. The deaths of his father and his brother Willie are part of foggy history. They are acquired memory rather than personal experience. Charlie's younger half-brother, Edward Rowbottom (he later took the Whittingham name), was mugged and beaten senseless in a New Orleans alley. The injuries left him mentally impaired and able to do little more than work at the stables for his brothers. He was killed at age sixty-four when a horse kicked him in the chest.

Big brother Joe Whittingham went from being Charlie's idol to his right-hand man. It was a hard road getting there, though. Joe was an admitted alcoholic who was also a brilliant horse trainer. Charlie has described him as "maybe better than me," which puts Joe Whittingham in sharp perspective. But his alcoholism prevented him from sustaining a career as a public trainer. He spent years doing odd jobs around the racetracks—parking cars, manning the stable gate—anything to stay close to the game.

When Charlie's business became successful enough to justify an expanded operation, he put his brother in charge of a string of horses at the San Luis Rey Downs training center, located about 30 miles inland from Del Mar. It was a perfect situation for Joe, with no one to answer to but Charlie. And Charlie only came around once a week, depending upon his schedule in the city. Combining a program of long, strong gallops with a calm yet structured environment, Joe would prepare two-year-olds for their first encounter with the hectic world they would be facing at the racetrack. When Charlie's stable became a haven for horses imported from Europe, South America and Australasia, Joe would handle their initial acclimatization at San Luis Rey. Charlie valued his brother's opinion. When Joe said "this one's a runner"—as he did during the early development of Turkish Trousers, Balzac, Tallahto, Top Command and dozens more—Charlie let himself get a little excited. With professional help for his alcoholism and faith from his brother, Joe Whittingham became a quiet legend as the man who supplied the foundation for a host of Charlie's stars.

Joe Whittingham's death from cancer at the age of seventy-two meant

Charlie had lost his only blood link to his early days in racing. Still, there were plenty of memories, most of them fond. Oldtimers still hailed Charlie as "one of them." Anyone Whittingham knew before World War II had an automatic entree into his good graces. If you could remember betting the option system at old Tanforan, or being in the crowd at Caliente the day Phar Lap ran, Whittingham considered you part of his extended family.

Taylor's death, on the other hand, rudely dashed his father's dreams. He saw in his youngest son nothing less than the spark of a natural-born horseman.

Taylor was, by all accounts, the most high-spirited, fun-loving, mischief-making kid in the Whittingham household. He was the kind of child who would put together a costume and perform a song and dance for company without need of encouragement, or, as his sister put it, "swing from a chandelier."

"Mike was quiet and I was shy," recalled Charlene. "Then Taylor came along. I'm sure my parents would have preferred another quiet one, but that wasn't Taylor. He was the most charismatic little kid you can imagine."

Michael was ten, Charlene was six and Taylor was a toddler when the Whittinghams made the Lowell Avenue house in Sierra Madre their permanent California home. There was always a nanny or a governess to help with the children.

"The three kids ate in the kitchen while Mom and Dad had their dinner in the den," Charlene continued. "We'd start making noise. Taylor would be under the table, or bouncing off the walls. And when we got too loud my dad would come to the door and push it open slowly, just a crack, and look at us without saying a word. Or sometimes he'd just knock at the door without even opening it. We shut up immediately."

Not surprisingly, Whittingham tolerated no questioning of his authority. He spent all morning and most of the day having orders followed at the barn. There was no reason things should be different at home.

"He never raised a hand to us, though," said Michael. "Really, he didn't even need to raise his voice. It never even occurred to you to disobey. He was never tested. I remember once at the beach as a kid he told me and some friends to clean up these tin cans we were playing with. I complained, and he lit into me with a verbal barrage I'll never forget. I don't think I questioned him again until I was in my twenties."

"My room was next to my parents' bedroom, so we all played in my brothers' room when my dad took his afternoon nap," Charlene said. "We'd be getting loud and crazy, and then suddenly Dad's voice would come out through the heater vent on the floor. 'Quiet down in there!' He'd be down on his knees in his room, yelling into the vent."

Both Michael and Charlene have memories of a playful father who would enjoy nothing more than horsing around on the floor.

"He'd swing from the door jamb, crack jokes and make funny faces," Charlene said. "My friends thought he was hilarious."

"We'd wrestle around," said Michael. "And you could tell how strong he was. I remember thinking how much he could hurt someone if he really intended to."

Michael went to work for his father before he was twelve years old.

"It was great fun," Michael said. "I got to know all the grooms and hear all their stories. Guys with names like Snake, Frog and Easy. I got fifty cents each for walking hots, then my dad thought I was making too much money. So he started paying me a flat two dollars a day."

Michael was eleven when he accompanied his father to Chicago for the Arlington Park summer meet. He remembers the segregated swimming pools, the mosquitoes ("big enough to hump a dog," as Charlie described them), and the instructions from his mother just before he left.

"Don't let your father drink too many martinis."

A few weeks later, the subject came up on a call from home. Young Michael was being watchful, as his mother had asked. But he needed some guidance.

"Is six too many?" he innocently wondered.

"When I turned sixteen and got my racing license, it was a great feeling," Michael went on. "Dad had to pay me the minimum of $36.95 a week from then on. Then I lined up a job at Arlington in the parking lot, so I was going to be rolling in money. On top of that, my dad sent his Alfa Romeo back to Chicago on the train. I even had a car to use."

That was the summer of 1962, when the Chicago-bound Whittingham stable included Black Sheep, winner of the Cinema Handicap at Hollywood Park, and Sir Ribot, winner of the California Derby Trial. The horses went by train and the family was going by air.

"You got your ticket?" a straight-faced Charlie asked Michael a few days before their scheduled departure. Michael didn't know if his father was kidding or not.

"Uh, well, no I don't."

"Well, you're a working man now, boy. If there's a job you need to get to, you've got to pay your own way. Oh well, I guess you can ride with the horses."

So Michael rode with the horses.

"It was a great experience," he said. "My mom didn't like it, but I know it was something I wanted to do all along. Part of it was a desire to do what my dad had done as a kid, when he rode the rails all over the place. This was the closest I would get to that experience.

"Mom fixed me a big basket of food to take along. We slept in the hay in the stalls. Sir Ribot was a nasty colt. You had to watch out. The way the car was set up, when you sat on the can he could reach over and bite you.

"There was a black guy and a white guy on the car with me looking after the horses. The black guy kept kidding me about being a rich kid. But he loved the stuff Mom had packed in that basket. The white guy was an ex-con, so I got to hear his stories. By the time we got to Chicago, I was so dirty we were all the same color."

Life for the Whittingham children meant travel, displacement, unpredictability and stretches of time with both mother and father on the road. In the 1990s, this would be a fairly common profile of the modern, two-professional, middle-class family, trying to stay one step ahead of a shaky economy. In the late 1950s and early 1960s, the Whittinghams were the exception to the stereotype. The popular American image was of June and Ward Cleaver or the placid Andersons of "Father Knows Best." The

Whittinghams, by comparison, were show business folks.

"It wasn't until I had a family of my own that I realized how weird it all was," Charlene said. "But as far as I was concerned, I had a very happy childhood. We went to private schools. We lived at the beach in the summer. We had a nice house, nice clothes, friends to play with. I felt really, really protected. That's a good feeling for a child, to feel safe.

"People would ask me how it felt to be Charlie Whittingham's daughter. I'd look at them and think, 'He's just my dad. How does it feel to be your dad's daughter?' Because my dad never acted like he was a big deal. He's very humble. Although he would tell us, 'I'm the Pope!' "

The Pope. Not the Bald Eagle. Not Sir Charles. Not the Tall Man from the West or any of the other obvious nicknames that came from the outside. "The Pope" came from within. And Whittingham, an occasional Catholic, was quite comfortable with an image of infallibility, especially when it came to his handling of Thoroughbreds. In most other matters he admitted to having feet of clay. The Ten Commandments were nowhere to be found in a condition book. Asked how long he would need for confession, the eighty-year-old Whittingham replied, "Too long."

Michael tested his father's capacity for tolerance when he entered into the "love generation" of the late 1960s, complete with long locks and full beard. On a rare visit home, mostly to see his mother, Michael was still there when Charlie got back from the track.

"Jesus Christ!" Charlie said with a shake of his head as he looked at his hairy son. He grabbed a knife and wrestled Mike's chin to the cutting board, where he threatened to start shaving.

"My mom thought he'd really do it," Michael said. "But I knew dad wouldn't touch so much as a hair. Later that day Sid Luft came over for dinner. He asked me where I was living. My dad was clear over at the bar, making drinks. But he didn't miss a beat. 'In a fuckin' cave. Where do you think?' "

Michael finally crawled out of that cave, as Charlie put it, to become an accomplished trainer in his own right.

"My mom didn't want me to be a trainer," Michael pointed out. "She wanted me to have a normal life. So I compromised and took some pre-veterinary study.

"There was one thing I overlooked, though. I hated to study. At least, I was bored by the lower level courses you had to take to get to the more interesting material. Anyway, I don't think I was meant to be a racetrack vet. When you come right down to it, their hours are just as crazy as a trainer's hours. And the work can be very tedious."

Michael worked for his father, then for Joe Whittingham at San Luis Rey. Finally, Charlie gave him a small "second string" of horses to train.

"I think I could have enjoyed being an assistant trainer forever," Michael said. "But Charlie booted me out. He said it was time to make it on my own. And he was probably right. I got some good owners from him and had some success right away."

Soon, though, the Whittingham name began to weigh heavily around Michael's neck.

"I had learned from my dad, so naturally my training style would be like my dad's," he pointed out. "But why would an owner go for second-generation Whittingham when the real thing is right over there?

"I suppose I could have handled it differently. Come on real strong or something. 'I'm a Whittingham and I can train better than anyone around!' But that's not me. I'm pretty low-key when it comes to finding owners."

Tom Tatham and his Oak Cliff Thoroughbreds found Mike Whittingham and struck gold. After winning back-to-back runnings of the Santa Margarita Invitational at Santa Anita in 1982 and '83, they hit the jackpot with a colt named Skywalker. In 1985, Mike beat his father to the Santa Anita Derby winner's circle when Skywalker came through. Then, in 1986, Mike and Skywalker took the Breeders' Cup Classic—a feat Charlie would not accomplish until 1987.

While Mike was struggling with his direction in the late 1960s, Taylor found his niche on horseback at the Judson School in Scottsdale, Arizona, a private institution best described as cowboy prep. He became a prize-winning bronc rider and calf-roper, known for his flamboyant style and custom-made Western wear. Standing well over six-feet tall, with his long, handsome face and golden hair, Taylor Whittingham looked and acted the part of a star.

Back in California, Taylor went to work at Whittingham's stable. He walked hots, did a little grooming, and accompanied horses to the track aboard his handsome white pony, Sierra Ghost.

"Taylor was very proud of that pony," said Peggy Whittingham. "He would wash him off with a bleach cleanser to keep his coat a bright white. After awhile the men at the barn started calling the pony 'Ajax.' "

"He could handle a horse, all right," said Charlie. "Did fine around the barn. Then he got in with the wrong people."

Wrong for Taylor, anyway. Recreational drug use was as common in the early 1970s as speakeasies were in the Roaring Twenties. Some people went through the marijuana-and-cocaine stage, survived and moved on. Others were not so fortunate. By the summer of 1974, Taylor had drifted away from working at the track, though he still moved in racing circles. He designed and sold jewelry, beautiful pieces mostly shaped from gold. Occasionally, he would pop up at racetrack scenes like the Del Mar summer yearling sale. Mary Jones, still giddy from the success of Cougar, introduced Taylor to everyone as "the next great trainer named Whittingham."

On Labor Day evening, barely two weeks after his father had been inducted into the horse racing Hall of Fame, Taylor shot himself under the chin with a pistol being passed around at a party in Escondido, a town just inland from Del Mar. Peggy rushed to the hospital, while Charlie stayed at their beach-front home until word came that his youngest son was dead. Then he went to work.

On that morning of Tuesday, September 3, 1974, the mood at the racetrack was eerie. It was as if a huge rock had been dropped at the center of the local racing community, and the ripples were being felt at even the most distant perimeters. There was an unusual hush in the stables that morning as word spread of Taylor's death. In the vicinity of Whittingham's Barn N, hard by the backstretch viewing stand, people lowered their voices and glanced over to catch a peek at Charlie. Charlie the tough Marine.

"That was the only time I ever saw Charlie wear sunglasses in the morning," recalled Francis Risco, who'd worked at the Whittingham stable since 1968. "I know he didn't want us to see his eyes. We just did our work— what else could we do? But nobody said much to anybody."

The next morning a funeral service was held for Taylor Whittingham, age twenty-one. That afternoon, while Taylor was being laid to rest, his father was at Del Mar to saddle a horse, his jaw set, his eyes steely blue. When a friend from out of town inquired casually, "How's things?" Whittingham folded open a *Racing Form* and pointed to Taylor's death notice.

Cold? Insensitive? Everyone took their crack at a dime-store psychoanalysis of Charlie's reaction. Peggy never really understood why he didn't rush to the hospital that night to be with her. Charlene called her father "a rock, our real strength" through the whole ordeal. And of course, that was what he did best: accepting the role of the strong man standing tall in the midst of chaos.

Other friends saw in Whittingham the beginnings of a deep and everlasting guilt. Both Charlie and Peggy focused on drugs as a major contributor toward Taylor's death.

"We didn't know much about that stuff back then," Charlie said. "None of us did. We didn't know how bad they get hooked and how they can lose control of their lives."

Two years after Taylor's death—not quite to the day but close enough— a long-haired kid wearing bib overalls and riding boots showed up at Whittingham's Santa Anita barn looking for a job. Rodney Ray Rash was sixteen years old, right off the plane from Maryland, and ready to take California racing by storm.

Rash proved to be a natural-born horseman, fearless and firm with the toughest customers in the barn. However, the fast and loose California lifestyle played havoc with the Maryland farm boy. As Rash dug himself into a hole of substance abuse, Whittingham kept throwing him lifelines until, one day, Charlie made a commitment that stunned almost everyone around him.

"I ended up in jail after one of my drunks," Rash recalled. "When I got out I figured I'd be fired for sure. I had embarrassed Charlie in front of all his friends and in front of my own peers. I followed Charlie around that morning just waiting for the ax to fall.

"As we walked back through the stable gate, some old guy asked Charlie to sign him in. Charlie looked over his shoulder and told me to do it. I said, 'Charlie, you know I can't do that. I don't have the license to do it.' He said, 'Well, goddammit, if you're gonna be my assistant you'd better get your ass over to the stewards' office and get your license.' " Rash was twenty-two.

As the years went by, Whittingham conceded that he saw a lot of Taylor in Rash, both the good and the bad. "I couldn't save Taylor," Charlie would say. "Maybe I can help Rodney."

In 1991, Rash went out on his own as a trainer after nine years as Whittingham's chief assistant. He had been sober for more than four years. After sending out his first stakes winner later that season, Rash did not hesitate to give credit where credit was due.

"Everything I've been able to do I owe to Charlie Whittingham," he said. "Everything."

CHAPTER 12

THE HOLY GRAIL

"If I'd known this was such a big deal, I would have done it a long time ago."

One damp August morning during the summer of 1985, Bill Albritton came pounding down Whittingham's shedrow at Del Mar, shaking his head and grinning to beat the band. Big Rudy Roberts, busy mucking out a stall, took one look at his fellow groom and knew something peculiar had gotten into his head.

"You won't believe what I just heard," Albritton said. "I just heard Charlie tell Shoemaker they were going to win the Derby with the big red colt."

Rudy rolled his eyes and sniffed.

"Sheeeit, man! Don't you know those two is too old to vote!"

Rudy had a right to be skeptical. Charlie Whittingham win the Kentucky Derby? Surely, the Berlin Wall would fall before that happened. He'd rather train a pack mule to do hand stands. Whittingham and the Derby had been like oil and water for nearly 30 years. He was going on 73. The Derby? Not likely.

Whittingham's antipathy toward the Derby had grown to mythic proportions. Most of the legend was pure exaggeration—sometimes fanned by Charlie himself—but there was some degree of substance. To that point, the summer of 1985, there were good reasons why Whittingham's most recent foray to the Derby was back in 1960 with a second-string colt named Divine Comedy. For one thing, he had geared the thrust of his operation toward older horses, because older horses were stronger, faster and more consistent. Such an equation invariably added up to more prize money. For the most part, his owners went along with the program.

Whittingham, as everyone knew, was never in a hurry. To be at the Derby, year after year, a trainer and an owner needed to operate with an urgency that Whittingham found illogical and downright distasteful. He believed the idea of the Derby—a mile and a quarter for animals barely turned three—was fundamentally unsound. As far as Whittingham was concerned, the foals in a given crop that truly qualified for such an ordeal were few and far between.

It was also a matter of pride. Stubborn, bull-headed pride. Whittingham would not, under any circumstances, expose himself to the widespread ridicule he felt some trainers and owners so richly deserved when they took their dangerously unseasoned animals to Churchill Downs for what amounted to ritual public sacrifice. He'd just as soon stay home and drink linament rather than roll the dice with a nice young prospect and take a chance on permanent damage—and loss of potential income.

Still, Whittingham is a red-blooded American horseman with the thrill of the game running through his veins. For years and years, Whittingham wanted to win a Kentucky Derby as much as the next guy. Working within the bounds of his conservative, long-range program for young horses, he was always on the lookout for that breakthrough colt who could stand the gaff of hard Derby training. His standards for taking a horse to the Derby were not necessarily higher than those of other trainers, just different. And the difference sometimes made Charlie seem like an outsider, an iconoclast, and a plain old party-pooper.

However, Whittingham's chronic absence from the Derby was not from lack of trying. Many times through the 1960s, '70s and early '80s he would get right to the threshold of the race, then something would go wrong. With a few breaks along the way, Whittingham would have had a dozen Derby starters and goodness knows how many wins.

From the very beginning, when he trained the precocious young talent bred and bought by Liz Whitney, Whittingham was thinking Derby. Porterhouse, his first stakes winner and the reigning champion of his generation, was the 2-to-1 future book favorite when he bruised his front feet at Keeneland only a few weeks before the 1954 Derby. Whittingham cursed his rotten luck, but Liz took it like a champ, expressing full confidence that Porterhouse would come back as good as ever. He did, for the next four seasons.

Nashville was better than Porterhouse, as far as Charlie was concerned, and a brilliant sprinting two-year-old of 1956. He was also chronically unsound, a real race-to-race proposition. Under the circumstances, Whittingham deemed him no match for the likes of Round Table, Bold Ruler, Gen. Duke, Gallant Man and Iron Liege as a three-year-old the following spring. Nashville was preserved and became a tough older sprinter.

Anyway, Whittingham said to anyone who would listen, there was a bona fide Derby colt just down the shedrow from Nashville. His name was Royal Heir, a son of Princequillo.

"I bought him for $17,500 from Luro, before he even broke his maiden," recalled Sid Luft, who raced as the Rainbow Stable with his wife, Judy Garland. "Charlie liked him so much he wanted to buy half, and right now. He was coming into Manhattan from Belmont Park to buy some shirts at Brooks Brothers. So I met him there, and he wrote me a check for $8,750 right on the counter."

Back in California during the winter of 1957, Royal Heir broke his maiden with a breathtaking stretch run, then finished a close fourth to Sir William, Swirling Abbey and Round Table in the Santa Anita Derby. Alas, Royal Heir became ill and missed the classic, then suffered a fatal injury in June while training for the Westerner Stakes at Hollywood Park.

(Some sad stories have happy endings . . . eventually. With the insurance money paid on Royal Heir, Luft and Whittingham bought three horses from the C. V. Whitney stable. One of them, a promising colt with the unfortunate name of Rover, broke down and had to be euthanized. At the same time, Luft was strapped for cash trying to bankroll a show for Garland at London's Dominion Theatre. Whittingham advanced Luft $15,000 on Rover's insurance policy, and the show went on.)

In 1960, Eagle Admiral was Whittingham's Derby colt for certain. The red son of Khaled was brought along slowly at Santa Anita that winter, then was sent to Florida, where he defeated heavily favored Bally Ache in the Fountain of Youth Stakes at Gulfstream Park. Barely a week before the Derby, Eagle Admiral injured a knee.

In April of 1965, Whittingham was eyeing the California Derby at Golden Gate Fields with Perfect Sky. "I'm throwing you a bone," Charlie said to cranky Frank Buckley, who booked mounts for journeyman Eddie Burns. "Don't screw it up." Perfect Sky and Burns won at odds of 10-to-1, but any thoughts of sending him on to the Derby were scrapped when Charlie learned the gelding had not even been nominated to the race by his owner, William du Pont Jr.

One year later, as Whittingham ushered in the first of his stakes winners for Howard B. Keck, Saber Mountain developed into a full-blown star. Whittingham trained the son of Bagdad precisely as he thought a Derby colt should be trained: long gallops, long works, and a series of races designed to increase confidence and competitiveness. Saber Mountain won his first five starts and was thought of as the West's budding answer to pre-Derby favorites Buckpasser and Graustark. Then he fractured a knee while finishing second to Boldnesian in the 1966 Santa Anita Derby.

The list goes on, effectively trashing the idea that Whittingham was fanatically gun-shy with two-year-olds and therefore predisposed against developing young talent into Derby material. Whittingham was merely weighing the risks of submitting immature knees and muscles to such crushing pressure. It was "pay now or pay later" when it came to taking the Derby route. Whittingham needed the equivalent of a certified check on deposit before he would take a chance at scrapping a colt's entire career.

Tumble Wind, for instance, was an early prodigy, nothing less than a latter-day Nashville. Yet Whittingham saw in him a hint of the classics. He took Tumble Wind to Kentucky in the spring of 1967, fully intending to run for the roses. The colt pulled up badly, though, after finishing eighth in the Blue Grass Stakes, but he was not lost for good. That same summer he won the Hollywood Derby. At age four he won a stakes at a mile and a half.

A decade later, Whittingham was sky high on Balzac, a fiery son of Buckpasser. "Our best shot since Saber Mountain," Whittingham told Keck, and the taciturn oilman allowed himself a small ration of excitement. Even though Balzac finished second to Affirmed in the 1978 Santa Anita Derby, Whittingham was not discouraged. He saved that until after the Hollywood Derby, in which Balzac broke a knee chasing Affirmed again.

Whittingham's careful side cropped up in 1972 with Quack, a king-sized son of T. V. Lark who won the California Derby in a breeze. "The Derby would knock this big colt for a loop," Whittingham told Quack's owner, Millard Waldheim. "If we treat him right now, he'll treat us right later." Not much later at that. In July of his three-year-old season, Quack beat older horses in the Hollywood Gold Cup, equaling the world's record for a mile and a quarter on dirt in the process.

As the 1986 season dawned, the Whittingham record in the Kentucky Derby was an unimposing 0-for-2. Gone Fishin', the colt Charlie called "a cute little devil," looked like a winner at the head of the Churchill Downs stretch in 1958. But Whittingham knew better. He was not at all surprised when Gone Fishin' ran out of gas and finished eighth to Tim Tam. Divine Comedy, the last-second replacement for Eagle Admiral in 1960, was a late bloomer (he won the Saranac Handicap at Aqueduct later that year) whose heart really was not in the Derby. He ran ninth, a furlong behind Venetian Way, prompting sports columnist Jim Murray to describe him as the horse "whose name is half right."

But the red colt that Bill Albritton rubbed during the summer of 1985 was different. The red colt—his name was Ferdinand—was bigger and stronger than most two-year-olds Whittingham had seen. He had a good head and a quiet demeanor that spoke of nothing but class. His only real physical flaw was in the hind legs, positioned as they were at an angle slightly more beneath the massive rump than was absolutely ideal. Whittingham figured he could work around that, since the rest of the package was so very, very choice.

Pretty soon, you could tell Whittingham held Ferdinand in special regard. When he arrived at the barn at four in the morning, he would wander over to the red colt's stall. Ferdinand would come to the webbing and nuzzle his trainer, sniffing for a piece of peppermint candy. When Ferdinand was on the track, galloping smoothly along for Janet Johnson, Whittingham would scan the horizon, on the lookout for loose horses or wild-riding bug boys. Usually, after supervising a set of horses in the Santa

Anita saddling enclosure and walking ring, Whittingham would bring up the rear as they strolled back to the barn. When Ferdinand was among them, Whittingham was always at his side, admiring the muscles dancing beneath the glowing red coat and glancing up at Johnson as she tried to hide her excitement.

There was a single, overriding reason for Whittingham's confidence that Ferdinand was Kentucky Derby material. The one major variable decidedly in his favor was quite simply the distance of the race—a mile and a quarter. No one knows what it takes to be a mile and a quarter horse better than Whittingham; and Whittingham loved nothing more than a horse who could still be going strong at the end of ten furlongs in top company. You win at a mile and a quarter, he figured, and you've earned your money, you've bred a good animal and you've trained him right. In fact, between the victory of Mister Gus in the 1956 Woodward Stakes and Strawberry Road's triumph in the Arcadia Handicap during that winter of 1986, nearly forty per cent of Whittingham's stakes winners had won at ten furlongs or more. That's almost a hundred horses.

Not only did Ferdinand have the physical scope for the Derby, he also had the right folks. His sire was Nijinsky, the most recent winner of the English Triple Crown in 1970. His dam was Banja Luka (after the Yugoslavian city), a daughter of the stamina sire Double Jay whose family included the high-class sisters Tallahto and Le Cle. This was Howard Keck's best female line, and Whittingham had trained them all. He knew what to expect in terms of health, soundness, rate of development and personality traits.

Tallahto, for instance, was a tightly-wrapped daughter of Nantallah who needed earmuffs at the end of her career to make it to the gate in one piece. Whittingham kept Tallahto's lid on long enough for her to defeat males in both the Carleton F. Burke Handicap at ten furlongs and the mile and a half Oak Tree Invitational in 1974. Le Cle, on the other hand, was the cool half-sister. Her best race over a testing distance was the 1973 Del Mar Handicap at eleven furlongs. She was stopped dead through the final eighth of a mile, yet she was beaten only a length by the tough East Coast gelding, Red Reality, while finishing fourth.

Ferdinand had a quiet two-year-old campaign through the fall of 1985. He broke his maiden on November 3 at Santa Anita under Wesley Ward— Shoemaker was home nursing his Breeders' Cup jet lag from the day before—then Ferdinand drew his first flutter of recognition by finishing third to Snow Chief in the Hollywood Futurity in December.

At that point, there was no real hurry. Whittingham was not even fazed when the colt came up short a few times at Santa Anita that winter. He lost one race going a mile after getting the lead. He wormed his way out of trouble to win a minor stakes race at a mile and one-sixteenth. Then he dropped back to a mile in the San Rafael Stakes and was beaten again when his mind wandered after getting the lead. Shoemaker was learning to deal with Ferdinand as if the big colt was an immature prodigy coming to grips with his singular talents. Whittingham was the patient headmaster.

In the nine-furlong Santa Anita Derby that winter, Ferdinand had no chance to catch Snow Chief, whose natural early speed carried to great lengths under the right conditions. Anyone else might have ripped out their hair after Ferdinand's third-place finish, seven lengths south of Snow Chief. But Whittingham, whose trade was in futures, liked everything about the race but the size of the check. "Just wait," he vowed, "til he gets to Kentucky."

On April 18, Ferdinand was shipped to Churchill Downs and deeply bedded in stall 22 of Barn 41. Also along for the ride was Hidden Light, a daughter of Tallahto who had won the Santa Anita Oaks for the Kecks and was by far the more accomplished of the Whittingham team. Ostensibly, she was there for the Kentucky Oaks, to be run the day before the May 3 Derby. In reality, she served herself up as the best workmate since Marie Curie helped Louis Pasteur. Were it not for Hidden Light, there may not have been a Ferdinand.

Whittingham descended upon Louisville in all his glory. He was enjoying the best possible situation. After a gap of twenty-six years since his Derby try with Divine Comedy, he was able to milk the "I'm back!" angle for all it was worth. He recited all the colts he had trained which might have made it to the Derby were it not for bad luck or lack of seasoning. He pointed out how many of those same colts ended up with long and profitable careers by avoiding the stress of the Derby. And he challenged anyone to describe how his life would have been one degree different if he'd have won a single Kentucky Derby instead of seven runnings of the Santa Anita Handicap.

"The Derby is a nice race to win"—how would he know?—"but it's also the biggest baloney race there is because of all the sportswriters who might not see another race all year."

Someone even made the mistake of asking Whittingham if he thought this was his last chance to win a Kentucky Derby. A few years earlier, when Whittingham kept a mental machete sharpened for those who delivered stupid questions, Charlie would have carved his initials in the guy's forehead. Instead, Whittingham raised an eyebrow and lightly replied, "Hell, I'm not figuring on dying anytime soon."

In truth, Whittingham couldn't lose. Expectations were low for Ferdinand, and Charlie liked it that way. The Vegas odds ignored the colt at 20-to-1 or more. Snow Chief drew most of the media. Wayne Lukas was in high gear with the Badger Land bandwagon. Broad Brush, Groovy, Mogambo and Rampage had their followers, as well. Ferdinand, noted Timothy Capps of the *Thoroughbred Record*, was "sort of like a building that is widely held to be an architectural masterpiece but has no occupants."

As far as his demeanor as a racehorse, Ferdinand had all the aggression of Big Bird, the lovable feather-duster of Sesame Street. His training was usually an exercise in compromise. His concentration was spotty. Whittingham kept the colt fit with long gallops and long works; but he could only sit and wait for Ferdinand to display a glimmer of the competitive mentality he would sorely need come the first Saturday in May.

Then came The Mile. Early on the morning of April 24, nine days before the Derby, Whittingham orchestrated an exercise of once around the Churchill Downs oval for Ferdinand, in company with Hidden Light. Shoemaker flew in late the night before and was in the saddle aboard the filly. Larry Gilligan, Whittingham's old jock of all trades, was strapped on Ferdinand. As the work began, Shoemaker sailed away first, leading Ferdinand by a few lengths as the pair rounded the clubhouse turn and headed for the backstretch. Turning into the homestretch, Hidden Light was still going strong, with Shoemaker sitting tight. Gilligan, also under wraps, was under instructions to wait until the final furlong before giving Ferdinand the signal. When he did, it was a sight to behold.

"Shoe peeked back at me and saw this big, red head and neck coming at him under a pull," Gilligan said later. "And his filly was still going strong."

Whittingham wanted Ferdinand to learn to make the lead and stay there. To that end, Gilligan allowed his colt to edge slightly ahead of Hidden Light and keep her measured. Lapped on each other, they tripped the clock at 1:38 4/5. "Just right," Whittingham thought. Ferdinand's move got the wiseguys wondering if maybe, just maybe, Whittingham had come to town for something other than the cuisine at the Executive West Hotel. Charlie just smiled and fingered his bankroll, then went back to the room where Peggy whipped up his daily lunch of peanut butter and jelly sandwich with bananas, apple juice and milk. Whittingham's head hit the pillow for his early afternoon nap filled with nothing but delightful Derby dreams.

To that point, Ferdinand was a living billboard for the Whittingham training technique. Get them sound, get them strong, then work them hard and long. You cannot, Whittingham insisted, baby a horse up to a race like the Kentucky Derby. Ferdinand was fresh—in fact he was still a little green—so he got nothing but searching, two-mile gallops to flesh out that fast mile work. On April 29, four days before the race, Ferdinand and Hidden Light were out for another spin; this time it was five furlongs in :58 3/5. The track was playing fast—Badger Land had turned in a :58 2/5 the day before—and Ferdinand, to be honest, was still a horse who had never won a race beyond a mile and one-sixteenth. But a few people were starting to dribble away from the obvious choices. Among them was Steve Nagler, an associate producer with ABC-TV who urged his producer to place one of only three isolated cameras on Ferdinand and Shoemaker during the running of the Derby.

"It wasn't really that difficult a decision," Nagler later recalled. "We did an interview with Charlie in which he all but said the horse was going to win. It was as if he was taking a megaphone and screaming, 'Watch out!' Yes, Ferdinand was coming off a fairly ugly third to Snow Chief in the

Santa Anita Derby. But that's where you had to be tuned in to Charlie. When a good trainer is doing something that doesn't seem at all logical, that's when you'd better take it even more seriously."

On the morning of the Derby, Ferdinand was out before dawn for an easy jog. Whittingham suppressed a grin as he watched the colt prance to and from the racetrack, coiled and ready to strike. Ferdinand jumped and played, giving Gilligan all he could handle.

"Charlie, this sucker had all four feet off the ground just walking to the track," Gilligan said as he muscled Ferdinand back to the barn. "If he doesn't win today, there ain't no cows in Texas."

Peter Lyons, Whittingham's traveling assistant, was a tad more cautious, though every bit as excited as Gilligan. "I can't brag that I told everyone I saw to bet the horse," conceded Lyons, a native Irishman who had come to Whittingham from Gainesway Farm. "But I damn well knew we wouldn't be embarrassed. It didn't matter if he was 17-to-1 or 70-to-1, he was going to be right there at the end."

The Louisville weather of May 3, 1986, made good on its promise of sunny and warm, with temperatures creeping into the seventies. Whittingham outfitted himself in a light blue oxford cloth dress shirt, tan slacks, a tie of red and white stripes on navy blue background, his favorite light gray, houndstooth sportcoat and a gray tweed hat. Shoemaker, whose three previous Derby winners had become faded history from the 1950s and '60s, donned Elizabeth Keck's pink and pale blue silks, the colors borne so boldly by Turkish Trousers, Pallisima, Tallahto and Le Cle. Ferdinand wore red.

Once friends and family were safely stationed in their box seats, Whittingham returned to the barn by mid-afternoon. Shedding his jacket, he paced the shedrow and generally made his already anxious crew edgy as cats on a steam grate. "Let's get it over with," Charlie mumbled to no one in particular. Ferdinand lolled in his stall, paying no heed to the tension in the air. His long, sexy forelock trickled down over the snowcone-shaped spot of white between his wide, dark eyes as he watched his keepers with gentle curiosity.

Finally, the Derby horses began filing through the stables on the way to the track. Antsy as he was, Whittingham nevertheless held back a few extra beats until the main opposition decamped. Wherever he races, he always prefers to sit tight for as long as possible before leaving the friendly confines of the barn. His people watch the other horses walking down the main road to the receiving barn, waiting until all of them are accounted for before heading out. Call it a trademark, call it gamesmanship, or call it an old habit that dies hard. "The last shall be first," preaches Whittingham. "But don't bet on the meek inheriting the earth."

As soon as Snow Chief and his entourage of media and groupies dove into the gauntlet of fans lining the path to the track, Whittingham issued a curt, "Let's go!" prompting Albritton to lead Ferdinand into the sunlight. Suddenly, finally, it was happening again. After an absence of twenty-six years, Whittingham was bringing a horse around the clubhouse turn at Churchill Downs and into the claustrophobic, wire-caged saddling paddock to prepare for the world's most famous horse race.

On that distant day in 1960, the California-bred Divine Comedy had encouraged little hope that he would do much better than his odds of 61-to-1 predicted. He didn't. As Whittingham followed Ferdinand past the stands, he was not thinking so much about Divine Comedy's ninth-place finish way back when. He thought more about the people, and the great gulf of time that had swallowed so many memories. Aligned alongside the Whittingham colt for the 1960 Derby were horses trained by Jimmy Jones, Tennessee Wright, Bob Wheeler, Marion Van Berg and fellow Californian Farrell Jones. Victoria Park, the horse who stood next to Divine Comedy in starting stall number twelve, was schooled by Horatio Luro himself. By 1986, nearly all of them were either dead or retired, although some hung on to the game in one way or another. Whittingham, still competitive as a wolverine, had outlasted them all. And now he was standing amidst another generation of horse trainers, men like LeRoy Jolley, Jack Van Berg, Wayne Lukas, Philip Gleaves, John Gosden and Phil Hauswald. They looked at Ferdinand and his odds of 17-to-1, then they focused on Whittingham. Wisely, they ignored the odds.

After an uneventful saddling ritual and post parade, Ferdinand entered post position number one at precisely 5:38 p.m. and stood there for a full two minutes, steady as a redwood, while the other fifteen horses were loaded one by one. Charlie, who had left his binoculars back at the hotel, craned his neck for a view of the gate and reconnoitered the tote board to make sure he could spot the fractional times of the race as they were displayed in lights. He had done all he could. Ferdinand was as ready as he would ever be. Whittingham had reached another of those moments shared by coaches and combat commanders: the ultimate results were out of his hands. He could only trust in Lady Luck and in the ability of his troops to carry out a battle plan.

Shoemaker's presence aboard Ferdinand had a calming affect on Whittingham. The two men were totally simpatico, sharing a self-confident, uncluttered approach to the execution of their respective crafts. They had been winning and drinking and laughing together for more than thirty years, with big race memories going back to October of 1955 when Shoemaker and Mister Gus set a Bay Meadows track record in the $100,000 William P. Kyne Handicap. Since that day, Shoemaker had won more than two hundred stakes races aboard horses prepared by Whittingham. The rider considered himself the natural extension of Whittingham's training. Whittingham always figured that if he had been a jockey, he would have been Shoemaker.

A deafening cheer pierced the azure skies above Churchill Downs as the field for the 112th Kentucky Derby spilled from the starting gates. Groovy—who would go on to become a star sprinter—blasted to the lead, with Zabaleta, Bachelor Beau and Snow Chief hot on his tail. Broad Brush, the Ack Ack colt who had won the Wood Memorial in New York, established a good position. Badger Land, who carried a ton of smart money as second choice to Snow Chief, was pinched back at the break and had to be steadied. And Ferdinand?

At the start, Shoemaker had angled his colt slightly to the right to compensate for the placement of the gate. A straight line from the inside post would take a horse and rider smack dab into the curve of the rail where it bends into the Churchill Downs straightaway. As a result, Ferdinand had an inconsequential brush with Mogambo, who broke from post number two. Icy Groom, coming out of post number five, made a beeline to the rail under Eddie Maple. Shoemaker had to pull hard on Ferdinand's reins to keep him safely off Icy Groom's heels. In the meantime, Keith Allen had maintained a tight line aboard Wise Times (post number three) in front and to the outside of Ferdinand, while Jacinto Vasquez let Mogambo work his way between Ferdinand and Wise Times. Ferdinand skinned the inside rail at least twice that Shoemaker recalled. It was no place for a claustrophobic racehorse.

As the field flashed past the finish line the first time around, Ferdinand was at the absolute back of the pack, running sixteenth. Shoemaker wasn't worried—or at least he said he wasn't worried—although he did offer up a quick prayer for a fast pace and a few breaks. Up in the stands, Whittingham yelled for Shoemaker to "get him out, get him out," advice the rider hardly needed. By the time they reached the beginning of the first turn, Ferdinand was in a race of his own. There was less than a mile left to run and fifteen horses to pass.

Shoemaker, cool as a sniper, began picking them off one at a time. In the middle of the first turn he shifted Ferdinand to the right of Wise Times and began to follow Mogambo. As they straightened onto the backstretch, Shoemaker sent his colt between Wise Times and Mogambo, left them behind, and took up a position inside longshot Fobby Forbes. About that time, Shoemaker spotted Badger Land up ahead, beginning to accelerate on the outside. "Fine," thought the wise old rider, "I'll let him run interference." They passed another longshot, Southern Appeal, and came up alongside Arkansas Derby winner Rampage.

Derby riders earn their money during the first quarter mile—when position is the key—and through the final three-eighths of a mile. That is when the pacesetters collapse and the closers attack, creating a messy confluence of the hopeful and the spent. As Ferdinand banked into the straightaway, 1,320 feet from the finish line, he had Rampage and Wheatly Hall to his immediate left, and to the front a four-horse spread comprised of a tiring Snow Chief, the resolute Broad Brush, the surprising English colt Bold Arrangement, and Badger Land. Whittingham, now surrounded by the screams of family and friends, tried to talk Shoemaker through the moving wall. "Damn it, jock, what're you gonna do from there—sprout wings?"

To that point, Ferdinand had given Shoemaker instant gratification every time the jockey needed a burst of speed or a change of course. A tired horse will feel sluggish to the rider, slow to respond and clumsy when switching the lead leg of his stride cycle. But while those around him were showing signs of weariness as the race wore on, Ferdinand appeared as if he had merely galloped an early morning mile. For a big horse, he was light and nimble. He had to be to deal with what came next.

Just inside the quarter pole, approaching the black-and-white pole measuring just three-sixteenths of a mile from the finish, two things happened at once. Pat Day, aboard Rampage, decided to gamble for a small opening on the inside, between the rail and Snow Chief. But Snow Chief was exhausted from chasing too close to the fast early pace. He lost his momentum and began to lean inward, closing the hole coveted by Day.

At that very instant, Shoemaker found himself with a miraculous gap three lanes to the left, between the retreating Snow Chief and Broad Brush. The only other horse with a chance to make the opening was Wheatly Hall, running to Ferdinand's immediate left. Ferdinand had just completed a smooth shift to his right lead, which made a quick dart toward the inside awkward at best. Shoemaker, the consummate horseman, deftly reined Ferdinand to port and shouted "Hee-ya." The colt responded like a Ferrari on a tight mountain road. Libby Keck's pink and blue silks slipped from view for an instant, then appeared in all their bright glory as Ferdinand spurted through the hole and into the clear. There was still more than a furlong to run, but the race, for all practical purposes, was over.

Shoemaker did not let up. Ferdinand was the kind of colt who saw no reason to win by a length when a nose would do just fine. But the jockey had lost too many heartbreakers in the Derby to let this one get away—standing up on Gallant Man, slaughtered on the first turn with Candy Spots, swamped by a huge field aboard Agitate, battered in the stretch aboard Avatar. As the crowd slowly began to understand exactly who was leading the race and drawing away, Shoemaker slapped Ferdinand left-handed with his whip and kept up a loud harangue into the colt's fuzzy red ears. This was no time to pull up, no two-bit Los Feliz Stakes or San Rafael. Shoemaker pestered Ferdinand all the way to the wire to win by two and a quarter lengths over Bold Arrangement. Broad Brush and Rampage were close behind in third and fourth.

Peggy Whittingham had been to the Derby twice before, first to watch Divine Comedy and then to be with Mike Whittingham when he saddled Skywalker in 1985. She had stood beside Charlie through Santa Anita Handicaps and Hollywood Gold Cups, gauging the progress of his horses by the number of "god damns" Whittingham hurled at the jockey. But the Derby—this Derby—was definitely a brand new experience. "Just when I thought it couldn't get any more exciting," Peggy said later, "Ferdinand got through and we knew he was going to win. I couldn't even hear myself screaming."

Charlie bolted out of the box seat and headed for the grandstand stairs, leaving Peggy and the Kecks in the dust. Peggy was used to Charlie racing off to meet his horses, so she had made a dry run through the stands the day before, just in case the dream came true. As Whittingham was engulfed by the crowd, shaking hands and smiling, Peggy and the Kecks were stopped at a key checkpoint and refused passage by an overly zealous Churchill Downs security guard. Charlie had breezed through without a hitch. But then, everybody knew Charlie.

"These people own the horse who just won the race!" Peggy protested.

"Sure they do, lady," the guard replied. "Don't they wish."

Luckily, Tom Meeker, president of Churchill Downs, came along to clear the air. He served as escort the rest of the way until the victorious party was reunited on the porch of the cupola overlooking the special Derby winner's circle in the racetrack infield. A hatless Whittingham beamed down at ABC's Jim McKay and allowed how "it took me twenty-six years to get here 'cause I said I wouldn't come 'til we got a good horse. We got one now."

The next twelve hours were a blur of celebration and unrestrained joy. Whittingham left his hat behind in the track directors' room and shrugged it off, saying, "It probably wouldn't fit my head now anyway." Drinks went on forever in the bar at the Executive West before Charlie finally sat down for a midnight meal. Of course, he was at the barn the next morning at four o'clock to check on his horse and bask in the admiration of the backstretch community. By the time the sun illuminated the twin spires and Sunday morning traffic picked up on Longfield Avenue, Charlie was in rare form:

—"Sleep's overrated," he said to a crowd of drowsy reporters. "You get all the sleep you need after you die. Got three hours last night, usually get about five. Never had a headache in seventy-three years."

—"The horse looks good to me. Don't know if I look so good to him this morning, though."

—"You tell people what business you've been in since 1934 and the first thing they ask you is, 'Did you ever win the Kentucky Derby?' When you tell them no, they walk away. Now, I guess they won't. If they ask."

The good luck continued back home. The day after the Derby, Palace Music won the John Henry Handicap at Hollywood Park, and Val Danseur finished in a dead-heat for first in the Golden Gate Handicap.

A few days later at Hollywood Park, Whittingham sat in his stable office fiddling with paperwork and answering the phone. Mary Bradley had dropped by to give Charlie a good-natured needle, just in case his ego had gotten a little out of hand.

"You seem awfully happy, Charlie. So what have you done lately?"

"Got the money on Sunday," Whittingham replied without a blink. "Up in San Francisco."

It is entirely possible Ferdinand gave Whittingham a bad case of Derby fever, although he would never admit it. At least, that's how it appeared when he showed up at Churchill Downs in both 1987 and '88 with colts who seemed to fall well shy of the Ferdinand standard.

Temperate Sil was a gray son of Belmont Stakes winner Temperence Hill. In 1987, he gave Whittingham his first victory in the Santa Anita Derby, then it was on to Kentucky, even though Charlie considered Temperate Sil a cut below Ferdinand's class. The colt shipped, got sick and missed the race, effectively providing Whittingham with an easy week. He killed time hanging around Jack Van Berg, who was preparing Alysheba for the Derby.

"Charlie's helping me train my horse," Van Berg announced. "Between the two of us we ought to be able to figure this thing out." Alysheba won, giving Van Berg his first Derby trophy, and Whittingham cashed at odds of 8-to-1.

In 1988, Whittingham went to Louisville with Lively One, a useful colt who had finished second in the Santa Anita Derby, and the filly Goodbye Halo, a candidate for the Kentucky Oaks. Lively One was a dark, cantankerous stretch-runner with a white blaze in the shape of a champagne glass. He needed the fast pace of Ferdinand's Derby to set up his run. Instead, he was handcuffed at the hind end of a tedious race won by the filly, Winning Colors, who led from start to finish. Lively One ran twelfth, but there were no hard feelings. At least Goodbye Halo won the Oaks.

A few days before the 1988 Derby, after Lively One and Goodbye Halo were through with their morning work, Whittingham proposed a field trip to his exercise rider, Pam Mabes.

"Let's go out to Arthur's place, gal. I've got some babies and mares out there to look at."

"Arthur" was the same Arthur B. Hancock III who'd first dealt with Whittingham some twenty-one years earlier at Arlington Park. Hancock owned Stone Farm, near Paris, Kentucky, where Cougar had served most of his stallion career and where Whittingham kept many of the horses he bred and owned with such partners as Sid Port, Mary Jones Bradley and Nancy Anne Chandler.

Among the "babies" were a sprinkling of two-year-olds. One of them was a lanky, nearly black colt by Halo—the same sire responsible for Lively One and Goodbye Halo—who sported a white blaze and stared at the world with the eye of a juvenile delinquent. He had just enough personality to warrant a second look, however, and then he turned around to jog away. Mabes gasped.

"My God, Charlie, his hocks almost touch! I can't believe he'll make it."

Whittingham, who had already paid Hancock $25,000 for a half-interest in the black colt, was noncommittal. But the thought had crossed his mind. He was already angling to sell half of his half to a friend, Ernest Gaillard, a surgeon from La Jolla, California.

"Sometimes they surprise you," Whittingham replied. "Let's see what he looks like after we've had him awhile."

The black colt already had a history that bordered on melodramatic. As a Stone Farm weanling he nearly died from severe diarrhea. After the colt failed to sell at a yearling auction, Hancock bought him from the breeders—the Oak Cliff Stable of Tom Tatham and partners—for $17,000 and tried to market him again in March of 1988 at Southern California's biggest sale of two-year-olds. No one would nibble at Hancock's bottom price of $50,000. In fact, the bidding did not get past $32,000.

"Let's take him home," Hancock said with a shake of his head. But on his way back to Kentucky, the colt and a filly traveling companion were upended when their van driver suffered a heart attack and careened off a north Texas highway. A local veterinary clinic patched up both horses and sent them on their way. By the time Pam Mabes laid eyes on him that afternoon in late April, the black colt—who had been given the name Sunday Silence—already had lived a pretty full life.

In nearly every respect, Sunday Silence was the diametric opposite of Ferdinand. They shared stable space for a few months during the summer and early fall of 1988, making their differences even more palpable. The only overlap was a common number of legs. Beyond that, they could have been two distinct species. Before long, however, Whittingham began to get an inkling that the torch would be passed . . . and it would not be traveling very far.

CHAPTER 13

SUNDAY'S CHILD

"A horse might have the look of eagles, but I've never seen an eagle who could run."

Life demands closure. Sometimes horse racing imitates life. On the afternoon of October 30, 1988, there were two places on this earth Charlie Whittingham desperately wanted to be. In California there was a beginning. In Kentucky there was an end. Whittingham, mindful of his debt to history, chose to be present at the end.

On that Sunday afternoon, the management of Churchill Downs offered its fans the opportunity to say farewell to Ferdinand during a public ceremony. The five-year-old chestnut was as proud and placid as ever, but his racing days were done. Rather than train him further in a last gasp attempt to defend his title in the Breeders' Cup Classic on November 5, Whittingham advised Keck to retire the son of Nijinsky and lay plans for his stallion career.

A melancholy Janet Johnson got a leg up from Frank Solis at the barn and rode slowly around the clubhouse turn, tracing the steps the big red horse had taken nearly thirty months before on his way to his date in the Derby. She cantered the colt up the stretch, turned, and then the two old friends made their way slowly back down Heartbreak Lane.

"People were cheering and clapping, and Ferdinand was enjoying it," Johnson recalled. "When we got to the winner's circle, Charlie was there. I couldn't see very good because of the tears. The announcer talked about Ferdinand. Charlie gave him a peppermint. Then they played 'My Old Kentucky Home.' Charlie didn't say much."

But he did wipe something from his eye.

Later that day, Whittingham got word from California that his near black two-year-old colt by Halo out of a mare named Wishing Well had finished second in his competitive debut at Santa Anita. It was a good race, reported assistant Rodney Rash. The colt had the lead and was caught right at the end by a Caro colt who looked like a nice prospect himself.

Four months earlier, the black colt was close to being a write-off. As far as Arthur Hancock was concerned, Sunday Silence was out of sight and out of mind. Long gone from Stone Farm, a two-time loser in the marketplace, the unlucky colt was finally in the hands of Whittingham. If there was even a hint of ability locked inside that ornery two-year-old carcass, Hancock figured Whittingham was about the only man who could find it. But he wasn't holding his breath.

One early afternoon in September of 1988, Hancock put in a routine phone call to Whittingham. They talked about broodmares and babies, and the yearling sales coming up. They were ready to ring off when Charlie offered one last little piece of information.

"You know, Arthur, this big black sonofabitch can run a little."

Hancock did some quick calculations. "My God," he thought, "he's talking about Sunday Silence." Such a terse evaluation from Whittingham regarding an unraced two-year-old was a rare commodity, tantamount to a ten-page endorsement from Wayne Lukas or a twenty-minute monologue from Woody Stephens. Hancock felt a flutter in his stomach. He tried hard not to get too excited.

Out West, there was more adventure than excitement. Whittingham and his crew were hip deep in a daily battle of wills with Sunday Silence. The colt was full of odd ideas about the behavior of a proper racehorse. Whether in his stall, on the tow-ring or on the racetrack, Sunday Silence was a certified troublemaker. His nickname became "Sunday Stop It."

All the while, Whittingham was cultivating the racehorse inside the rogue. After more than half a century in the close company of Thoroughbreds, he could recognize raw potential no matter how it was shrouded by physical defects or mental immaturity. Whittingham drew a large circle around Sunday Silence and allowed him the latitude to be himself, within reason. He reminded his people to be patient, firm and kind. This one, he told them, could be worth the trouble.

Each morning at dawn, Sunday Silence would buck and rear and spoil for trouble as Whittingham's first set of horses waited for the five-thirty opening of the main track. By the time the barriers came down, Sunday Silence was a nervous wreck. Pam Mabes, his exercise rider, tried in vain to follow Whittingham's prescribed routine—first walk, then jog, then gallop smoothly into the day's exercise. But that was all too polite for Sunday Silence. As Mabes fought for control one morning, Whittingham finally yelled, "Just let him go!" With a burst of energy, Sunday Silence left his well-mannered stablemates in the dust.

Mabes, a freckle-faced female version of actor Michael J. Fox, was the latest in a long line of top women exercise riders employed by Whittingham. She had done well with the morning work aboard Lively One, another dark-coated son of Halo with a strong personality. Whittingham, a man who prefers proven patterns to experimentation, thought Mabes and the newest Halo colt would be the right match. Before long, Mabes was recommending otherwise.

"Charlie, are you sure you don't want somebody else on this horse?" she pleaded. "Somebody who can cowboy him maybe? He's going a hundred miles an hour with me, and he's got his head turned! Tell you the truth, I'm kind of afraid of him."

"Naw, girl, you're doing just fine," Whittingham replied with half a smile. "Don't fight him. Just go with him."

Soon, Mabes discovered the key was keeping Sunday Silence in some kind of constant motion. He never stood completely still. Little wonder he never made much of an impression in a sales setting. What he really wanted to do was run—run just as fast as he could and all of the time until he dropped from delicious exhaustion. He was like a kid on the first day of summer vacation, or a new Corvette fresh off the showroom floor. There was nothing classic or traditional about Sunday Silence, as far as Whittingham could tell, and no inclination toward behavior modification. The colt seemed to be some kind of prehistoric throwback, a living legacy of the days when horses were hunted, when fear and hunger ruled their lives. In a classy stable full of calm, earnest animals, Sunday Silence was Al Capone singing with the Vienna Boys Choir.

Under the strong, no-nonsense touch of his groom, Charles Clay, the black colt would at least mind his own business as he continued to blossom in the fall of 1988. The harder he worked, the better he acted. Whittingham loved to watch Sunday Silence in full, wide-open gallops, stretching his legs in joyous abandon. When Mabes geared down, the colt would protest by dipping his head between his legs and bucking to a stop. "Sunday, stop it! Stop it!" she'd cry, and Whittingham would chime in as the horse and rider barreled their way through the Santa Anita grandstand tunnel and into the paddock. "Whoa now . . . just relax horse!"

One morning, walking back to the stables from the Santa Anita paddock, Sunday Silence scrambled off the dirt path and onto the slick pavement. Shod as they are with aluminum plates, horses are liable to slip and fall on such a surface if they do not quietly tiptoe back to safer ground. Sunday Silence, of course, began to panic. He was lunging and leaping, threatening to do himself serious harm. Whittingham planted himself in front of the colt and tried to flag him down, but Sunday Silence kept right on going. Charlie jumped out of the way before his horse could charge through him.

Soon, the colt began to build up a reputation outside the Whittingham barn. One day, as Sunday Silence's first race approached, Whittingham put an unsuspecting Bill Shoemaker aboard for a workout. Shoemaker was fifty-seven and only a year from retirement. After Sunday Silence got through with him, he was even closer.

"Don't you ever put me on this half-broke sonofabitch again," Shoemaker called to Whittingham as they walked through the paddock. "Take this horse back to the ranch."

"Getting a little old for this?" Whittingham needled. "Not getting scared, are you?"

In mid-October Sunday Silence worked a full mile in company for the first time. Mabes, her eyes wide, could not hide her enthusiasm. Whittingham looked up at her and deadpanned, "I think we might have ourselves a runner."

Even before Sunday Silence made his first start, the New York-based colt Easy Goer already had won two major stakes races at Belmont Park and was acting like the second coming of Secretariat. At the beginning of 1989, Easy Goer was a prohibitive favorite in Kentucky Derby future book betting, while Sunday Silence was barely a blip on the screen, boasting only a maiden win and two second-place finishes. That was just fine with Whittingham, though. He preferred to lay low while the racing press focused on Easy Goer, and then Houston, the $2.9-million son of Seattle Slew who had narrowly beaten Sunday Silence in a Hollywood Park allowance race in December.

On March 2, 1989, an overcast Thursday, Whittingham slipped Sunday Silence quietly into his three-year-old campaign at Santa Anita. The track was muddy, but Sunday Silence hardly noticed. He was quick and efficient in dusting off six undistinguished opponents. Two days later, the three-year-old Easy Goer was unveiled at Gulfstream Park, where he won a minor stakes event with ease. Whittingham took notice, but just barely. He was contemplating the next jump with Sunday Silence. It promised to be a big one.

By then it was apparent Whittingham thought he had a Kentucky Derby colt. He said as much to Hancock, who still was incredulous, and to Dr. Ernest Gaillard, who had purchased half of Whittingham's half-interest in Sunday Silence the previous summer. It was a typical Whittingham hedge—Gaillard, a retired surgeon, paid $25,000 for a quarter share, allowing Whittingham to break even at worst. Hancock sat chilly on his half interest, willing to gamble on the next roll of the dice.

"Here's a colt who was rated a 'triple zero' by a lot of people who saw him in the sale as a yearling," Hancock recalled. "I'm sure Charlie didn't even like him much the first time he saw him as a two-year-old. After he won that first race at three, I'd had some offers to sell part of him. But I kept thinking that if Charlie had faith, I had no business doubting him."

How much faith? Enough to throw Sunday Silence directly into proven three-year-old competition over a distance of ground in his very next start.

The San Felipe Handicap on March 19 provided Whittingham with just about every answer he needed. The colt broke poorly, appeared disoriented around the first turn, pulled himself into contention on the backstretch, and then caught the leaders in the stretch to take command. At the end Sunday Silence was a little dazed and confused, but he was also an easy winner. Pat Valenzuela, nauseous and dizzy from a bout with the flu, alighted from the colt full of wonder. It was an awesome display of raw talent focused just enough to accomplish the task at hand—a classic piece of Whittingham training. Next stop, the Santa Anita Derby.

After the San Felipe, Whittingham modestly appraised Sunday Silence as being in the top five or six Derby contenders. Privately, he knew he had them all beat but one, and he wasn't so sure Easy Goer could withstand Sunday Silence's combination of quick acceleration and naked aggression. Hancock, twenty-five hundred miles away and getting more nervous by the day, was receiving a flood of offers for part of the colt.

"What do you think I should do, Charlie?" Hancock wondered during a call to his partner. "How do you feel about it?"

"Do whatever you want," Whittingham said. "You know as well as anybody that anything could happen to the horse between now and his next race. They're like fresh strawberries—they can spoil overnight."

With Sunday Silence fully exposed as a Kentucky Derby contender, Whittingham was being asked to make the inevitable comparisons with Ferdinand. "Faster and quicker," Whittingham said of Sunday Silence. "But he still could use some seasoning. I've got plenty of time for that, though."

In fact, he was running out of time. Sunday Silence was still a pony-mounting basket case most mornings. Every trip to the starting gate was an adventure in the afternoons. But Whittingham resisted the temptation to made radical adjustments. Charlie continued to indulge the colt's flighty psyche while honing his natural power. Sunday Silence may have been a screwball between the ears, but he was rapidly becoming an admirable physical specimen. Though admittedly not a poster boy for ideal conformation—those hocks still came perilously close to brushing—

he had attained a full-chested, well-muscled masculinity, with a certain swagger to go along with his height. In short, Sunday Silence had become his own prototype.

Saturday, April 8, 1989. Destinies mingled from far corners of the continent. In the space of an hour and a half, two bombshells landed squarely at the nerve center of horse racing. Bulletins whizzed back and forth across the land. Stories overlapped, intertwined and became confused. It was a day to remember where you were, what you wore, and who you were with when the word came down.

At a quarter past four, Eastern Standard Time, beneath the flight path of JFK International Airport at Aqueduct Race Course on Long Island, Easy Goer made a shambles of the one-mile Gotham Stakes. The chestnut son of Alydar won by thirteen lengths and came within a snap of the fingers of equaling the game's most hallowed speed record, held by Dr. Fager.

Easy Goer was barely cooled out and bedded down when, three thousand miles away, Sunday Silence pranced into the saddling paddock to prepare for the Santa Anita Derby. News of Easy Goer's Gotham was spreading like wildfire out West. Maybe he was a superhorse after all, some mumbled. Maybe the Californians should stay home. Valenzuela cocked an eyebrow and said, "Wait and see." Whittingham, busy saddling his black tornado, paused long enough to praise Easy Goer and wonder aloud, "The last time I checked, the Derby was a mile and a quarter." Then Sunday Silence went out and won by eleven lengths.

In the sport of horse racing, the moments of natural rivalry are rare. There are no home teams, no franchises, and no alma maters. There are no schedules that require traditional confrontations. Racing history is filled with individual achievements, accumulated helter-skelter, and relying upon the framework of a few very special events—the Triple Crown, a sprinkling of ancient handicaps, more recently the Breeders' Cup. Only by sheer chance, sweet accident, will a true racing rivalry materialize. Two horses will emerge unexpectedly to collide in a series of unforgettable events. Citation and Noor, Kelso and Gun Bow, Affirmed and Alydar. Each time they met, their legends grew until the rivalry became the heart of the game. Everything else was just waiting.

Twelve days after the Santa Anita Derby, Whittingham headed to Kentucky with Sunday Silence, Charles Clay and Pam Mabes. They set up camp in the same barn and same stall that served Ferdinand so well in 1986. They found Alex Hassinger, a former Whittingham aide, on the scene with some horses for Dick Lundy and asked him to pony Sunday Silence to the track. Then they hunkered down to train their horse while the Derby carnival slowly assembled.

Late on the afternoon of April 22, the phone rang in Mabes' room at the Executive West Motel. She knew who it was before answering.

"So, what did you think?" Whittingham was on the other end, fresh from watching Easy Goer win the Wood Memorial at Aqueduct by three lengths.

"He looked awful good, Charlie," she answered. "Did it pretty easy."

"Yeah," Whittingham replied. "But he wasn't beating nothing but a bunch of moo cows."

Derby week 1989 was a study in contrasts. Shug McGaughey, the soft-spoken Kentuckian who trained Easy Goer, sincerely believed his colt was the best and said as much, but he preferred to let the horse do the talking. The racing press, both East and West, banged the drum loudly for Easy Goer's impending coronation as the next Secretariat. Over in the next barn, bundled up in down jackets and high-collared sheepskin, Whittingham broadly hinted at a Sunday Silence surprise in the face of public opinion.

"What's with Charlie?" wondered a veteran writer. "It's not like him to get cocky."

"Aw, he's getting old," came the answer. "He's been back here three straight years since he won in '86. Got a bad case of Derby fever late in life."

In the meantime, Arthur Hancock was riding his own emotional roller-coaster. He was being bombarded with offers to sell part of Sunday Silence, offers that no sensible commercial breeder should rightfully ignore. "I was in a quandary," Hancock said. "I finally put it to Charlie, 'The guy wants to buy a quarter interest. How about I put up twelve and a half percent of my share and you do the same?' Charlie shoots back, 'I'm not selling!' That answered my question."

Running a contender in the Derby was nothing new to Hancock—he was co-owner of 1982 winner Gato Del Sol—but the scenario of 1989 was especially bittersweet. Easy Goer was owned by Ogden Phipps, the same Ogden Phipps who had swung his support to Arthur Hancock's younger brother, Seth, when control of Claiborne Farm was up for grabs upon the death of Bull Hancock in 1972. Arthur reacted badly to the loss of what he thought was his birthright by diving head first into booze and bad company.

"My life then was a joke," Hancock recalled. "But there were a few friends who cared, and one of them was Charlie Whittingham. He liked me before and he liked me after. His loyalty was a lifeline."

Seared into his memory, like a scar from a noble wound, was an evening at the Whittinghams some sixteen years before. Mary Jones was there with Arthur and Charlie. The mood was decidedly mellow.

"Charlie," announced Arthur, his words a bit slurred, "one of these days, we're gonna win the Kentucky Derby together."

Whittingham reached for a handy bottle of bourbon and said with a laugh, "Here, Arthur. We'll drink to it."

In the days leading up to the Derby, Hancock spent much of his time scanning the landscape for omens. He spied a white cat on a guide post not far from his farm, an odd sight that must have meant something. Three days before the race, a rabbit appeared outside his office window, munching grass. Got to be a lucky sign, he thought. Got to be.

As it turned out, the only signal worth a damn was delivered by Whittingham shortly after Sunday Silence breezed a half mile on the morning entries were taken for the Derby. Whittingham clicked off his stopwatch, glanced down, then wandered off a few steps as Sunday Silence glided to a stop around the clubhouse turn. Charlie's mind was whirring. The equation was becoming crystal clear. Nearby, Hancock waited anxiously for Whittingham's evaluation of the work. Just right? A bit too fast? C'mon, Charlie, what's the word?

"We will get the money."

Hancock blinked hard against the chilly wind and stared at his partner.

"What are you saying, Charlie? How can you—"

"My boy"—Whittingham had that twinkle in his eye—"we will GET the money."

A little while later, as Hancock was walking through the Churchill Downs stables to the track kitchen, he found a penny hiding off to the side of the path. It was heads up, a keeper.

"Wouldn't it be something if it was a 1982," said a friend walking along-side. They had been reminiscing about Gato Del Sol.

"That'd be almost too much to ask," laughed Hancock. But just in case, he checked. There it was, worn but clear, above the capital "D" marking the Denver mint: 1982.

Luck had nothing to do with Sunday Silence's two and a half length victory in the 1989 Kentucky Derby. As Whittingham had predicted, his tough-minded colt dominated a difficult situation from the start. The race-time temperature of forty-three degrees was the coldest in forty years, setting the horses on edge and numbing their handlers. There was a nine-minute delay in the start of the race while Triple Buck, a longshot, had a shoe replaced. Valenzuela dismounted and Sunday Silence stood like a pro for Hassinger, who was alongside on the pony.

"I had never ponied a horse to the post in the afternoon before in my life," Hassinger recalled. "So here I am doing it in the Kentucky Derby, with a horse who I think is going to win, and before we load into the gate the jock jumps off. Was I nervous? Hell yes! When I finally let him go into the gate, my hand was numb."

At the start of the race, Sunday Silence and Triple Buck bumped briefly. Whittingham saw it and shrugged it off. "He's tough," he said later. "He's got a lot of pride. He'll kick your brains out if he has a chance." Valenzuela used the colt's natural speed to establish position behind the pace of Houston and in front of Easy Goer. With a quarter of a mile to run, Sunday Silence moved for the lead and set sail down the long Churchill Downs stretch into the teeth of a twenty mile an hour head wind. Just as Whittingham began counting his money, Valenzuela went to the whip to keep the colt from leaning on Northern Wolf to his inside. Sunday Silence swerved right, then left, then right again, depending on where he was hit. Valenzuela said the colt was shying from the sights and sounds of the throng lining the stretch. Whittingham would have preferred to see the jockey forget his whip and steer with his hands. Either way, Easy Goer still finished second.

Whittingham's second Derby was different from the first. In 1986, the horse took a backseat to the people involved. The story was Whittingham and Shoemaker, two old dudes and one last hurrah. When Whittingham showed up in the winner's circle again just three years later, attention shifted to the animal and to the work that went into his development. What kind of creature was this Sunday Silence, so thoroughly rejected and poorly constructed that even his venerable trainer sold off part of his share? "We really didn't know what we had until he started working. Then it was clear he was a runner," Whittingham said. "That happens sometimes. They come along slower than others. I wouldn't have sold any of him if he'd breezed a couple of times first."

Easy Goer's defeat in the Derby was written off to the muddy racetrack. The Preakness, maintained his backers, would be different. Sunday Silence would need to be at his best to beat Easy Goer the next time around. Even then, they said, it was doubtful.

"Sunday Silence may well turn out to be the best colt in the land," wrote Steven Crist in The New York *Times*. "But few will believe that until he beats Easy Goer again."

As usual, Whittingham was focused on his own horse. "Didn't pay any attention to how the other horse trained in Kentucky," he said. "And why should I? Wouldn't make any difference how I trained my horse." On the Monday after the Derby, Whittingham had Sunday Silence back on the track for a gallop. The colt was feeling frisky, despite his tough race over an exhausting surface. Whittingham wanted to shave a little off the edge before sending Sunday Silence to Baltimore.

"It was a strange feeling, really neat," recalled Mabes. "The place was practically deserted. The reporters had all left. It was just Charlie watching, and me and Sunday out there alone, galloping under those twin spires. I was thinking, 'My God, we won the Derby just two days ago.' It all seemed like a dream."

Five days later, the dream went wrong. After cooling out from a routine gallop over the Pimlico main track, Sunday Silence was favoring his right front foot. Whittingham took a look and suspected a bruised hoof. Just to make sure it was nothing worse, he put in a call to Alex Harthill in Louisville. The veterinarian dropped what he was doing and jumped the next flight to Baltimore without packing a bag. "As it turned out," Harthill recalled, "I had to stay longer than I thought. Had to buy a toothbrush and a razor. Charlie said he would have lent me a comb—if he had one to lend."

Fortunately, there were no fractures in the foot and the knee was sound. Harthill found nothing more than bruises causing the painful pressure. Dr. Ric Redden, blacksmith to the stars, flew in from Kentucky with a pair of custom-made horseshoes, fitted with a bar across the open end to provide more support. Harthill applied a compress to the foot to promote healing. When the compress fell off, as it often did, Charles Clay was right there to resume his own therapy—a constant relay of hot soaks to draw the bruise and cold soaks to toughen the hoof. Night after night.

Sunday Silence did nothing but walk around the barn for three straight days. Each morning when the Easy Goer crew arrived, Whittingham, Harthill, Mabes and Clay would already be on the scene, haggard and red-eyed from another night of worry. McGaughey's people would regale Whittingham and company with a replay of their night on the town. "Too bad you couldn't be there," they would chirp. "Great band. Great food. Unbelievable crabs."

On the Wednesday before the Preakness, Whittingham decided to test the foot. "He was walking all right," Whittingham recalled. "But you don't really know until you ask them to do something. If he'd favored it after that gallop, I don't think we would have run."

No chance of that, though. When Sunday Silence hit the track for that

Wednesday gallop, he fairly exploded with pent-up energy. "He gave me the shivers," Mabes recalled. "He was so glad to be out there training again. He never took a bad step before they found the bruise, and once he went back he never took a bad step after. That's the great thing about working for Charlie—you never had any fear something would happen to you because there might be something wrong with your horse. Even when other people might say your horse is lame, if Charlie said he was okay, I trusted him completely."

Harthill continued to tinker with the foot through the end of the week, cutting away bits of dead tissue as they surfaced. On Thursday morning, as entries for the race were about to be drawn, Harthill and Clay decided there had been enough press scrutiny and plenty of photos taken of Sunday Silence lolling around his stall. "The horse needed some quiet time," Harthill said. "Everybody does now and then."

Clay was more to the point. "I can't keep you people from hanging around," he announced in the general direction of the gathered press. "But I sure as hell can remove the view." With that, the groom pulled the dutch doors shut on stall number forty. Rumors flew. Sunday Silence napped. And Whittingham was breathing easier for the first time in five days. But, once again, Hancock was feeling uneasy.

"Charlie, there's nobody who likes Sunday Silence." Hancock was on the phone, room-to-room at the hotel, and reading from a poll of a hundred sports writers that favored Easy Goer about ninety-seven to three. "They say the only reason Easy Goer didn't win the Derby is because he didn't like the mud. Are you telling me none of them know what they're talking about?"

Whittingham was the last man who would train by opinion polls. Even in his "mellow" seventies, he still harbored a deep and abiding contempt for amateurs and dilettantes who dared pass judgment on his work. As usual, Charlie was able to cut through the fog with one clean slice.

"Arthur, those bastards don't even know what color our horse is."

Hancock was somewhat relieved. "I felt better," he later recalled, "and then I turned on the television. Not five seconds into this fellow's report on the Preakness he says, 'No one gives the chestnut son of Halo much of a chance.' I swear to God that's exactly what he said. At that moment I felt like the private going into battle, trembling with fear until his general reassures him that the enemy doesn't even know how to fire their cannon."

Whittingham was right again, but not by much. The race was as exciting as a horse race can get—certainly the greatest Preakness ever run. Easy Goer, back on his game, got the jump on Sunday Silence around the final turn. Valenzuela had to steady his colt then move to the outside in order to take up the chase. With a breathtaking leap, Sunday Silence caught Easy Goer deep in the stretch and appeared to be on his way to a clear-cut victory. But Easy Goer fought back, as Trevor Denman's call of the race echoed above the screams of the record crowd of more than ninety thousand fans.

"Head and head, nose and nose . . . what a horse race this is! Here's. . . the . . . finish"—dramatic pause—"Sunday Silence wins it by a nose!"

After the Derby, Whittingham had predicted Sunday Silence would win the Triple Crown. After the Preakness, the uncharacteristically brash statement was looking pretty good. "Why not say it if it's what I believe?" Whittingham said when asked about his blatant display of public confidence.

By the time Sunday Silence arrived at Belmont Park to prepare for the Belmont Stakes, the Triple Crown grind was beginning to take its toll. The colt had run the race of his life to win the Preakness, following hard on the heels of a testing Kentucky Derby. Under normal circumstances, Whittingham would have packed him up and shipped him home to California for a brief rest. But Sunday Silence was sound, the foot problem was behind them, and, well, there was that $5-million Chrysler-sponsored bonus for winning the Triple Crown. And if he finished at least third, he would earn a million-dollar consolation prize.

If Sunday Silence was tired from the Triple Crown grind, he didn't act it. Through the unseasonable heat and steaming rains of a Long Island spring, he continued to gobble up his two-mile gallops and give Mabes and Clay all they could handle. Clay, who lived with the colt, was hoping Whittingham would back off a bit on the gallops. "Look at the Preakness,"

Clay recalled. "He didn't hardly get no training for that and look how he ran." But Whittingham knew he would need a fit horse to handle Easy Goer at a mile and a half on his home court.

Descending upon New York with a potential Triple Crown winner, Whittingham never gave so many interviews, never faced so many cameras and microphones in his life. His New York memories—more than forty years strong—were summoned up and rehashed until Whittingham felt like a walking relic of a dead era. In private, he and Peggy reminisced about the old days living on the Geary Estate, closing the bar at the hotel they called the "Bucket of Blood" and the time when baby Michael crawled out onto an apartment window railing and scared the daylights out of the people below. For public consumption, Whittingham trotted out tales of Porterhouse and Mister Gus, Mab's Choice and Oil Royalty, Buddy Hirsch, Kay Jensen and Woody Stephens, and posed for pictures and a chat with Horatio Luro and Stephens.

"Who do you like to win the race?" Luro was asked as he stood next to Charlie.

"You've got the mark on the wall," The Senor cryptically replied. Whittingham just smiled.

Through it all, Sunday Silence stayed in character. On the day before the race, as Whittingham led him through the Belmont grandstand tunnel from the paddock to the track for a routine gallop, the colt spooked from some imagined demon and reared high into the air. On his way up, the colt's left front foot struck out in Whittingham's direction. Charlie ducked and dodged, never letting go of the shank, and was grazed just above the right temple.

"Oh, my God, Charlie!" cried Mabes, who was hanging on for dear life. "Are you okay?"

"Go on with him, go dammit. Go on!" snapped Whittingham as he unleashed the horse.

The cut was superficial—"A long way from my heart," Whittingham cracked—but Mabes was still shaken. "Clay, I think I just killed Charlie," she said as she returned to the barn.

"After all his years of head-butting, he's got so much scar tissue up there you can't hurt him," Peggy reassured Pam.

Whittingham got a little first aid, then topped off the incident with the words everyone was waiting for:

"I just hope he didn't hurt his foot banging on my noggin that way."

As it turned out, Sunday Silence gave a performance that would have won most Belmonts. He followed the pace of the fresh French colt, Le Voyageur, through the first turn and down the long backstretch, then edged to the lead approaching the exit of the vast final turn. Suddenly, from the outside, Easy Goer unleashed a powerful move. He whisked past the two colts on the lead and set off in a race of his own. At the finish of the mile and a half, the red colt was eight lengths in front of Sunday Silence. The Triple Crown was down the drain.

"I'm trying to feel bad," Whittingham said later. "But they handed me this check for a million dollars, the horse is fine, and I plan on wakin' up tomorrow. Anyway, we beat the other horse two out of three. We just couldn't handle him on his home ground."

That night, Whittingham and McGaughey hooted with the owls at the Garden City Hotel. Mabes gave up around midnight, but Charlie and Shug were still going strong. At three in the morning they said their loud goodbyes in front of the hotel. A little before five, Mabes was downstairs, waiting for Whittingham because Whittingham *had* to have Sunday Silence out of his stall and walking early.

At five o'clock sharp Whittingham sailed through the lobby doors, and they were off to the racetrack. Later, as reporters began dribbling in, Whittingham entertained them with tales of cross-eyed coyotes, riding the rails, and sliding down bedsheets to dodge the rent. While everyone wanted to talk about Sunday Silence and Easy Goer, he summoned up names like Home Burning and Porterhouse, Talon and Dandy. He painted scenes filled with characters called Apples, Bananas, Snake and Highball. And everyone laughed.

The crowd of reporters finally cleared away. At last, the Triple Crown was over. It was time for a rest, for the horse and the people. Mabes grabbed her jacket, anxious to get back to her room, while Whittingham gathered his newspapers and gave Sunday Silence one last look. As they slid into their rental car, Charlie got that twinkle in his eye, the look that said the day should never end, and there was no place he would rather be.

"Girl, let's go get us a cold one down at Hirsch's cottage."

EPILOGUE

"I taught him everything he knows. I didn't teach him everything I know."

Jimmy Kilroe had Charlie Whittingham in his sights from the start. Kilroe watched him in action, morning and afternoon. He measured the results against a checklist of names that included Plain Ben Jones, Sunny Jim Fitzsimmons and Max Hirsch. He separated the fact from the fiction, the jealousy from the praise. When it all boiled down, Kilroe had him pegged:

"All the stuff about hard work is one thing, but many people work very hard and don't know what they're doing. Whittingham knows. He's the perfect example of genius rising to its rightful level."

The level remains incredibly high. Five weeks before he turned eighty, on a sparkling March day at the races, Whittingham saddled and sent out the winner of the Santa Anita Handicap for the ninth time in his career. This was no champion horse from Europe, no Triple Crown winner turned four. This was a stubborn old customer named Sir Beaufort, a rogue at the gate and a real head case otherwise. In other hands he would have been gelded and sold for day money. But Charlie saw a spark, and he gave the spark enough light and fresh air to catch fire at just the right time.

Sir Beaufort's accomplishment should not have been a surprise to anyone. Whittingham has been dedicated to overachievement all his life. Barefoot runaways from border towns are not supposed to go this far. His horses followed suit.

"If you look at the record," observed a Whittingham patron, "you'll notice that Charlie's horses rarely make successful stallions. The reason is simple. Charlie can make mediocre horses do great things. What they achieve is not necessarily because of their breeding. It's because of Charlie's training. When they retire, they are on their own again. Charlie can't help them at stud."

Don't worry about Whittingham going all soft. He may move a step slower and the voice might crack. But beware if he says, "Try to choke me . . . if you can." Just take a step back. Keep the hands very quiet. Hopefully, no one will get hurt. This is, after all, the fellow who once was asked to feel happy for a small-time trainer's success. Grinding a toe into the dirt, he replied, "Step on an ant early and he'll never bite you."

Then turn to a moment early in 1972. Barely a week before he was scheduled to accept his first Eclipse Award, celebrating his season with Ack Ack, Cougar and Turkish Trousers, Whittingham received a copy of the following telegram:

"Wednesday I buried my daughter, Ada Denise Chapman. During the brief span of her young life she loved the horses. And her last wish was for me to contact or wire Mr. Charlie Whittingham or Uncle Bill Shoe. Mr. Whittingham had sent her the shoes of Ack Ack and Cougar. When she died Tuesday night all she wanted besides her cross were the horses' shoes from Ack Ack and Cougar. She sent her love and wishes to Mr. Whittingham and Uncle Bill Shoe. I think as her father that they should be recognized, as millionaires, to take the time to give an eleven-year-old girl this brief pleasure of their solicitude. Thomas Chapman."

It is a strange business, horse racing, that allows a rough ex-Marine to touch so many people in so many ways. Ada Chapman would have cowered in fear at the sight of her kindly Mr. Whittingham spewing bile at a rider who had messed up a work. She would have cried at the tales of Riot in Paris and Denodado, grand animals even Charlie couldn't save. But she would have giggled and pointed at the Whittingham who, when properly lubed, would jump on a dance floor and do the twist to "Tequila."

Whittingham was, is and ever shall be a wild-hearted, horse-training sonofagun. He learned early to lose gracefully and win with aplomb, and how to celebrate life no matter what the outcome. Picture Charlie at dawn, squinting into the rising sun, or on a bright afternoon at the races, winning all the money. And remember, this is the same guy who took the floor at his wedding party and delivered to Peggy and his friends a toast for all time:

> *"Here's to fast horses and beautiful women,*
> *The two things I like best.*
> *And when I die I hope from my hide*
> *They will make a side saddle*
> *So I will always rest*
> *Next to the two things I love best—*
> *Fast horses, and beautiful women."*

APPENDIX

Career and Stakes History for Charlie Whittingham, 1953-'93

1953
15 wins, 3 stakes wins, $194,120
Champion: PORTERHOUSE, 2-year-old colt

Horse	Owner	Stakes
Porterhouse	Llangollen Farm	Christiana S
		Futurity S
		National Stallion S

1954
22 wins, 1 stakes win, $163,545

Horse	Owner	Stakes
Mab's Choice	R. S. Howard	Distaff H

1955
35 wins, 4 stakes wins, $348,692

Horse	Owner	Stakes
Mister Gus	Llangollen Farm	William P. Kyne H
Porterhouse	Llangollen Farm	Lakes and Flowers H
		San Carlos H
Tipper	Llangollen Farm	La Centinela S

1956
35 wins, 11 stakes wins, $704,875

Horse	Owner	Stakes
Mister Gus	Llangollen Farm	Arlington H
		San Antonio H
		Woodward S
Porterhouse	Llangollen Farm	Californian S
		Lakes and Flowers H
		Palos Verdes H
		San Carlos H
		Santa Barbara H
Social Climber	Llangollen Farm	Cinema H
		El Dorado H
		San Felipe H

1957
45 wins, 9 stakes wins, $718,855

Horse	Owner	Stakes
Corn Husker	Llangollen Farm	San Gabriel H
		San Juan Capistrano H
		Santa Anita H
Guide Line	Llangollen Farm	Selima S
Nashville	Llangollen Farm	Lakes and Flowers H
		Palos Verdes H
Porterhouse	Llangollen Farm	Hollywood Express H
		Los Angeles H
Social Climber	Llangollen Farm	Californian S

1958 38 wins, 4 stakes wins, $549,593

Horse	Owner	Stakes
Nooran	Mrs. Leslie Fenton	Santa Maria H
Restless Wind	Llangollen Farm	Arlington Futurity
		Prairie State S
		Washington Park Futurity

1959 41 wins, 4 stakes wins, $367,940

Horse	Owner	Stakes
Clandestine	Charles H. Wacker & Mrs. Winston Guest	Palos Verdes H
Eagle Admiral	Llangollen Farm	Golden Gate Futurity
Royal Living	Llangollen Farm	San Juan Capistrano H
Tender Size	Llangollen Farm	Vanity H

1960 30 wins, 5 stakes wins, $271,977

Horse	Owner	Stakes
Clandestine	Charles H. Wacker & Mrs. Winston Guest	San Carlos H
Divine Comedy	Llangollen Farm	Roamer H
		Saranac H
Eagle Admiral	Llangollen Farm	Fountain of Youth S
Restless Wind	Llangollen Farm	San Bernardino H

1961 19 wins, 1 stakes win, $124,880

Horse	Owner	Stakes
Scotland	W. M. Ingram	Del Mar H

1962 35 wins, 5 stakes wins, $332,545

Horse	Owner	Stakes
Black Sheep	C R Mac Stable	American Derby
		Cinema H
		San Vicente H
Oil Royalty	John R. Gaines	Las Flores H
Sir Ribot	Mr. & Mrs. Fred Turner Jr.	California Derby Trial

1963 24 wins, 4 stakes wins, $379,514

Horse	Owner	Stakes
Denodado	Flying M Stable	San Felipe H
Oil Royalty	John R. Gaines	Beldame H
		Vineland H
Rablero	C. R. McCoy	San Marcos H

1964 325 starts, 29 wins, 4 stakes wins, $210,088

Horse	Owner	Stakes
Count Charles	Flying M Stable	Santa Catalina S
		Will Rogers S
Now Buck	Mrs. William G. Gilmore	Burlingame S
Oil Royalty	John R. Gaines	Santa Barbara H

1965
316 starts, 33 wins, 2 stakes wins, $263,815

Horse	Owner	Stakes
Calgary Brook	Mrs. Howard B. Keck	Peninsula H
Perfect Sky	Foxcatcher Farm	California Derby

1966
261 starts, 52 wins, 15 stakes wins, $550,103

Drin	Howard B. Keck	Cinema H
		Del Mar Derby
		Gold Rush S (1st div)
Maintain	Llangollen Farm & Hemacinto Stable	Hillsborough H
Pelegrin	Howard B. Keck	San Marino H (2nd div)
Perfect Sky	Foxcatcher Farm	San Gabriel H
Pretense	Llangollen Farm	Palos Verdes H
Restless Song	Rock Spring Farm Stable	Cabrillo S
Saber Mountain	Howard B. Keck	Los Feliz S (2nd div)
		San Felipe H
		San Vicente S
Title Game	Oxford Stable	Howard S
		Portola S
Tumble Wind	Llangollen Farm & Rock Spring Farm	Haggin S
		Westchester S

1967
339 starts, 56 wins, 13 stakes wins, $1,038,208

Drin	Howard B. Keck	Charles H. Strub S
Forli	Arthur Hancock Jr.	Coronado S
Pretense	Llangollen Farm	American H
		Gulfstream Park H
		Inglewood H
		San Antonio H
		San Pasqual H
		Santa Anita H
Saber Mountain	Howard B. Keck	Sierra Madre H
Spinning Around	Oxford Stable	Honeymoon S
Tumble Wind	Llangollen Farm & Rock Spring Farm	Argonaut S
		Hollywood Derby
		San Vicente S

1968
517 starts, 84 wins, 12 stakes wins, $846,431

Deck Hand	Forked Lightning Ranch	Pomona H
Fiddle Isle	Howard B. Keck	Baldwin S (2nd div)
Pinjara	Howard B. Keck	Cabrillo H
		Cinema H
		El Dorado H
Pretense	Llangollen Farm	Bing Crosby H
Racing Room	Llangollen Farm	Hollywood Express H
Rich Desire	L. P. Doherty	Brentwood Claiming S
Scoop Time	Llangollen Farm	Ramona H

Horse	Owner	Stakes
Super Breeze	Llangollen Farm	Nursery S
Tumble Wind	Llangollen Farm & Rock Spring Farm	San Gorgonio H
		San Luis Obispo H (2nd div)

1969 — 537 starts, 80 wins, 13 stakes wins, $1,053,491

Horse	Owner	Stakes
Deck Hand	Forked Lightning Ranch	San Marcos H
Fiddle Isle	Howard B. Keck	Carleton F. Burke Invitational H
Noholme, Jr.	Forked Lightning Ranch	Caballero S
		Cinema H
Pinjara	Howard B. Keck	Century H
		San Bernardino H
Sailors Mate	Bwamazon Farm	Anoakia S
Tell	Mrs. Howard B. Keck	Argonaut S
		Autumn Days S
		Baldwin S
		Hollywood Derby
		Volante H
		Will Rogers S

1970 — 551 starts, 82 wins, 22 stakes wins, $1,302,354

Horse	Owner	Stakes
Ack Ack	Mr. & Mrs. E. E. Fogelson	Autumn Days H
		Los Angeles H
Bargain Day	Forked Lightning Ranch	Bing Crosby H
		Brentwood Claiming S
Beja	Mrs. Howard B. Keck	Del Mar Oaks
		Linda Vista H
Colorado King Jr.	Forked Lightning Ranch	Argonaut S
		Santa Catalina S
Daryl's Joy	R. K. C. Goh	Del Mar H
		Oak Tree S
Fiddle Isle	Howard B. Keck	American H
		Carleton F. Burke Invitational H
		Hollywood Park Invitational Turf H
		Lakeside H
		San Juan Capistrano Invitational H
		San Luis Rey H (1st div)
Lime	Charlie Whittingham & Mary Jones	Will Roger S (1st div)
Pinjara	Howard B. Keck	Coronado S
Queen Janine	Dr. Jock Jocoy	Osunitas S
T. V. Commercial	Bwamazon Farm	San Diego H
		San Marino H
Whittingham	Charlie Whittingham & Mary Jones	Will Rogers S (2nd div)

1971 — 393 starts, 77 wins, 33 stakes wins, $1,737,115
Eclipse Award as Outstanding Trainer
Champions: ACK ACK, Horse of the Year, sprinter, handicap horse
TURKISH TROUSERS, 3-year-old filly

Horse	Owner	Stakes
Ack Ack	Mr. & Mrs. E. E. Fogelson	American H

Horse	Owner	Stakes
		Hollywood Express H
		Hollywood Gold Cup Invitational H
		San Antonio S
		San Carlos H
		San Pasqual H
		Santa Anita H
Advance Guard	Burt Bacharach	Cortez H
		Inglewood H
		San Diego H
Bargain Day	Forked Lightning Ranch	San Bernardino H (1st div)
Cougar	Mary Jones	Californian S
		Ford Pinto Invitational Turf H
		Oak Tree Invitational
		San Gabriel H
		San Juan Capistrano Invitational H
		San Marcos H
Daryl's Joy	R. K. C. Goh	Arcadia H
		San Luis Obispo H
House of Porter	Forked Lightning Ranch	Graduation S
Pinjara	Howard B. Keck	Del Mar H
		Crenshaw S
		Sierra Madre H
Restless Runner	Llangollen Farm	Baldwin S
		Marina Del Rey S
Turkish Trousers	Mrs. Howard B. Keck	Del Mar Oaks
		Hollywood Oaks
		Honeymoon S
		Princess S
		Railbird S
		Santa Susana S
		Santa Ynez S
		Senorita S (2nd div)

1972
429 starts, 79 wins, 20 stakes wins, $1,734,020
Champion: COUGAR, turf horse

Horse	Owner	Stakes
Buzkashi	Everett & Talley	American H
		Arcadia H (1st div)
Cougar II	Mary Jones	Californian S
		Carleton F. Burke H
		Century H
		Oak Tree Invitational S
Groshawk	Mr. & Mrs. Quinn Martin	Del Mar Futurity
		Norfolk S
Le Cle	Mrs. Howard B. Keck	Honeymoon S
		Princess S
Lord Derby	Llangollen Farm	San Luis Obispo H (2nd div)
Pallisima	Mrs. Howard B. Keck	Hollywood Oaks
		Linda Vista H
Practicante	Claiborne Farm	San Juan Capistrano Invitational H
		San Luis Obispo H (1st div)

193

Horse	Owner	Stakes
Quack	Bwamazon Farm	California Derby Hollywood Gold Cup Invitational H Will Rogers S
Turkish Trousers	Mrs. Howard B. Keck	Santa Margarita Invitational H Santa Maria H

1973 — 423 starts, 85 wins, 22 stakes wins, $1,865,385

Horse	Owner	Stakes
Belle Marie	Kinship Stable	Palomar H (2nd div) Santa Susana S (gr. II) Santa Ysabel S
Cougar II	Mary Jones	Century H (gr. I) Santa Anita H (gr. I) Sunset H (gr. I)
Groshawk	Mr. & Mrs. Quinn Martin	La Jolla Mile H (gr. III) Will Rogers H (gr. II)
Grotonian	Marjorie L. Everett	Chula Vista H
Kennedy Road	Mrs. Arthur W. Stollery	Cabrillo H Hollywood Gold Cup Invitational H (gr. I) San Antonio S (gr. I) San Diego H
La Zanzara	Aaron U. Jones	Linda Vista H (gr. III)
Le Cle	Mrs. Howard B. Keck	Beverly Hills Handicap (gr. II)
Manitoulin	Mrs. J. M. Galbreath	Cortez H
New Moon	Charlie Whittingham & Mary Jones	Autumn Days H (gr. III)
Quack	Bwamazon Farm	Californian S (gr. I) San Bernardino H (gr. II)
Star of Kuwait	Marjorie L. Everett	El Monte H
Tallahto	Mrs. Howard B. Keck	La Centinela S (2nd div) Santa Ynez S (gr. II)

1974 — 542 starts, 92 wins, 24 stakes wins, $1,925,020

Horse	Owner	Stakes
Belle Marie	Kinship Stable	Santa Ana H
El Rey	Charlie Whittingham & Mary Jones	South Bay H
El Seetu	Charles Wacker III	Coronado S
Greco II	E. E. Fogelson	Sunset H (gr. I)
La Zanzara	Aaron U. Jones	Beverly Hills H (gr. II)
Matun	Marjorie L. Everett	Lakeside H (gr. II) San Diego H San Simeon H (gr. III)
Miss Musket	Aaron U. Jones	Fantasy S Hollywood Oaks (gr. II) Santa Susana S Santa Ysabel S
Quack	Bwamazon Farm	Californian S (gr. I)
Sphere	Claiborne Farm	Palomar H
Star of Kuwait	Marjorie L. Everett	Leland Stanford H
Tallahto	Mrs. Howard B. Keck	Carleton F. Burke H (gr. II) Hawthorne H

Horse	Owner	Stakes
		Oak Tree Invitational S (gr. I)
		Santa Barbara H (gr. I)
		Vanity H (gr. I)
		Wilshire H
Tree of Knowledge	Pin Oak Stable	Hollywood Gold Cup Invitational H (gr. I)
Within Hail	Bwamazon Farm	El Cajon S
		Volante H (gr. III)

1975   487 starts, 93 wins, 23 stakes wins, $2,437,244

Horse	Owner	Stakes
Blue Times	Aaron U. Jones	Eddie Read H
Crumbs	Burt Bacharach	El Cajon S
Dulcia	Mrs. Arthur W. Stollery	National Championship H
		Ramona H (gr. III)
		Vanity H (gr. I)
Gay Style	John Sikura Jr.	Inglewood H (2nd div)
		Santa Barbara H (gr. I)
		Santa Maria H (gr. II)
La Zanzara	Aaron U. Jones	Beverly Hills H (gr. II)
		San Juan Capistrano H (gr. I)
Royal Glint	Dan Lasater	San Bernardino H (gr. II)
Snap Apple	Howard B. Keck	Del Mar Invitational Oaks (gr. III)
Stardust Mel	Marjorie L. Everett	Bel Air H (gr. II)
		Charles H. Strub S (gr. I)
		San Fernando S (gr. II; 1st div)
		Santa Anita H (gr. I)
Terete	Marjorie L. Everett	Cinema H (gr. II)
Thermal Energy	E. E. Fogelson	Sunny Slope S (gr. III)
Top Command	Mr. & Mrs. Quinn Martin & Murty Farm	Carleton F. Burke H (gr. II; 1st div)
		Oak Tree Invitational S (gr. I)
Trojan Bronze	Adrian B. Roks	San Luis Rey S (gr. I)
		San Marcos H (gr. III)
Victorian Prince	Grovetree Stable	Lakeside Turf H (gr. II; 2nd div)

1976   410 starts, 67 wins, 24 stakes wins, $2,248,783

Horse	Owner	Stakes
Bynoderm	Marjorie L. Everett	Coronado H
Caucasus	Cardiff Stock Farm	Manhattan H (gr. II)
		South Bay H
		Sunset H (gr. I)
Dahlia	Nelson Bunker Hunt	Hollywood Invitational H (gr. I)
Gay Style	John Sikura Jr.	Santa Maria H (gr. II)
		Santa Monica H (gr. II)
King Pellinore	Cardiff Stock Farm	American H (gr. II)
		Carleton F. Burke H (gr. II)
		Champions Invitational H (gr. I)
		Inglewood H (2nd div)
		Oak Tree Invitational H (gr. I)
Riot in Paris	Charlie Whittingham & Mary Jones	Bel Air H (gr. II)
		Del Mar Invitational H (gr. II)

Horse	Owner	Stakes
		Inglewood H (1st div)
Royal Derby II	E.E. Fogelson & Charlie Whittingham	Henry P. Russell H
Stravina	Mrs. Arthur W. Stollery	Santa Barbara H (gr. I)
Strong	Mr. & Mrs. Quinn Martin	San Marino H (1st div)
Swingtime	Geraldine A. Riley	Brentwood S (1st div)
		Hawthorne H (1st div)
Thermal Energy	E. E. Fogelson	San Vicente S (gr. III)
Vagabonda	Arno D. Schefler	Las Palmas H (gr. III)
		Ramona H (gr. III)
		San Rafael S

1977   362 starts, 57 wins, 15 stakes wins, $1,573,070

Horse	Owner	Stakes
Balzac	Mrs. Howard B. Keck	Norfolk S (gr. II)
Caucasus	Cardiff Stock Farm	Arcadia H (gr. III)
		San Luis Rey S (gr. I)
Glenaris	Mrs. Arthur W. Stollery	Hollywood Oaks S (gr. II)
		Senorita S
Kulak	Mary Jones Bradley, Charlie Whittingham	El Cajon S
	and Dr. Buck Wynne Jr.	Volante H (gr. III)
Pikehall	Howard B. Keck	Escondido H
Riot in Paris	Mary Jones Bradley & Charlie Whittingham	San Gabriel H (gr. III)
Royal Derby II	E.E. Fogelson & Charlie Whittingham	San Luis Obispo H (gr. II)
		San Marcos H (gr. III)
Stone Point	Howard B. Keck	Oceanside S (2nd div)
		La Jolla Mile S (gr. III)
Swingtime	Mary Jones Bradley & Charlie Whittingham	Beverly Hills H (gr. II)
		Las Palmas H (gr. III)

1978   356 starts, 63 wins, 15 stakes wins, $2,273,823

Horse	Owner	Stakes
Cheraw	Mr. & Mrs. Quinn Martin & Murty Farm	Henry P. Russell H (2nd div)
Donna Inez	Howard B. Keck	California Jockey Club H
		Torrey Pines S
Exceller	Nelson Bunker Hunt	Arcadia H (gr. III)
		Hollywood Gold Cup H (gr. I)
		Hollywood Invitational H (gr. I)
		Jockey Club Gold Cup S (gr. I)
		Oak Tree Invitational S (gr. I)
		San Juan Capistrano (gr. I)
		Sunset H (gr. I)
Fact	Mary Bradley, Dr. Buck Wynne & Whittingham	Osunitas S
Star of Erin II	Mr. & Mrs. Quinn Martin	Carleton F. Burke H (gr. II; 1st div)
		Inglewood H (2nd div)
Swingtime	Mary Bradley and Charlie Whittingham	Beverly Hills H (gr. II)
		Santa Maria H (gr. II)

1979   396 starts, 71 wins, 21 stakes wins, $2,216,627

Horse	Owner	Stakes
Ancient Art	Howard B. Keck	Market Basket S

196

Horse	Owner	Stakes
		San Clemente S
Balzac	Mrs. Howard B. Keck	Oak Tree Invitational S (gr. I)
Camarado	Nelson Bunker Hunt	Monrovia H (1st div)
Celine	Howard B. Keck	La Habra S
El Fantastico	Mary Bradley & Leone J. Peters	San Marino H (1st div)
Farnesio	Epsom Horse Inc.	Premiere H
Good Lord	Michael L. Hines	Eddie Read H
Guadanini	Joseph Kaida	Caballero H
Hyannis Port	Bell Bloodstock & Charlie Whittingham	Alibhai H
		Volante H (gr. III)
		Westwood S
More So	Nelson Bunker Hunt	Children's Hospital H
		Palomar H
Our Suiti Pie	Mary Bradley	Del Mar Oaks (gr. II)
Sanedtki	Serge Fradkoff	Santa Margarita Invitational H (gr. I)
		Sierra Madre H (2nd div)
Sirlad	Abram S. Hewitt	Bel Air H (gr. II)
		Sunset H (gr. I)
Stellar Envoy	E. E. Fogelson	Miss Todd S
White Rammer	Mr. & Mrs. J. C. H. Bryant	Triple Bend H

1980   386 starts, 56 wins, 16 stakes wins, $2,561,907

Horse	Owner	Stakes
A Thousand Stars	Alan Clore	Palomar H
Bold Tropic	Mr. & Mrs. Cyril Hurvitz	American H (gr. II)
		Carleton F. Burke H (gr. II)
		Lakeside H (gr. II)
Borzoi	Charles A.B. St. George, Wm. McDonald, J.R. Fluor & Dr. R.B. Chesne	Seaside H
Caro Bambino	Mary Bradley	Citation H (gr. III)
El Fantastico	Mary Bradley and Leone Peters	Caballero H
Exploded	Mary Bradley, Mrs. Nancy Wynne & Whittingham	Del Mar Derby H (gr. III)
Fast	Nelson Bunker Hunt	Tanforan H (gr. III)
Fiestero	Red Bee Ranch & Charlie Whittingham	San Marino H
Galaxy Libra	A. Shead	Chula Vista H
High Counsel	Nelson Bunker Hunt	Norfolk S (gr. I; 2nd div)
Inkerman	Ed Hudson	Sunset H (gr. I)
Lunar Probe	Mr. & Mrs. Quinn Martin	El Monte S
Queen to Conquer	Wimborne Farm	Ramona H (gr. II)
Teddy Doon	I.W. Allan	Cabrillo H

1981   372 starts, 74 wins, 23 stakes wins, $3,991,277

Horse	Owner	Stakes
Bold Tropic	Mr. & Mrs. Cyril Hurvitz	American H (gr. II)
		Inglewood H
Borzoi	Charles A.B. St. George et al (see 1980)	San Bernadino H (gr. II)
Captain General	Lowell T. Hughes	San Marino H
Forlion	Mr. & Mrs. Seymour W. Brown	Morvich H
Galaxy Libra	Louis R. Rowan	Man o' War S (gr. I)
		Rolling Green H (gr. III)

Horse	Owner	Stakes
		San Marcos H (gr. III)
		Sunset H (gr. I)
Handsome One	Mary Bradley & Nancy Wynne	Spotlight H
Kilijaro	Serge Fradkoff & Edward A. Seltzer	Autumn Days H
		Gamely H (gr. II)
		Matriarch S
		Monrovia H
		Palomar H (gr. III)
		San Gorgonio H
Northern Fable	Michael G. Rutherford	Torrey Pines S
Obraztsovy	W.T. Pascoe III & Brian Sweeney	San Juan Capistrano H (gr. I)
Providential	Serge Fradkoff	Hollywood Turf Cup H
		Washington, D.C., International S (gr. I)
Queen to Conquer	Wimborne Farm	Ramona H (gr. II)
		Santa Ana H (gr. III)
Rose of Morn	Meadow Stable	Curious Clover S

1982

409 starts, 62 wins, 18 stakes wins, $4,586,077
Eclipse Award as Outstanding Trainer
Champion: PERRAULT, turf horse

Horse	Owner	Stakes
Ask Me	Mrs. Howard B. Keck	Bay Meadows Derby
Castilla	Mary Bradley	Del Mar Oaks (gr. II)
		Honeymoon H (gr. II)
		Matriarch S
		Yellow Ribbon Invitational (gr. I)
Craelius	Mrs. Howard B. Keck	El Cajon S
		Oceanside S
Erins Isle	Brian Sweeney	Californian S (gr. I)
		Sunset H (gr. I)
Exploded	Mary Bradley, Nancy Wynne & Whittingham	Hollywood Invitational H (gr. I)
Flying Partner	Buckland Farm	Fantasy S (gr. I)
		Santa Ynez S (gr. II)
High Counsel	Lowell T. Hughes	Sierra Nevada H
Northern Fable	Michael G. Rutherford	Palomar H (gr. III)
Perrault	Serge Fradkoff & Baron Thierry von Zuylen	Arcadia H (gr. III)
		Budweiser Million S (gr. I)
		Hollywood Gold Cup H (gr. I)
		San Luis Rey (gr. I)

1983

445 starts, 75 wins, 19 stakes wins, $4,018,913

Horse	Owner	Stakes
Bohemian Grove	Robert E. Sangster	Santa Gertrudes H (1st div)
Castilla	Mary Bradley	Las Palmas H (gr. II)
		San Gorgonio H (gr. III)
Craelius	Mrs Howard B. Keck	Sunset H (gr. I)
Dr. Daly	Mary Bradley, Nancy Wynne & Whittingham	Oceanside S (2nd div)
Erins Isle	Brian Sweeney	Hollywood Invitational H (gr. I)
		San Juan Capistrano H (gr. I)
		San Luis Rey S (gr. I)
Estupendo	Mary Bradley & Charlie Whittingham	La Puente S

Horse	Owner	Stakes
Handsome One	Mary Bradley & Nancy Wynne Chandler	Caballero H
Little Hailey	Dr. W. O. Seabaugh	La Habra S
Lucence	Wimborne Farm	Exceller S
Mademoiselle Forli	Penowa Farm	Wilshire H (gr. II)
Palikaraki	Sidney L. Port	Arlington H (gr. I)
Pelerin	L.P. Doherty & Harold Snowden	San Luis Obispo (gr. II)
Re Ack	C. Cole	Bradbury S
The Wonder	Alain du Breil	Californian S (gr. I)
		Century H (gr. I)
		San Bernadino H (gr. II)

1984 — 428 starts, 53 wins, 17 stakes wins, $3,168,012

Horse	Owner	Stakes
Air Distingue	Sheikh Mohammed	Wishing Well S
Auntie Betty	Green Thumb Farm Stable	Pink Pigeon S
Craelius	Mrs. Howard B. Keck	Caballero H
Dancing	Mrs. Howard B. Keck	Askmenow S
Fact Finder	Nelson Bunker Hunt	California Jockey Club H (gr. III)
		Yerba Buena H (gr. III)
Galant Vert	Baron Guy de Rothschild	San Marino H
Greinton	Mary Jones, Howell Wynne & Whittingham	Princequillo H
Honeyland	Sidney Port & Summa Stable	Portrero Grande H
Lido Isle	J. R. Fluor	Sangue S
Load the Cannons	Summa Stable	San Juan Capistrano Invitational H (gr. I)
Lord At War	Peter M. Perkins	Citation H (gr. III)
		Goodwood H
		Native Diver H (gr. III)
Lucence	Wimborne Farm	San Marcos H (gr. II)
Prince Florimund	E. W. Miller	San Gabriel H (gr. III; 1st div)
Prince True	Mrs. Howard B. Keck	Cinema H (gr. II)

1985 — 464 starts, 68 wins, 27 stakes wins, $5,895,873

Horse	Owner	Stakes
Banner Bob	Sharon & William Walsh	Malibu S (gr. II)
Champion Pilot	Summa Stable	El Monte H
Craelius	Mrs. Howard B. Keck	Marina Del Rey H
Dahar	Summa Stable	Century H (gr. I)
		San Gabriel H (gr. III)
		San Marcos H (gr. III)
Dr. Daly	Mary Bradley, Nancy Chandler & Whittingham	Golden Act S
Estrapade	Summa Stable	Gamely H (gr. I)
		Las Palmas H (gr. II)
		Santa Ana H (gr. I)
		Yellow Ribbon S (gr. I)
Fact Finder	Nelson Bunker Hunt	Matriarch Invitational S (gr. I)
		San Gorgonio H (gr. II)
		Santa Barbara H (gr. I)
Gato Del Sol	Arthur Hancock III & Leone J. Peters	Caballero H
Greinton	Mary Bradley, Howell Wynne & Whittingham	Californian H (gr. I)
		Hollywood Gold Cup (gr. I)

Horse	Owner	Stakes
		San Bernardino H (gr. II)
Hail Bold King	Due Process Stable	Genesis H
Lord At War	Peter Perkins	Goodwood H (gr. III)
		San Antonio H (gr. I)
		Santa Anita H (gr. I)
Prince True	Mrs. Howard B. Keck	San Juan Capistrano Invitational H (gr. I)
		San Luis Rey S (gr. I)
Temerity Prince	Justin R. Querbes III	Ancient Title H
		Hollywood Turf Sprint Championship
Val Danseur	Bradley Brown, Cynthia Cogswell	Johnny's Image H
	& Lawrence Ensor III et al	

1986
541 starts, 95 wins, 36 stakes wins, $8,801,284
Champion: ESTRAPADE, turf filly/mare

Horse	Owner	Stakes
Dahar	Summa Stable	San Juan Capistrano Invitational H (gr. I)
		San Luis Rey S (gr. I)
Epidaurus	Howard B. Keck	Pomona Invitational H
Estrapade	Allen Paulson	Beverly Hill H (gr. II)
		Budweiser-Arlington Million S (gr. I)
		Oak Tree Invitational S (gr. I)
Ferdinand	Mrs. Howard B. Keck	Kentucky Derby (gr. I)
		Malibu S (gr. II)
		Santa Catalina S
Forlitano	Evergreen Farm	Seabiscuit Claiming S
Glaros	Enemy Stables & Mandysland Farm	Henry P. Rusell H
Greinton	Mary Bradley, Howell Wynne & Whittingham	Santa Anita H (gr. I)
Hail Bold King	Due Process Stable	San Francisco Mile H
Hidden Light	Mrs. Howard B. Keck	Del Mar Oaks (gr. II)
		Hollywood Oaks (gr. I)
		La Habra S
		Santa Anita Oaks (gr. I)
Infinidad	Arthur B. Hancock III	Princess Rooney S
Kraemer	Nelson Bunker Hunt	Bay Meadows Oaks (gr. III)
Le Belvedere	Allen Paulson	Bay Meadows Derby (gr. III)
Louis Le Grand	Allen Paulson	Carleton F. Burke H (gr. I)
Mazaad	Sheikh Mohammed	Spotlight S
		Will Rogers H (gr. III)
Miraculous	Mary Jones Bradley	Providencia S
Palace Music	Nelson Bunker Hunt & Allen Paulson	Bay Meadows H (gr. II)
		Col. F. W. Koester H
		John Henry H (gr. I)
Rivlia	Nelson Bunker Hunt	Caballero H
Strawberry Road	Allen Paulson & Summa Stable	Arcadia H (gr. II)
Sweettuc	Nelson Bunker Hunt	Hoist the Flag S (gr. III; 2nd div)
Temperate Sil	Frankfurt Stable and Charlie Whittingham	Balboa S (gr. III)
		Hollywood Futurity (gr. I)
Thrill Show	M. Bradley, R.L. Duchossois & Whittingham	Hollywood Derby (gr. I; 1st div)
Val Danseur	Bradley Brown et al (see 1985)	Golden Gate H (gr. II)
		Rolling Green H (gr. III)
		Santa Gertrudes H

1987

483 starts, 90 wins, 38 stakes wins, $9,415,097
Champion: FERDINAND, Horse of the Year, older male

Horse	Owner	Stakes
Barbarina	Henryk de Kwiatkowski	Great Lady M. Stakes
Bold Second	Dr. William Seabaugh & Whittingham	De Anza S
		Sunny Slope S
Bolder Than Bold	Mary Bradley, Nancy Chandler, & Whittingham	San Simeon H (gr. III)
Epidaurus	Howard B. Keck	Native Diver H (gr. III)
		San Pasqual H (gr. II)
Ferdinand	Mrs. Howard B. Keck	Breeders' Cup Classic (gr. I)
		Cabrillo H
		Goodwood H (gr. III)
		Hollywood Gold Cup H (gr. I)
Forlitano	Evergreen Farm	Citation H (gr. II)
		Rolling Green H (gr. III)
		San Jacinto H
Goodbye Halo	Arthur B. Hancock III	Hollywood Starlet S (gr. I)
Ifrad	Sidney Port & Charlie Whittingham	Arlington H (gr. I)
Infinidad	Arthur B. Hancock III	Chula Vista H (gr. II)
		Vanity H (gr. I)
Judge Angelucci	Olin B. Gentry	Bay Meadows Budweiser Breeders' Cup H
		Bel Air H (gr. II)
		Californian S (gr. I)
		Longacres Mile H (gr. II)
		San Bernardino H (gr. II)
Le Belvedere	Allen Paulson	Inglewood H (gr. II)
Lord Ruckus	Tabb & Triple M Farms	Governor's Cup H
		Hollywood Turf Express H
Louis Le Grand	Allen Paulson	San Luis Obispo (gr. II)
Reloy	Nelson Bunker Hunt	Santa Ana H (gr. I)
		Santa Barbara H (gr. I)
Rivlia	Nelson Bunker Hunt	Carleton F. Burke H (gr. I)
		Golden Gate H (gr. II)
		Hollywood Invitational H (gr. I)
Rosedale	Nelson Bunker Hunt	San Juan Capistrano Invitational H (gr. I)
		San Marino H
Swink	Nelson Bunker Hunt	Del Mar Invitational H (gr. II)
		Sunset H (gr. I)
Temperate Sil	Frankfurt Stable and Charlie Whittingham	Santa Anita Derby (gr. I)
		Swaps S (gr. I)
Thrill Show	M. Bradley, R.L. Duchossois, & Whittingham	Arcadia H (gr. II)

1988

519 starts, 88 wins, 25 stakes wins, $6,195,079

Horse	Owner	Stakes
Epidaurus	Howard B. Keck	San Carlos H (gr. II)
Fiction	Evergreen Farm	Santa Gertrudes H
Fitzwilliam Place	Kewton USA & Summa Stable	Beverly Hills H (gr. I)
Forlitano	Evergreen Farm	Citation H (gr. II)
Goodbye Halo	Arthur B. Hancock III & Alex Campbell Jr.	Coaching Club American Oaks (gr. I)
		Kentucky Oaks (gr. I)
		Las Virgenes S (gr. I)

Horse	Owner	Stakes
		Mother Goose S (gr. I)
		Santa Ynez S (gr. III)
Ifrad	Sidney Port & Charlie Whittingham	All-American H (gr. III)
		San Francisco Mile H (gr. III)
		Turf Paradise H
Jeanne Jones	Golden Eagle Farm	Autumn Days H
		Fantasy S (gr. I)
		Santa Ysabel S
Judge Angelucci	Olin B. Gentry	Mervyn LeRoy H (gr. I)
		San Antonio H (gr. I)
Lively One	John Sikura	Santa Catalina S
		Swaps S (gr. I)
Motley	Thomas J. Curnes	Caballero H
Nasr El Arab	Sheikh Mohammed	Carleton F. Burke H (gr. I)
Pattern Step	Evergreen Farm	Hollywood Oaks (gr. I)
		Providencia S
Peace	Olin B. Gentry	Cinema H (gr. II)
Rivlia	Narvick International	San Luis Rey S (gr. I)

1989
436 starts, 86 wins, 39 stakes wins, $11,402,231
Eclipse Award as Outstanding Trainer
Champion: SUNDAY SILENCE, Horse of the Year, 3-year-old colt

Horse	Owner	Stakes
Claire Marine	Sidney Port & Charlie Whittingham	Beverly D. Stakes
		Beverly Hills H (gr. I)
		Matriarch S (gr. I)
		Palomar H (gr. II)
		Santa Anita Budweiser Breeders' Cup H
		Wilshire H (gr. II)
Daloma	Enemy Stable & Mandysland Farm	A Gleam H (gr. III)
		Monrovia H
Delegant	Evergreen Farm	Santa Gertrudes H
Fitzwilliam Place	Kewton USA & Summa Stable	Gamely H (gr. I)
Forlitano	Evergreen Farm	Bougainvillea H (gr. II)
Frankly Perfect	Wayne Gretzky, Summa Stable	Golden Gate H (gr. II)
	& Sylvester Stallone	Hollywood Turf Cup H (gr. I)
		San Luis Rey S (gr. I)
Goodbye Halo	Arthur B. Hancock III & Alex Campbell Jr.	Chula Vista H (gr. II)
		El Encino S (gr. III)
		La Canada S (gr. I)
Live the Dream	Mary Bradley, Nancy Chandler & Whittingham	Henry P. Russell H
		Hollywood Derby (gr. I)
Lively One	John Sikura	Cabrillo H (gr. III)
		San Diego H (gr. III)
Nasr El Arab	Sheikh Mohammed	Charles H. Strub S (gr. I)
		San Juan Capistrano Invitational H (gr. I)
Payant	Ignacias Correas & Dr. William Seabaugh	Del Mar Invitational H (gr. II)
Peace	Olin B. Gentry	John Henry H (gr. I)
		Premiere H (gr. III)
River Master	Cardiff Stud Farm, Red Baron's Barn	Ascot H (gr. III)

Horse	Owner	Stakes
	& Timestable	La Jolla H (gr. III)
Ruhlmann	Mr. & Mrs. Jerome S. Moss	Mervyn LeRoy H (gr. I)
		Native Diver H (gr. III)
		San Bernardino H (gr. II)
		Viking Spirit S
Seven Rivers	Enemy Stable & Mandysland Farm	Volante H (gr. II)
Sunday Silence	Dr. Ernest Gaillard, Arthur Hancock III,	Breeders' Cup Classic (gr. I)
	& Charlie Whittingham	Kentucky Derby (gr. I)
		Preakness S (gr. I)
		San Felipe S (gr. II)
		Santa Anita Derby (gr. I)
		Super Derby (gr. I)

1990 — 383 starts, 58 wins, 18 stakes wins, $5,691,735

Horse	Owner	Stakes
Frankly Perfect	Wayne Gretzky & Summa Stable	San Luis Obispo H (gr. III)
Girl of France	Baron Thierry von Zuylen	Admirably H
Golden Pheasant	Wayne Gretzky & Summa Stable	Arlington Million S (gr. I)
		John Henry H (gr. II)
Lively One	John Sikura	Goodwood H (gr. II)
		Kensington H
Live the Dream	Mary Jones, Nancy Chandler & Whittingham	Del Mar Invitational H (gr. II)
		Fiesta H
Petalia	Howard B. Keck	Dahlia H (gr. II; 1st div)
River Master	Cardiff Stud Farm, Red Baron's Barn	All-American H (gr. III)
	& Timestable	Khaled H
Rosadora	Mary J. Bradley	Matinee S
Ruhlmann	Mr. & Mrs. Jerome S. Moss	San Bernardino H (gr. II)
		Santa Anita H (gr. I)
Shining Steel	Wayne Gretzky & Summa Stable	Shoemaker H (gr. II)
Sir Beaufort	Victoria Calantoni	La Puente S
Sunday Silence	Dr. Ernest Gaillard, Arthur Hancock III	Californian S (gr. I)
	Zenya Yoshida & Charlie Whittingham	
Warcraft	Mary Jones, Nancy Chandler & Whittingham	Native Diver H (gr. III)

1991 — 443 starts, 61 wins, 17 stakes wins, $5,378,204
Champion: MISS ALLEGED, female turf

Horse	Owner	Stakes
Anshan	Sheikh Mohammed	Pinjara H
		San Bernadino H (gr. II)
Campagnarde	Allen Paulson	Ramona H (gr. I)
Compelling Sound	Mr. & Mrs. Jerome S. Moss	Silver Screen H (gr. III)
		Will Rogers H (gr. III)
Flawlessly	Harbor View Farm	Del Mar Oaks (gr. III)
		Harold C. Ramser Sr. H (gr. III)
		Matriarch S (gr. I)
		San Clemente S
		Street Dancer S
Golden Pheasant	Wayne Gretzky & Summa Stable	Japan Cup (Jpn-I)
Miss Alleged	Fares Farm	Hollywood Turf Cup S (gr. I)
River Traffic	Evergreen Farm	Majestic Light S

Horse	Owner	Stakes
River Warden	Sheikh Mohammed	San Marino H
Royal Touch	Sheikh Mohammed	San Gorgonio H (gr. II)
Taffeta and Tulle	Sheikh Mohammed	Buena Vista H (gr. III)
The Prime Minister	Mary Bradley, Nancy Chandler & Fred Seitz	Goodwood H (gr. II)

1992 — 368 starts, 38 wins, 9 stakes wins, $3,213,025
Champion: FLAWLESSLY, female turf

Horse	Owner	Stakes
Flawlessly	Harbor View Farm	Beverly Hills H (gr. I)
		Matriarch S (gr. I)
		Ramona H (gr. I)
Golden Pheasant	Zenya Yoshida	Inglewood H (gr. II)
Luna Elegante	Trans Media Park Stud	Run for the Roses S
Qathif	Mr. & Mrs. Jerome Moss	Miramontes H
		Sunset H (gr. II)
Sir Beaufort	Victoria Calantoni	Native Diver H (gr. III)
		Royal Owl H

1993 — 269 starts, 25 wins, 7 stakes wins, $2,312,729
(through October 4)

Horse	Owner	Stakes
Campagnarde	Allen Paulson	Honey Fox H
		Hurry Countess S
Flawlessly	Harbor View Farm	Beverly D. Stakes (gr. I)
		Beverly Hills H (gr. I)
		Ramona H (gr. I)
Sir Beaufort	Victoria Calantoni	San Carlos H (gr. II)
		Santa Anita H (gr. I)

CAREER — 2,436 wins, 638 stakes wins, career earnings of $104,308,311 (includes 68 victories and $244,755 from 1950-'52; previous information unavailable Source: *The Blood-Horse, American Racing Manual*)

INDEX